UNDER THE GENERAL EDITORSHIP OF

JOHN HENRY RALEIGH & IAN WATT

13635

AUG 31 96
SEP 26 96   aug 36

1

SEVEN OLD ENGLISH POEMS

THE LIBRARY OF LITERATURE

SEVEN OLD ENGLISH
POEMS

·

CÆDMON'S HYMN

THE BATTLE OF BRUNANBURH

THE DREAM OF THE ROOD

THE BATTLE OF MALDON

THE WANDERER

THE SEAFARER

DEOR

·

EDITED WITH COMMENTARY AND GLOSSARY

by JOHN C. POPE

YALE UNIVERSITY

THE BOBBS-MERRILL COMPANY, INC.

INDIANAPOLIS · NEW YORK

Copyright © 1966 by The Bobbs-Merrill Company, Inc.
Library of Congress Catalog Card Number 66–26804
Printed in the United States of America
Designed by Joseph P. Ascherl
Second Printing

Preface

This edition has grown out of my needs as the teacher of an elementary course in Old English for graduate students. The poems are those I have found it most profitable to read early in the year, as a preliminary to the study of *Beowulf*. They are arranged in the order in which I usually take them up with the class. There is nothing sacred about this order, except that *The Wanderer* and *The Seafarer* offer difficulties of interpretation beyond the rest, since they exhibit a more richly metaphorical and connotative use of language in accordance with their intellectually complicated themes; while *Deor*, with its allusions to heroic legends, stands in that respect closer than the others to the world of *Beowulf*.

The text and glossary have been my principal concern. The text is normalized very much according to the system of Professor F. P. Magoun, Jr., whose normalized text, *The Anglo-Saxon Poems in Bright's Anglo-Saxon Reader* (Department of English, Harvard University, 1960) has been a staple of my course for several years; and I might have rested content with this if I had not wished to include the whole of *The Dream of the Rood* and *The Seafarer*, and to treat all seven poems somewhat more intensively than his edition allowed. I have decided to adopt as my norm a somewhat less archaic version of Early West Saxon than Magoun's, which follows the spellings of Holthausen's *Altenglisches etymologisches Wörterbuch*. These spellings are excellent for the student of etymology and phonology, but in certain respects (notably the rounded *œ*, long and short, and the distinction between *io* and *eo*) they go beyond the spellings most frequently encountered in the literary manuscripts, especially those of the poetry, and beyond the spellings adopted as standard by the leading grammars. I have retained the *e* of the poetical manuscripts for the *i*-mutation of *o*, and have included what was historically *io* under the generalized *eo* of many, though by no

means all, of the manuscripts. The most conspicuous mark of
Early West Saxon, the *ie*, long and short, though it became
archaic during the tenth century and was obsolete by the time
of *The Battle of Maldon*, is too helpful to the student to be
abandoned.

In a few other particulars I have departed from Holthausen
and Magoun, generally in favor of less drastic alteration of the
manuscript records and in accord with the forms given precede-
ence in the grammars of Sievers-Brunner and Campbell. Here
and there (like Magoun) I have allowed variant forms to stand
for fear of disturbing the meter, and at least once (*sleaht* in *The
Wanderer* for *slieht* in *Brunanburh*) for fear of too drastic an
alteration of the phonetic pattern—though in this matter we
must generally resign ourselves to the probability that our in-
herited texts are very far from faithful to the dialectal forms and
other details of the poet's own speech. At all events the full
record and cross-references of the glossary should render my few
inconsistencies harmless. I have deliberately refrained from
normalizing the pronominal forms *mē*, *þē*, *ūs*, *ēow*, so that the
reader must decide whether they are dative or accusative, or con-
sult my guesses in the glossary. Similarly, I have not normalized
the endings in the manuscripts for the nominative and accusative
plural of adjectives. The generalized ending *-e* is very common
and is allowed to stand even if the noun modified is feminine or
neuter. Consequently there is no instance in the ensuing texts
of the specifically feminine *-a*, and only two of the neuter *-u*
(*Wanderer* 85, *īdlu* and 100, *wæl-ġīfru*).

Partly to let the reader know precisely how I have modified
these texts, and partly to keep the student aware of the irregulari-
ties he will encounter as soon as he turns to our standard editions
of Old English poetry, I have put at the foot of the page the
full record of the manuscript readings insofar as they differ from
the normalized text. Outright emendations (most of which are
the work of previous editors) are distinguished from mere varia-
tions in spelling—though sometimes a grammatical ending in the
manuscript is susceptible of more than one interpretation, and
the normalizer must make an editorial choice.

The glossary has been an even greater concern than the text.

It is planned for a double purpose. On the one hand, it enables the beginner to make considerable progress toward gaining a general control of the poetic vocabulary. All nominal and adjectival compounds, if distinctly recognizable as such, are separated into their two components by hyphens in the text of the poems, and each component is separately defined in its alphabetical place in the glossary. In this way the student, following a plan recommended by Professor Magoun, can learn a relatively small number of simple words out of which a rather large number of compounds are formed by the poets, and can usually understand the compounds for himself, as the poets themselves, freely compounding words as they wished, expected their audiences or readers to do. On the other hand, the student of poetry wants not only to increase his general command of the vocabulary but to understand the subtleties of his text. For this reason I have defined the compounds as well as their components, and tried as far as possible to give, for all words, the meanings most applicable to their particular occurrences.

My own practice is to return to the standard editions, with their unnormalized texts, as soon as the student has acquired a grounding in the grammar and has begun to build a substantial vocabulary. Those who wish to continue the use of normalized texts can with very slight adjustment proceed to those of Professor Magoun, which are published by the Department of English at Harvard. Besides the poems in Bright's Reader, he has normalized *Beowulf* and *Judith* in one volume (1959) and the poems of the Vercelli Book in another (1960). His own device for building vocabulary is the *Grouped Frequency Word-List of Anglo-Saxon Poetry*, prepared jointly with John F. Madden, C.S.B. (Second corrected printing, 1960). An almost essential companion to these texts is Jess B. Bessinger, Jr., *A Short Dictionary of Anglo-Saxon Poetry*, Toronto University Press: Toronto, Ontario, 1960.

NOTE TO THE REVISED EDITION: The first edition of this book was reproduced photographically from typescript for the use of my own students. In preparing it for general use I have corrected many small errors and omissions, rewritten several portions of the commentary, augmented others, and added a section on versification. The bibliographical suggestions in the commentary have been extended but remain highly selective. The older bibliography is amply represented in the special editions to which I have referred. I must rely upon teacher and student to make further exploration and to add fresh items year by year.

I am grateful to many of my present and former students for calling attention to inconsistencies and oversights. To Dr. Robert B. Burlin I am indebted for valuable bibliographical suggestions and for generously given assistance in editorial tasks. To Dr. Frances Randall Lipp, who tried out the first edition with her classes, I owe searching criticism on several matters pertaining to the interpretation of the texts and further help on bibliography.

J. C. P.

New Haven, Connecticut
1966

CONTENTS

AIDS TO PRONUNCIATION

Þ, þ represent the voiceless *th* in *thin*.

Ð, ð represent the voiced *th* in *this*.

ċ is pronounced like *ch* in *chin*.

ċċ is the same sound prolonged or doubled.

ġ is pronounced like *y* in *year* or *day*.

nġ is pronounced like the *ng* in *hinge* (but not if the *n* belongs to a separable element, as in an-ġinn or on-ġinnan).

cg (not specially marked) is always like *dge* in *edge*.

sc (not specially marked) when initial or final is like *sh* in *shall*, *English*; when medial, as in *āscian*, it is like *sk* in *ask*.

SEVEN OLD ENGLISH POEMS

Cædmon's Hymn

The Northumbrian Version of MS M, *dated 737*
(*The Moore* MS, *University Library, Cambridge,*
Kk. 5. 16, f. 128ᵛ)

Nu scylun hergan   hefaenricaes uard,
metudæs maecti   end his modgidanc,
uerc uuldurfadur,   sue he uundra gihuaes,
eci dryctin,   or astelidæ.

5 He aerist scop   aelda barnum
heben til hrofe,   haleg scepen;
tha middungeard   moncynnæs uard,
eci dryctin,   æfter tiadæ,
firum foldu,   frea allmectig.

Variants in MS L (Leningrad, Public Library, MS Lat. Q. v. I.
18, f. 107, dated 746 or earlier): **1** scilun. herga. hefenricæs.
2 mehti. and. modgithanc. **3** gihuæs. **5** ærist. ældu. **6** hefen to
hrofæ halig sceppend. **7** middingard. **9** allmehtig.

Cædmon's Hymn

The Hymn Normalized in West-Saxon Spelling
Based on the Northumbrian Version of MSS M *and* L

Nū sculon herian   heofon-rīċes Weard,
Metodes meahta   and his mōd-ġeþanc,
weorc Wuldor-Fæder,   swā hē wundra ġehwæs,
ēċe Dryhten,   ōr astealde.

5   Hē ǣrest scōp   ielda bearnum
heofon to hrōfe,   hāliġ Scieppend;
þā middan-ġeard   mann-cynnes Weard,
ēċe Dryhten,   æfter tēode—
fīrum foldan   Frēa ælmihtiġ.

Substantive variants in MS T (Bodleian Library, Tanner 10, f. 100), the best of the West-Saxon texts, included in the Old English version of Bede's *Historia Ecclesiastica:*
4 onstealde. **5** eorðan *for* ielda.

Spelling variants in T compared with the normalized text:
1 herigean. **2** meotodes. meahte. **4** drihten. **5** sceop.
6 scyppend. **7** moncynnes. **8** drihten.
Among variants in some of the later copies are: **1** we *before* sculon. **4** ord *for* or. **5** gesceop *for* scop.

The Battle of Brunanburh

(The Anglo-Saxon Chronicle)

Hēr Æðelstān cyning, eorla dryhten,
beorna bēag-ġiefa, and his brōðor ēac,
Ēadmund æðeling, ealdor-langne tīr
ġeslōgon æt sæċċe sweorda ecgum
5   ymbe Brūnanburh. Bord-weall clufon,
hēowon heaðu-linda hamora lāfum
eaforan Ēadweardes, swā him ġe-æðele wæs
fram cnēo-māgum þæt hīe æt campe oft
wiþ lāðra ġehwone land ealgoden,
10   hord and hāmas. Hettend crungon,
Scotta lēode and scip-flotan,
fǣġe fēollon. Feld dennode

A = Corpus Christi College, Cambridge, MS 173 (the Parker
Chronicle), ff. 26ʳ–27ʳ. B = British Museum, MS Cotton Tiberius
A. vi, ff. 31ʳ–32ʳ. C = British Museum, MS Cotton Tiberius B. i,
f. 141ʳ⁻ᵛ. D = British Museum, MS Cotton Tiberius B. iv, ff.
49ʳ–50ʳ. A was copied at Winchester soon after 955; B and C are
copies of a MS at Abingdon, now lost; B after 977, C eleventh
century. D was copied from a northern MS after 1016.

1 B æþestan. BC cing. BCD drihten. 2 ACD beah-. ABD -gifa;
C -gyfa. 3 C ealdorlagne. D tyr. 4 B geslogan. B sake; D secce.
C swurda. B ecggum. 5 BC embe. BC brunnan- (AD brunan, *but* A
corrected to brunnan).   bord-] D heord-. AD -weal. ABD clufan.
6 ABD heowan. ABCD heapo-. A -linde; B -lina; D -linga *altered to* -linda.
D hamera. A lafan. 7 A afaran; C aforan; D eoforan *altered to*
eaforan. D eadweardes. 8 A from. ACD -mægum. ACD hi.
9 ACD gehwæne; B gehwane. AC ealgodon; B ealgodan; D gealgodon.
10 D heted. A crungun. 11 A sceotta. A leoda. C scyp-.
12 ABC feollan. A dænede *corrected to* dænnede; BC dennade.

5

secga swāte   siþþan sunne upp
on morgen-tīd,   mǣre tungol,
15   glād ofer grundas,   Godes candel beorht,
ēċes Dryhtnes,   oþ sēo æðele ġesceaft
sāg to setle.   Þǣr læġ secg maniġ
gārum aġīeted,   guma Norðerna
ofer scield scoten,   swelċe Scyttisc ēac,
20   wēriġ, wīġes sæd.

               West-Seaxe forþ
andlangne dæġ   ēorod-cystum
on lāst leġdon   lāðum þēodum,
hēowon here-flīeman   hindan þearle
mēċum mylen-scearpum.   Mierċe ne wierndon
25   heardes hand-plegan   hæleða nānum
þāra-þe mid Anlāfe   ofer ēar-ġebland
on lides bōsme   land ġesōhton,
fǣġe to ġefeohte.   Fīfe lāgon
on þam camp-stede   cyningas ġeonge,
30   sweordum aswefede,   swelċe seofone ēac
eorlas Anlāfes,   unrīm herġes,
flotena and Scotta.   Þǣr ġeflīemed wearþ
Norþ-manna bregu,   nīede ġebǣded,
to lides stefne   lȳtle weorode;

13 A secgas hwate. AD up.   15 A Condel.   16 ABCD drihtnes. oþ] B þæt.
A sio; D se.   17 ABCD sah. D sætle. A mænig; CD monig.   18 ACD ageted;
B forgrunden. BCD guman. BC norðerne; D norþærne.   19 A scild;
BCD scyld. BD sceoten. AC swilce; BD swylce. A scittisc.   20 BC
wigges. D ræd. AD wesseaxe; B westsexe; C and wessexe.   21 A ondlongne.
BCD eored-. A -cistum.   22 A legdun; D lægdon. C ðeodon.   23 ABD
heowan. A herefleman; B hereflyman; C hereflymon; D heora flyman.   24 A
mylenscearpan; D mycelscearpum. ABCD myrce. ABCD wyrndon.   25 A
heeardes. A hond-.   26 þara-þe] A þæ; D þæra þe. A æra-.   27 C
liþes. A gesohtun; B gesohtan.   28 D fage. D feohte. A lægun.
29 B þæm. A cyninges; B ciningas; C cingas. A giunge; D iunga.
30 C aswefde. ABC swilce; D swylce. AD scofene; C vii.   31 unrim]
C and unrim. A heriges.   32 ABCD flotan. A sceotta. A geflemed;
BCD geflymed.   33 BCD brego. AB nede; CD neade. A gebeded.   34 D
stæfne. A litle. C werode.

35 crēad cnearr on flot, cyning ūt ġewāt
on fealone flōd, feorh ġenerede.
Swelċe þær ēac se frōda mid flēame cōm
on his cȳþþe norþ, Constantīnus,
hār hilde-rinc. Hrēman ne þorfte
40 mēċa ġemānan; hē wæs his māga sceard,
frēonda ġefielled on folc-stede,
beslæġen æt sæċċe, and his sunu forlēt
on wæl-stōwe wundum forgrunden,
ġeongne æt gūðe. Ġielpan ne þorfte
45 beorn blanden-feax bill-ġesliehtes,
eald inwitta, nē Anlāf þȳ mā;
mid hira here-lāfum hliehhan ne þorfton
þæt hīe beadu-weorca beteran wurdon
on camp-stede cumbol-ġehnāstes,
50 gār-mittunge, gumena ġemōtes,
wæpen-ġewrixles, þæs hīe on wæl-felda
wiþ Ēadweardes eaforan plegodon.
Ġewiton him þā Norþ-menn næġled-cnearrum,
drēoriġ daroða lāf, on Dinges mere
55 ofer dēop wæter Dyflin sēċan,

35 D creat. cnearr on] BCD cnear on; A cnearen. D flod. B cing;
C cining. D *omits 35b and 36a.* **36** A fealene. CD generode. **37**
AC swilce; BD Swylce. **38** A costontinus. **39** har] D hal. A hildering;
D hylderinc. D hryman. **40** meca] A mæcan; B mecea; D mecga. he]
BC her. AD mæga. **41** ABCD gefylled. on] C on his. **42** beslægen]
A beslagen; C beslegen; B forslegen. B sace; D sæcge. D forlæt.
43 A wundun. A fergrunden. **44** A giungne. A gelpan; BCD gylpan.
45 BC -fex. A bil-. A geslehtes; B geslyhtes; CD geslihtes. **46** A
inwidda; D inwuda. þy] BD þe. **47** AB heora; CD hyra. D -leafum.
A hlehhan; BC hlihhan; D hlybban. AC þorftun; BD þorftan. **48** A
heo; CD hi. BCD beado-. A wurdun; B wurdan. **49** A culbod-,
cumbel- *over line.* A -gehnades. **50** ABC -mittinge. **51** þæs] D þæs þe.
ACD hi. **52** AD afaran; C aforan. AB plegodan. **53** AB gewitan.
C hym. A normen *altered to* norþmen; D norðmen. C negledcnearrum;
D dæg gled on garum. **54** C dreori. A daraða; C darepa; D dareða.
B dynges; D dyniges. **55** D deopne. A difelin; B dyflen; D dyflig.
B secean.

eft Īra land   ǣwisc-mōde.

Swelċe þā ġebrōðor   bēġen ætsamne,

cyning and æðeling,   cȳþþe sōhton,

West-Seaxna land,   wīġes hrēmġe.

60   Lēton him behindan   hrǣw bryttian

sealwiġ-pādan,   þone sweartan hræfn

hyrned-nebban,   and þone hasu-pādan,

earn æftan hwīt,   ǣses brūcan,–

grǣdiġne gūþ-hafoc,   and þæt grǣġe dēor,

65   wulf on wealda.

              Ne wearþ wæl māre

on þȳs īġ-lande   ǣfre ġīeta

folces ġefielled   beforan þissum

sweordes ecgum,   þæs-þe ūs secgaþ bēċ,

ealde ūþwitan,   siþþan ēastan hider

70   Engle and Seaxe   upp becōmon,

ofer brād brimu   Britene sōhton,

wlance wīġ-smiðas,   Wēalas ofercōmon,

eorlas ār-hwæte   eard beġēaton.

56 eft] A and eft, *the* and *added later above the line*. Īra] A hira;
CD yra.   **57** AC swilce; B Swylce; D swylce. A gebroþer; C broðor.
D bege. BC ætsomne; D æt runne.   **58** BC cing. D eaðeling. B sohtan.
59 A wesseaxena; C wessexena. BC wigges. A hramige *altered to*
hremige; BCD hremige.   **60** AB letan; D læton. C hym. C behindon.
A hræ *with* w *added over line;* B hraw; CD hra. B bryttigean; C brittigan;
D bryttinga.   **61** A saluwig; BCD salowig. C hrefn.   **62** D hyrnet-.
A þane. A hasewan-; B haso-. D -wadan.   **64** D cuðheafoc. D grege.
65 ABCD wealde.   **66** A þis; D þisne. A eiglande; B eglande. A æfer.
BC gyta; D gita.   **67** ACD gefylled; B afylled. BCD þyssum.
68 C swurdes. B secggeaþ.   **69** B syþþan.   **70** B sexan; C sexe. AD up. AB
becoman.   **71** BCD brade. AB brytene; C bretene. AB sohtan.   **72** A
weealles. AB ofercoman.   **73** ABC arhwate. A begeatan.

The Dream of the Rood

(Vercelli Book, ff. 104^v^–106^r^)

   Hwæt, iċ swefna cyst   secgan wille,
hwæt mē ġemǣtte   to midre nihte,
siþþan reord-berend   reste wunodon.
Þūhte mē þæt iċ ġesāwe   seldlīcre trēo

5   on lyft lǣdan   lēohte bewunden,
bēama beorhtost.   Eall þæt bēacen wæs
begoten mid golde;   ġimmas stōdon
fæġere æt foldan sċēatum,   swelċe þǣr fīfe wǣron
uppe on þam eaxl-ġespanne.   Behēoldon þǣr enġel-dryhta fela,

10   fæġere þurh forþ-ġesċeaft;   ne wæs þǣr hūru fracuðes ġealga,
ac hine þǣr behēoldon   hālġe gāstas,
menn ofer moldan   and eall þēos mǣre ġesċeaft.
Seldlīċ wæs se siġe-bēam,   and iċ synnum fāg,
forwundod mid wammum.   Ġeseah iċ wuldres trēo

15   wǣdum ġeweorðod   wynnum scīnan,
ġeġiered mid golde;   ġimmas hæfdon
bewriġen weorþlīċe   Wealdendes trēo.
Hwæðre iċ þurh þæt gold   onġietan meahte
earmra ǣr-ġewinn,   þæt hit ǣrest ongann

20   swǣtan on þā swīðran healfe.   Eall iċ wæs mid sorgum ġedrēfed;
forht iċ wæs for þǣre fæġeran ġesihþe.   Ġeseah iċ
                         þæt fūse bēacen

Emendations: **2** hwæt] MS hæt. **9** eaxl] MS eaxle. engel-dryhta fela]
MS engel dryhtnes ealle. **15** geweorðod] MS geweorðode. **17** bewrigen]
MS bewrigene. Wealdendes] MS wealdes. **20** sorgum] MS surgum.

Variant spellings in the MS: **1** wylle. **3** syðþan. wunedon.
4 syllicre. treow. **8** swylce. **10** fracodes. **11** halige. **12** men.
13 Syllic. fah. **14** forwunded. wommum. treow. **16** gegyred. **17** treow.
18 ongytan. **19** gewin. ongan. **21** fægran. gesyhðe.

wendan wǣdum and blēoum: hwīlum hit wæs mid wǣtan
                                                            bestīemed,
beswiled mid swātes gange,   hwīlum mid since ġeġierwed.

    Hwæðre iċ þǣr licgende   lange hwīle
25   behēold hrēow-ċeariġ   Hǣlendes trēo,
oþ-þæt iċ ġehīerde   þæt hit hlēoðrode;
ongann þā word sprecan   wudu sēlesta:

    "Þæt wæs ġēara ġeö   —iċ þæt ġīeta ġeman—
þæt iċ wæs ahēawen   holtes on ende,
30 astyred of stefne mīnum.   Ġenāmon mē þǣr strange fēondas,
ġeworhton him þǣr to wǣfer-sīene,   hēton mē hira
                                                            weargas hebban.
Bǣron mē þǣr beornas on eaxlum,   oþ-þæt hīe mē on
                                                            beorg asetton;
ġefæstnodon mē þǣr fēondas ġenōge.   Ġeseah iċ þā
                                                            Frēan mann-cynnes
efstan elne miċle   þæt hē mē wolde on ġestīgan.

35   Þǣr iċ þā ne dorste   ofer Dryhtnes word
būgan oþþe berstan   þā iċ bifian ġeseah
eorðan scēatas.   Ealle iċ meahte
fēondas ġefiellan,   hwæðre iċ fæste stōd.

    Onġierede hine þā ġeong Hæleþ   —þæt wæs God ælmihtiġ—,
40 strang and stīþ-mōd;   ġestāg hē on ġealgan hēanne,
mōdiġ on maniġra ġesihþe,   þā hē wolde mann-cynn līesan.
Bifode iċ þā mē se Beorn ymbclypte;   ne dorste iċ
                                                            hwæðre būgan to eorðan,
feallan to foldan scēatum.   Ac iċ scolde fæste standan.

    Rōd wæs iċ arǣred;   ahōf iċ rīċne Cyning,
45 heofona Hlāford;   hieldan mē ne dorste.

Variant spellings: **22** bleom. bestemed. **23** beswyled. gegyrwed.   **25** treow.
26 gehyrde.   **27** ongan.   **28** geo] iu. gyta.   **30** genaman.   **31** -syne.
heora. wergas.   **33** man-.   **34** mycle.   **37** mihte.   **38** gefyllan.
39 Ongyrede.   **40** Gestah.   **41** gesyhðe. mancyn. lysan. **43** sceolde. **45** hyldan.

Þurhdrifon hīe mē mid deorcum næġlum: on mē sindon
                    þā dolg ġesīene,
opene inwitt-hlemmas;   ne dorste iċ hira ǣnigum scieþþan.
Bismerodon hīe unc bū-tū ætgædere.   Eall iċ wæs mid
                    blōde bestīemed,
begoten of þæs Guman sīdan   siþþan hē hæfde his
                    gāst onsended.
50   Fela iċ on þam beorge   ġebiden hæbbe
        wrāðra wyrda.   Ġeseah iċ weoroda God
        þearle þenian.   Þīestru hæfdon
        bewriġen mid wolcnum   Wealdendes hrǣw,
        scīrne scīman;   scadu forþ ēode
55   wann under wolcnum.   Wēop eall ġesceaft,
        cwīðdon Cyninges fiell;   Crīst wæs on rōde.
        "Hwæðre þǣr fūse   feorran cōmon
        to þam Æðelinge.   Iċ þæt eall behēold.
Sāre iċ wæs mid sorgum ġedrēfed,   hnāg iċ hwæðre þam
                    secgum to handa,
60   ēaþ-mōd, elne miċle.   Ġenāmon hīe þǣr ælmihtiġne God,
ahōfon hine of þam hefigan wīte.   Forlēton mē þā hilde-rincas
standan stēame bedrifenne;   eall iċ wæs mid strǣlum forwundod.
Aleġdon hīe þǣr lim-wēriġne;   ġestōdon him æt his
                    līċes hēafdum;
behēoldon hīe þǣr heofones Dryhten,   and hē hine þǣr
                    hwīle reste,
65   mēðe æfter þam miċlan ġewinne.   Ongunnon him þā
                  mold-ærn wyrċan
beornas on banan ġesihþe,   curfon hīe þæt of beorhtan stāne;

Emendations: **47** ænigum] MS nænigum.   **59** sorgum] *not in* MS.

Variant spellings: **46** -drifan. hi. deorcan. syndon.   **47** inwid-.
sceðð an.   **48** Bysmeredon. bestemed.   **50** Feala.   **51** weruda.
52 Þystro.   **54** sceadu.   **55** eal.   **56** fyll.   **57** Hwæðere. cwoman.
60 mycle.   **61** hefian.   **63** Aledon.   **64** heofenes.   **65** moldærn
altered to moldern.   **66** gesyhðe.

ġesetton hīe þǣr-on sigora Wealdend.   Ongunnon him þā
                                sorg-lēoþ galan,
earme on þā ǣfen-tīde,   þā hīe woldon eft sīðian,
mēðe fram þam mǣran þēodne;   reste hē þǣr mǣte weorode.

70   Hwæðre wē þǣr grēotende   gōde hwīle
        stōdon on staðole.   Stefn upp ġewāt
        hilde-rinca.   Hrǣw cōlode,
        fæġer feorh-bold.   Þā ūs man fiellan ongann
        ealle to eorðan.   Þæt wæs eġeslīċ wyrd!

75   Bedealf ūs man on dēopan sēaðe.   Hwæðre mē þǣr
                              Dryhtnes þeġnas,
        frēondas ġefrugnon   *   *   *
          ġieredon mē   golde and seolfre.

         "Nū þū meaht ġehīeran,   hæleþ mīn se lēofa,
        þæt iċ bealu-wara weorc   ġebiden hæbbe,

80   sārra sorga.   Is nū sǣl cumen
        þæt mē weorðiaþ   wīde and sīde
        menn ofer moldan   and eall þēos mǣre ġesceaft,
        ġebiddaþ him to þissum bēacne.   On mē Bearn Godes
        þrōwode hwīle;   for-þon iċ þrymm-fæst nū

85   hlīfie under heofonum,   and iċ hǣlan mæġ
        ǣġhwelċne ānra,   þāra-þe him biþ eġesa to mē.
        Ġeō iċ wæs ġeworden   wīta heardost,
        lēodum lāðost,   ǣr-þon iċ him līfes weġ
        rihtne ġerȳmde,   reord-berendum.

90   Hwæt, mē þā ġeweorðode   wuldres Ealdor
        ofer holt-wudu,   heofon-rīċes Weard,
        swelċe swā hē his mōdor ēac,   Mārian selfe,
        ælmihtiġ God,   for ealle menn

Emendations: **70** greotende] MS reotende.   **71** stefn] MS syððan.
91 holt-] MS holm-.

Variant spellings: **67** sorh-.   **70** Hwæðere.   **71** up.   **73** feorg-.   fyllan.
ongan.   **76** gefrunon.   **77** gyredon.   **78** miht. gehyran.   **83** þyssum.
84 forþan. þrym-.   **85** hlifige. heofenum.   **86** æghwylcne.   **87** Geo] Iu.
88 ærþan.   **92** swylce. sylfe.

ġeweorðode   ofer eall wīfa cynn.

95   "Nū iċ þē hāte,   hæleþ mīn se lēofa,
þæt þū þās ġesihþe   secge mannum;
onwrēoh wordum   þæt hit is wuldres bēam,
sē-þe ælmihtiġ God   on þrōwode
for mann-cynnes   manigum synnum
100   and Ādames   eald-ġewyrhtum.
Dēaþ hē þær bieriġde;   hwæðre eft Dryhten arās
mid his miċlan meahte   mannum to helpe.
Hē þā on heofonas astāg.   Hider eft fundaþ
on þisne middan-ġeard   mann-cynn sēċan
105   on dōm-dæġe   Dryhten selfa,
ælmihtiġ God   and his englas mid,
þæt hē þonne wile dēman,   sē āg dōmes ġeweald,
ānra ġehwelċum,   swā hē him æror hēr
on þissum lænan   līfe ġe-earnaþ.
110   Ne mæġ þær æniġ   unforht wesan
for þam worde   þe se Wealdend cwiþ:
friġneþ hē for þære meniġe   hwær se mann sīe,
sē-þe for Dryhtnes naman   dēaðes wolde
biteres onbierġan,   swā hē ær on þam bēame dyde.
115   Ac hīe þonne forhtiaþ,   and fēa þenċaþ
hwæt hīe to Crīste   cweðan onġinnen.
Ne þearf þær þonne æniġ   anforht wesan
þē him ær on brēostum bereþ   bēacna sēlest.
Ac þurh þā rōde sceal   rīċe ġesēċan
120   of eorþ-weġe   æġhwelċ sāwol,
sēo-þe mid Wealdende   wunian þenċeþ."

Emendation: 117 anforht] MS unforht *(either a misleading spelling or an error).*

Variant spellings: 96 gesyhðe. 99 man-. manegum. 100 Adomes.
101 byrigde. hwæðere. 102 mihte. 103 heofenas. 104 þysne. man-.
105 sylfa. 107 ah. 108 gehwylcum. ærur. 109 þyssum. lænum.
111 cwyð. 112 frineð. mænige. man. 114 onbyrigan. 118 on] in.
120 æghwylc. sawl.

Ġebǣd iċ mē þā to þam bēame   blīðe mōde,
elne miċle, þǣr iċ āna wæs
mǣte weorode; wæs mōd-sefa
125 afȳsed on forþ-weġ; fela ealra ġebād
langung-hwīla. Is mē nū līfes hyht
þæt iċ þone siġe-bēam sēċan mōte,
āna oftor þonne ealle menn
wēl weorðian; mē is willa to þām
130 miċel on mōde, and mīn mund-byrd is
ġeriht to þǣre rōde. Nāg iċ rīċra fela
frēonda on foldan. Ac hīe forþ heonan
ġewiton of weorolde drēamum, sōhton him wuldres Cyning;
libbaþ nū on heofonum mid Hēah-Fædere,
135 wuniaþ on wuldre; and iċ wēne mē
daga ġehwelċe hwonne mē Dryhtnes rōd,
þē iċ hēr on eorðan ǣr scēawode,
on þissum lǣnan līfe ġefeċċe,
and mē þonne ġebringe þǣr is bliss miċel,
140 drēam on heofonum, þǣr is Dryhtnes folc
ġeseted to symble, þǣr is singāl bliss;
and mē þonne asette þǣr iċ siþþan mōt
wunian on wuldre, wēl mid þam hālgum
drēames brūcan. Sīe mē Dryhten frēond,
145 sē-þe hēr on eorðan ǣr þrōwode
on þam ġealg-trēowe for guman synnum:
hē ūs onlīesde, and ūs līf forġeaf,
heofonlīcne hām. Hyht wæs ġenīewod

Emendations: **125** -weg] MS -wege.   **142** me] MS he.

Variant spellings: **122** þan.   **123** mycle.   **124** werede.   **128** men.
129 well.   **130** mycel.   **131** Nah. feala.   **132** heonon.   **133** worulde.
134 lifiaþ. heofenum.   **136** gehwylce. hwænne.   **138** þysson. gefetige.
139 blis. mycel.   **141** symle. blis.   **142** syþþan.   **143** well.
144 Si.   **147** onlysde.   **148** Hiht. geniwad.

mid blǣdum and mid blisse, þām-þe þǣr bryne þolodon.
150 Se Sunu wæs sigor-fæst on þam sīþ-fǣte,
mihtiġ and spēdiġ, þā hē mid meniġe cōm,
gāsta weorode, on Godes rīċe,
Anwealda ælmihtiġ, englum to blisse,
and eallum þam hālgum þām-þe on heofonum ǣr
155 wunodon on wuldre, þā hira Wealdend cōm,
ælmihtiġ God, þǣr his ēðel wæs.

Variant spellings: **149** bledum. þolodan. **150** -fate. **151** manigeo.
155 wunedon. heora. cwom.

The Battle of Maldon

(*Bodleian Library, MS Rawlinson B. 203, pp. 7–12,
a transcript made about 1724 by John Elphinston
from the incomplete eleventh-century manuscript,
Cotton Otho A. xii, burned in 1731.*)

* * * brocen wurde.

Hēt þā hyssa hwone   hors forlǣtan,
feorr afȳsan   and forþ gangan,
hycgan to handum   and to hyġe gōdum.

5 Þā þæt Offan mǣġ   ǣrest onfunde,
þæt se eorl nolde   iergþe ġeþolian,
hē lēt him þā of handum   lēofne flēogan
hafoc wiþ þæs holtes   and to þǣre hilde stōp;
be þām man meahte oncnāwan   þæt se cniht nolde
10 wācian æt þam wīġe   þā hē to wǣpnum fēng.

Ēac him wolde Ēadrīċ   his ealdre ġelǣstan,
frēan to ġefeohte,   ongann þā forþ beran
gār to gūðe.   Hē hæfde gōd ġeþanc
þā hwīle þe hē mid handum   healdan meahte
15 bord and brād sweord;   bēot hē ġelǣste
þā hē ætforan his frēan   feohtan scolde.

Þā þǣr Byrhtnōþ ongann   beornas trymian,
rād and rǣdde,   rincum tǣhte
hū hīe scoldon standan   and þone stede healdan,

Emendations and restorations (E = Elphinston's transcript):
4*b* to] E t.   5 Þa] E þ.   10 wige] E w . . . ge.

Variant spellings: 2 hwæne.   3 feor.   4 hicgan. hige   6 yrhðo.
7 handon.   9 mihte.   10 w(ig)ge.   12 ongan.   14 mihte.   15 swurd.
16 sceolde.   17 ongan.   19 sceoldon.

20 and bæd þæt hira randas rihte hēolden
  fæste mid folmum and ne forhtoden nā.
  Þā hē hæfde þæt folc fægere ġetrymed,
  hē līehte þā mid lēodum þǣr him lēofost wæs,
  þǣr hē his heorþ-weorod holdost wisse.

25 Þā stōd on stæðe, stīþlīċe clipode
  wīċinga ār, wordum mǣlde,
  sē on bēot abēad brim-līðendra
  ǣrende to þam eorle þǣr hē on ōfre stōd:
  "Mē sendon to þē sǣ-menn snelle,
30 hēton þē secgan þæt þū mōst sendan hræðe
  bēagas wiþ ġebeorge; and ēow betere is
  þæt ġē þisne gār-rǣs mid gafole forġielden
  þonne wē swā hearde hilde dǣlen.
  Ne þurfe wē ūs spillan ġif ġē spēdaþ to þām;
35 wē willaþ wiþ þam golde griþ fæstnian.
  Ġif þū þæt ġerǣdest, þe hēr rīċost eart,
  þæt þū þīne lēode līesan wille,
  sellan sǣ-mannum on hira selfra dōm
  feoh wiþ frēode and niman friþ æt ūs,
40 wē willaþ mid þam sceattum ūs to scipe gangan,
  on flot fēran, and ēow friðes healdan."

  Byrhtnōþ maðelode, bord hafenode,
  wand wācne æsc, wordum mǣlde
  ierre and anrǣd, aġeaf him andsware:
45 "Ġehīerst þū, sǣ-lida, hwæt þis folc sæġeþ?
  Hīe willaþ ēow to gafole gāras sellan,

Emendations and restorations: 20 randas] E randan. 33 þonne] E þon.
hilde] E . .ulde. 36 þæt] E þat.

Variant spellings: 20 hyra. heoldon. 21 folman. forhtedon. 22 getrymmed.
23 lihte. leodon. 24 -werod. wiste. 25 clypode. 28 ærænde. 29 -men.
30 raðe. 32 forgyldon. 33 dælon. 36 Gyf. 37 leoda. lysan. 38 syllan.
hyra. sylfra. 40 scype. 44 yrre. 45 Gehyrst. segeð. 46 Hi. syllan.

ǣtrenne ord   and ealde sweord,
þā here-ġeatwe   þe ēow æt hilde ne dēag.
Brim-manna boda,   abēod eft ongēan,
50   sæġe þīnum lēodum   miċle lāðre spell,
þæt hēr stent unforcūþ   eorl mid his weorode,
þe wile ealgian   ēðel þisne,
Æðelrēdes eard   ealdres mīnes,
folc and foldan.   Feallan sculon
55   hǣðne æt hilde.   Tō hēanlīċ mē þynċeþ
þæt ġē mid ūrum sceattum   to scipe gangen
unbefohtne,   nū ġē þus feorr hider
on ūrne eard   inn becōmon.
Ne scule ġē swā sōfte   sinc ġegangan;
60   ūs sceal ord and ecg   ǣr ġesēman,
grimm gūþ-plega,   ǣr wē gafol sellen."
     Hēt þā bord beran,   beornas gangan
þæt hīe on þam ēa-stæðe   ealle stōden.
Ne meahte þǣr for wætere   weorod to þam ōðrum;
65   þǣr cōm flōwende   flōd æfter ebban,
lucon lagu-strēamas.   Tō lang hit him þūhte
hwonne hīe togædere   gāras bǣren.
Hīe þǣr Pantan strēam   mid prasse bestōdon,
Ēast-Seaxna ord   and se æsc-here.
70   Ne meahte hira ǣniġ   ōðrum derian
būtan hwā þurh flānes flyht   fiell ġenāme.
     Se flōd ūt ġewāt.   Þā flotan stōdon ġearwe,
wīċinga fela,   wīġes ġeorne.
Hēt þā hæleða hlēo   healdan þā brycge

Emendations and restorations: **61** we] E þe

Variant spellings: **47** ættrynne. swurd.   **48** -geatu. deah.   **50** sege.
miccle.   **51** stynt. werode.   **52** gealgean. þysne.   **54** sceolon.
55 hæþene. þinceð.   **56** scype. gangon.   **57** unbefohtene. feor   **58** in.
59 sceole.   **61** grim. gofol. syllon.   **63** hi. -steðe. stodon.   **64** mihte. werod.
67 hwænne. hi. beron.   **68** Hi.   **69** -seaxena.   **70** mihte. hyra.   **71** buton. fyl.
72 gearowe.   **74** bricge.

75 wigan wīġ-heardne —sē wæs hāten Wulfstān—
cāfne mid his cynne; þæt wæs Ċēolan sunu,
þe þone forman mann mid his francan ofscēat
þe þǣr bealdlīcost on þā brycge stōp.
Þǣr stōdon mid Wulfstāne wigan unforhte,
80 Ælfhere and Maccus, mōdġe twēġen;
þā noldon æt þam forda flēam ġewyrċan,
ac hīe fæstlīċe wiþ þā fīend weredon
þā hwīle þe hīe wǣpna wealdan mōston.
   Þā hīe þæt onġēaton and ġeorne ġesāwon
85 þæt hīe þǣr brycg-weardas bitere fundon,
ongunnon lytiġian þā lāðe ġiestas,
bǣdon þæt hīe upp-gang āgan mōsten,
ofer þone ford faran, fēðan lǣdan.
   Þā se eorl ongann for his ofermōde
90 alīefan landes tō fela lāðre þēode.
Ongann ċeallian þā ofer ċeald wæter
Byrhthelmes bearn —beornas ġehlyston—:
"Nū ēow is ġerȳmed; gāþ recene to ūs,
guman to gūðe. God āna wāt
95 hwā þǣre wæl-stōwe wealdan mōte."
   Wōdon þā wæl-wulfas —for wætere ne murnon—
wīċinga weorod, west ofer Pantan,
ofer scīr wæter scieldas wǣgon,
lid-menn to lande linda bǣron.
100 Þǣr onġēan gramum ġearwe stōdon
Byrhtnōþ mid beornum; hē mid bordum hēt

Emendations: 87 upp-gang] E upgangan.
97 west] E pest (?—*Dobbie thinks* west *was intended*).

Variant spellings: 77 man. 78 baldlicost. bricge. 80 Ælfere.
modige. 82 hi. fynd. 83 hi. 84 hi. 85 hi. bricg-.
86 lyteġian. gystas. 87 hi. moston. 89 ongan. 90 alyfan.
laþere. 91 ongan. cald. 92 Byrhtelmes. 93 ricene. 97 werod.
98 scyldas. wegon. 99 -men. linde. 100 gearowe.

wyrćan þone wīġ-hagan   and þæt weorod healdan
fæste wiþ fēondum.   Þā wæs feohte nēah,
tīr æt ġetohte.   Wæs sēo tīd cumen
105   þæt þǣr fǣġe menn   feallan scoldon.
Þǣr wearþ hrēam ahafen,   hræfnas wundon,
earn ǣses ġeorn.   Wæs on eorðan ćierm.

Hīe lēton þā of folmum   fēol-hearde speru,
grimme ġegrundne   gāras flēogan.
110   Bogan wǣron bisiġe,   bord ord onfēng.
Biter wæs se beadu-rǣs,   beornas fēollon
on ġehwæðere hand,   hyssas lāgon.

Wund wearþ Wulfmǣr,   wæl-reste ġećēas,
Byrhtnōðes mǣġ;   hē mid billum wearþ,
115   his sweostor sunu,   swīðe forhēawen.
Þǣr wearþ wīćingum   wiðerlēan aġiefen.
Ġehīerde ić þæt Ēadweard   ānne slōge
swīðe mid his sweorde,   swenġes ne wiernde,
þæt him æt fōtum fēoll   fǣġe cempa;
120   þæs him his þēoden   þanc ġesæġde,
þam būr-þeġne,   þā hē byre hæfde.

Swā stefnetton   stīþ-hycgende
hyssas æt hilde,   hogodon ġeorne
hwā þǣr mid orde   ǣrest meahte
125   on fǣġan menn   feorh ġewinnan,
wigan mid wǣpnum;   wæl fēoll on eorðan.
Stōdon stede-fæste;   stihte hīe Byrhtnōþ,
bæd þæt hyssa ġehwelć   hogode to wīġe,

Emendations: **103** feohte] E fohte.   **109** grimme] *not in* E.
113 wearþ] E weard.   **116** wearþ] E wærd.

Variant spellings: **102** wi-. werod.   **103** neh.   **105** men. sceoldon.
106 hremmas.   **107** cyrm.   **108** Hi. folman.   **109** gegrundene.
110 bysige.   **113** -ræste.   **115** swuster-.   **116** agyfen.   **117** gehyrde.
118 swurde. wyrnde.   **120** gesæde.   **121** -þene.   **122** stemnetton.
-hicgende.   **123** hysas.   **124** ærost. mihte.   **125** fægean. men.   **126** feol.
127 stæde-. hi.   **128** gehwylc.

þe on Denum wolde   dōm ġefeohtan.

130 Wōd þā wīġes heard,   wǣpen upp ahōf,
bord to ġebeorge,   and wiþ þæs beornes stōp.
Ēode swā anrǣd ˙eorl to þam ċeorle,
ǣġðer hira ōðrum   yfeles hogode.
Sende þā se sǣ-rinc   sūðerne gār,

135 þæt ġewundod wearþ   wiġena hlāford.
Hē scēaf þā mid þam scielde   þæt se sceaft tobærst
and þæt spere sprenġde   þæt hit sprang onġēan.
Ġegremed wearþ se gūþ-rinc;   hē mid gāre stang
wlancne wīċing   þe him þā wunde forġeaf.

140 Frōd wæs se fierd-rinc;   hē lēt his francan wadan
þurh þæs hysses heals,   hand wīsode
þæt hē on þam fǣr-scaðan   feorh ġerǣhte.
Þā hē ōðerne   ofostlīċe scēat
þæt sēo byrne tobærst;   hē wæs on brēostum wund

145 þurh þā hring-locan,   him æt heortan stōd
ǣterne ord.   Se eorl wæs þȳ blīðra,
hlōg þā mōdiġ mann,   sæġde Metode þanc
þæs dæġ-weorces   þe him Dryhten forġeaf.
Forlēt þā drenga sum   daroþ of handa

150 flēogan of folman,   þæt sē tō forþ ġewāt
þurh þone æðelan   Æðelrēdes þeġn.
Him be healfe stōd   hyse unweaxen,
cniht on ġecampe,   sē full cāflīċe
brǣġd of þam beorne   blōdiġne gār,

155 Wulfstānes bearn,   Wulfmǣr se ġeonga
forlēt forheardne   faran eft onġēan;
ord inn ġewōd   þæt sē on eorðan læġ
þe his þēoden ǣr   þearle ġerǣhte.

Variant spellings: **129** Denon.   **130** up.   **133** hyra.   **136** scylde.
138 Gegremod.   **140** fyrd-.   **141** hals.   **142** -sceaðan.   **143** ofstlice.
146 ætterne.   þe.   **147** hloh.   modi.   man.   sæde.   **148** Drihten.
151 þegen.   **154** brǣd.   **157** in.

Ēode þā ġesierwed   secg to þam eorle;
160 hē wolde þæs beornes   bēagas ġefeċċan,
rēaf and hringas   and ġereġnod sweord.
Þā Byrhtnōþ bræġd   bill of sċēaðe,
brād and brūn-ecg,   and on þā byrnan slōg.
Tō hræðe hine ġelette   lid-manna sum
165 þā hē þæs eorles   earm amierde.
Fēoll þā to foldan   fealu-hilte sweord,
ne meahte hē ġehealdan   heardne mēċe,
wǣpnes wealdan.   Þā-ġīet þæt word ġecwæþ
hār hilde-rinc,   hyssas bielde,
170 bæd gangan forþ   gōde ġefēran;
ne meahte þā on fōtum lenġ   fæste ġestandan.
Hē to heofonum wlāt:
"Iċ ġeþancie þē,   þēoda Wealdend,
ealra þāra wynna   þē iċ on weorolde ġebād.
175 Nū iċ āg, milde Metod,   mǣste þearfe
þæt þū mīnum gāste   gōdes ġe-unne,
þæt mīn sāwol to þē   sīðian mōte
on þīn ġeweald, Þēoden engla,
mid friðe ferian.   Iċ eom frymdiġ to þē
180 þæt hīe hell-scaðan   hīenan ne mōten."
Þā hine hēowon   hæðne scealcas,
and bēġen þā beornas   þe him bī stōdon,
Ælfnōþ and Wulfmǣr   bēġen lāgon,
þā on-efen hira frēan   feorh ġesealdon.

Emendations: **171** gestandan] E ge stundan.   **173** Ic geþancie] E ge
þance (*but there is probably a considerable loss here*).

Variant spellings: **159** gesyrwed.   **160** gefecgan.   **161** gerenod.   swurd.
162 brǣd.   sceðe.   **163** -eccg.   sloh.   **164** raþe.   **165** amyrde.
166 fealo-.   swurd.   **167** mihte.   **168** -gyt.   **169** bylde.   **171** mihte.
172 heofenum.   **173** Waldend.   **174** þǣra.   worulde.   **175** ah.
177 sawul.   **179** frymdi.   **180** hi.   helsceaðan.   hynan.   moton.   **181** hæðene.
182 big.   **183** Wulmǣr.   **184** onemn.   hyra.

185   Hīe bugon þā fram beadwe þe þǣr bēon noldon.
      Þǣr wearþ Oddan beárn ǣrest on flēame,
      Godrīc fram gūðe, and þone gōdan forlēt
      þe him maniġne oft mearh ġesealde;
      hē ġehlēop þone eoh þe āhte his hlāford,
190   on þām ġerǣdum þe hit riht ne wæs,
      and his brōðru mid him bēġen ærndon,
      Godwine and Godwīġ, gūðe ne ġīemdon,
      ac wendon fram þam wīġe and þone wudu sōhton,
      flugon on þæt fæsten and hira feore burgon,
195   and manna mā þonne hit ǣniġ mǣþ wǣre,
      ġif hīe þā ġe-earnunga ealle ġemunden
      þe hē him to duguðe ġedōn hæfde.
      Swā him Offa on dæġ ǣr asæġde
      on þam mæðel-stede þā hē ġemōt hæfde,
200   þæt þǣr mōdiġlīce maniġe sprǣcon
      þe eft æt þearfe þolian noldon.

      Þā wearþ afeallen þæs folces ealdor,
      Æðelrēdes eorl; ealle ġesāwon
      heorþ-ġenēatas þæt hira hearra læġ.
205   Þā þǣr wendon forþ wlance þeġnas,
      unearge menn efston ġeorne;
      hīe woldon þā ealle ōðer twēġa:
      līf forlǣtan oþþe lēofne ġewrecan.
      Swā hīe bielde forþ bearn Ælfrīces,
210   wiga wintrum ġeong, wordum mǣlde;
      Ælfwine þā cwæþ, hē on ellen sprǣc:

Emendations: **186** wearþ] E wurdon.   **191** ærndon] E ærdon.
192 Godwine] E godrinc. **201** þearfe] E þære. **208** forlǣtan] E for
lætun.

Variant spellings: **185** Hi. beaduwe. **188** mænigne. mear. **192** gymdon.
194 hyra. **196** gyf. hi. gemundon. **198** asæde. **199** meþel-. **200** modelice.
mancga. **204** hyra. heorra. **205** þegenas. **206** men.
207 hi. **209** hi. bylde.

"Gemunaþ þāra mǣla   þe wē oft æt medu sprǣcon,
þonne wē on benċe   bēot ahōfon,
hæleþ on healle,   ymbe heard ġewinn;
215   nū mæġ cunnian   hwā cēne sīe.
Iċ wille mīne æðelu   eallum ġecȳðan,
þæt iċ wæs on Mierċum   miċles cynnes;
wæs mīn ealda fæder   Ealhhelm hāten,
wīs ealdor-mann   weorold-ġesǣliġ.
220   Ne sculon mē on þǣre þēode   þeġnas ætwītan
þæt iċ of þisse fierde   fēran wille,
eard ġesēċan,   nū mīn ealdor liġeþ
forhēawen æt hilde.   Mē is þæt hearma mǣst;
hē wæs ǣġðer mīn mæġ   and mīn hlāford."
225   Þā hē forþ ēode,   fǣhþe ġemunde,
þæt hē mid orde   ānne ġerǣhte
flotan on þam folce,   þæt sē on foldan læġ
forweġen mid his wǣpne.   Ongann þā winas manian,
frīend and ġefēran,   þæt hīe forþ ēoden.
230   Offa ġemǣlde,   æsc-holt ascōc:
"Hwæt þū, Ælfwine, hafast   ealle ġemanode
þeġnas to þearfe.   Nū ūre þēoden liġeþ,
eorl on eorðan,   ūs is eallum þearf
þæt ūre ǣġhwelċ   ōðerne bielde
235   wigan to wīġe,   þā hwīle þe hē wǣpen mæġe
habban and healdan,   heardne mēċe,
gār and gōd sweord.   Ūs Godrīċ hafaþ,
earg Oddan bearn,   ealle beswicene.
Wēnde þæs formaniġ mann,   þā hē on mēare rād,
240   on wlancan þam wicge,   þæt wǣre hit ūre hlāford.

Emendations: 212 Gemunaþ þara] E ge munu þa.   224 ægðer] E ægder.
Variant spellings: 212 meodo.   215 sy.   216 wylle. æþelo.   217 Myrcon.
miccles.   218 Ealhelm.   219 -mann.   woruld-.   220 sceolon. þegenas.
221 fyrde.   228 Ongan.   229 frynd. hi. eodon.   230 asceoc.   232 þegenas.
lið.   234 æghwylc. bylde.   237 swurd. hæfð.   238 earh.
239 formoni. man.

For-þon wearþ hēr on felda   folc totwǣmed,
scield-burh tobrocen.   Abrēoðe his anġinn,
þæt hē hēr swā maniġne   mann aflīemde!"
      Lēofsunu ġemǣlde   and his linde ahōf,
245 bord to ġebeorge;   hē þam beorne oncwæþ:
"Iċ þæt ġehāte,   þæt iċ heonan nylle
flēon fōtes trem,   ac wille furðor gān,
wrecan on ġewinne   mīnne wine-dryhten.
Ne þurfon mē ymbe Stūrmere   stede-fæste hæleþ
250 wordum ætwītan,   nū mīn wine ġecrang,
þæt iċ hlāford-lēas   hām sīðie,
wende fram wīġe;   ac mē sceal wǣpen niman,
ord and īren."   Hē full ierre wōd,
feaht fæstlīċe,   flēam hē forhogode.
255   Dunnere þā cwæþ,   daroþ acweahte,
unorne ċeorl,   ofer eall clipode,
bæd þæt beorna ġehwelċ   Byrhtnōþ wrǣce:
"Ne mæġ nā wandian   sē-þe wrecan þenċeþ
frēan on folce,   nē for feore murnan."
260 Þā hīe forþ ēodon,   feores hīe ne rōhton;
ongunnon þā hīred-menn   heardlīċe feohtan,
grame gār-berend,   and God bǣdon
þæt hīe mōsten ġewrecan   hira wine-dryhten
and on hira fēondum   fiell ġewyrċan.
265   Him se ġīsel ongann   ġeornlīċe fylstan;
hē wæs on Norþ-Hymbrum   heardes cynnes,
Ecglāfes bearn;   him wæs Æscferhþ nama.
Hē ne wandode nā   æt þam wīġ-plegan,
ac hē fȳsde forþ   flān ġeneahhe;

Variant spellings: 241 -þan.   242 scyldburh.   angin.   243 man.   aflymde.
246 heonon.   nelle.   247 trym.   248 -drihten.   249 embe.   hælæð.
250 gecranc.   253 ful.   yrre.   255 acwehte.   256 clypode.   257 gehwylc.
260 hi.   hi.   261 -men.   263 hi.   moston.   hyra.   -drihten.   264 hyra.   fyl.
265 gysel.   ongan.   266 Norðhymbron.   267 Æscferð.   269 genehe.

270   hwīlum hē on bord scēat,   hwīlum beorn tǣsde,
        ǣfre ymbe stunde   hē sealde sume wunde
        þā hwīle þē hē wǣpna   wealdan mōste.

        Þā-ġīet on orde stōd   Ēadweard se langa,
        ġearu and ġeornfull,   ġielp-wordum sprǣc
275   þæt hē nolde flēogan   fōt-mǣl landes,
        ofer bæc būgan,   þā his betera læġ.

        Hē bræc þone bord-weall   and wiþ þā beornas feaht
        oþ-þæt hē his sinc-ġiefan   on þam sǣ-mannum
        weorþlīċe wræc   ǣr hē on wæle lāge.

280   Swā dyde Æðelrīċ,   æðele ġefēra,
        fūs and forþ-ġeorn   feaht eornoste;
        Siġebyrhtes brōðor   and swīðe maniġ ōðer
        clufon cellod bord,   cēne hīe weredon.

           *   *   *   *

        Bærst bordes læriġ,   and sēo byrne sang
285   gryre-lēoða sum.   Þā æt gūðe slōg
        Offa þone sǣ-lidan   þæt hē on eorðan fēoll,
        and þǣr Gaddes mǣġ   grund ġesōhte.

        Hræðe wearþ æt hilde   Offa forhēawen;
        hē hæfde þēah ġeforðod   þæt hē his frēan ġehēt,
290   swā hē bēotode ǣr   wiþ his bēag-ġiefan,
        þæt hīe scolden bēġen   on burg rīdan
        hāle to hāme   oþþe on here cringan,
        on wæl-stōwe   wundum sweltan;
        hē læġ þeġnlīċe   þēodne ġehende.

295   Þā wearþ borda ġebræc.   Brim-menn wōdon,
        gūðe ġegremede;   gār oft þurhwōd
        fǣġes feorh-hūs.   Forþ þā ēode Wīstān,

Emendations: **283** *No sign of loss after this line in E, but the context indicates that some lines describing a viking's attack on Offa are missing.* **292** cringan] E crintgan (*for* crincgan). **297** Forþ þa] E forða.

Variant spellings: **270** hwilon. hwilon. **271** embe. **273** -gyt. **274** gearo. geornful. gylp-. **276** leg. **278** -gyfan. **279** wurðlice. wrec. læge. **282** Sibyrhtes. mænig. **283** hi. **285** sloh. **288** raðe. **290** beahgifan. **291** hi. sceoldon. burh. **294** ðegenlice. **295** -men. **296** gegremode.

Þurstānes sunu, wiþ þās secgas feaht;
hē wæs on ġeþrange hira þrēora bana
300 ǣr him Wīġhelmes bearn on þam wæle lāge.
Þǣr wæs stīþ ġemōt; stōdon fæste
wigan on ġewinne, wīġend crungon
wundum wērġe. Wæl fēoll on eorðan.

Ōswold and Ēadwold ealle hwīle,
305 bēġen þā ġebrōðru, beornas trymedon,
hira wine-māgas wordum bǣdon
þæt hīe þǣr æt þearfe þolian scolden,
unwāclīċe wǣpna nēotan.

Byrhtwold maðelode, bord hafenode—
310 sē wæs eald ġenēat— æsc acweahte;
hē full bealdlīċe beornas lǣrde:
"Hyġe sceal þȳ heardra, heorte þȳ cēnre,
mōd sceal þȳ māre þȳ ūre mæġen lȳtlaþ.
Hēr liġeþ ūre ealdor eall forhēawen,
315 gōd on grēote. Ā mæġ gnornian
sē-þe nū fram þȳs wīġ-plegan wendan þenċeþ.
Iċ eom frōd feores; fram iċ ne wille,
ac iċ mē be healfe mīnum hlāforde,
be swā lēofum menn licgan þenċe."
320 Swā hīe Æðelgāres bearn ealle bielde,
Godrīċ to gūðe. Oft hē gār forlēt
wæl-spere windan on þā wiċingas;
swā hē on þam folce fyrmest ēode,
hēow and hīende, oþ-þæt hē on hilde ġecrang.
325 Næs þæt nā sē Godrīċ þe þā gūðe forbēag * * *

Emendations: 299 geþrange] E geþrang. 300 Wighelmes]
E wigelines (defended as a name by Dobbie, but very
likely a misreading of wigelmes). 324 oþ-] E oð. 325 guðc] E gude.

Variant spellings: 298 suna. 299 hyra. 300 læge. 302 cruncon.
303 werige. feol. 306 hyra. wordon. 307 hi. sccoldon. 310 acwehte.
311 ful. baldlice. 312 Hige. þc. þe. 313 þe. þe. 314 lið.
316 þis. 319 leofan. men. 320 hi. bylde. 324 hynde. gecranc.
325 forbeah.

The Wanderer

(*Exeter Book*, ff. 76ᵛ–78ʳ)

"Oft him ān-haga āre ġebīdeþ,
Metodes mildse, þēah-þe hē mōd-ċeariġ
ġeond lagu-lāde lange scolde
hrēran mid handum hrīm-ċealde sǣ,

5   wadan wræc-lāstas. Wyrd biþ full arǣd."
—Swā cwæþ eard-stapa earfoða ġemyndiġ,
wrāðra wæl-sleahta, wine-māga hryre.—
"Oft iċ scolde āna ūhtna ġehwelċe
mīne ċeare cwīðan; nis nū cwicra nān

10   þe iċ him mōd-sefan mīnne durre
sweotule asecgan. Iċ to sōðe wāt
þæt biþ on eorle indryhten þēaw
þæt hē his ferhþ-locan fæste binde,
healde his hord-cofan, hycge swā hē wille.

15   Ne mæġ wēriġ-mōd wyrde wiþstandan
nē se hrēo hyġe helpe ġefremman.
For-þon dōm-ġeorne drēoriġne oft
on hira brēost-cofan bindaþ fæste.
   "Swā iċ mōd-sefan mīnne scolde,

20   oft earm-ċeariġ, ēðle bedǣled,
frēo-māgum feorr, feterum sǣlan,

Emendations: **14** healde] MS healdne.

Variant spellings in the MS: **2** metudes. miltse. **3** longe. sceolde.
4 hondum. **5** ful. **6** earfeþa. **7** -mæga. **8** sceolde. gehwylce. **12** in.
13 ferð-. **15** -stondan. **18** in. hyra. **19** sceolde. **20** bidæled.
21 -mægum. feor.

28

siþþan ġēara ġeō   gold-wine mīnne
hrūsan heolstre bewrāh,   and iċ hēan þanan
wōd winter-ċeariġ   ofer waðuma ġebind,
25   sōhte sele-drēoriġ   sinces bryttan
hwǣr iċ feorr oþþe nēah   findan meahte
þone-þe on medu-healle   mīne wisse
oþþe meċ frēond-lēasne   frēfran wolde,
wēman mid wynnum.—   Wāt sē-þe cunnaþ
30   hū slīðen biþ   sorg to ġefēran
þam-þe him lȳt hafaþ   lēofra ġeholena.
Waraþ hine wrǣc-lāst,   nealles wunden gold,
ferhþ-loca frēoriġ,   nealles foldan blǣd.
Ġeman hē sele-secgas   and sinc-þeġe,
35   hū hine on ġeoguðe   his gold-wine
wenede to wiste.   Wynn eal ġedrēas.
   "For-þon wāt sē-þe sceal   his wine-dryhtnes
lēofes lār-cwidum   lange forþolian,
þonne sorg and slǣp   samod ætgædere
40   earmne ān-hagan   oft ġebindaþ,
þynċeþ him on mōde   þæt hē his mann-dryhten
clyppe and cysse   and on cnēo lecge
handa and hēafod,   swā hē hwīlum ǣr
on ġēar-dagum   ġief-stōles brēac.
45   Þonne onwæcneþ eft   wine-lēas guma,
ġesiehþ him beforan   fealwe wǣgas,
baðian brim-fuglas,   brǣdan feðra,
hrēosan hrīm and snāw   hæġle ġemenġed.
   "Þonne bēoþ þȳ hefiġran   heortan benna,
50   sāre æfter swǣsne.   Sorg biþ ġenīewod

Emendations: 22 minne] MS mine.   24 waðuma] MS waþena.
28 -leasne] MS -lease.
   Variant spellings: 22 geo] iu.   23 biwrah. þonan.   26 feor.   27 in.
meodu-.   32 nales.   33 ferð-.   nalæs.   34 gemon.   36 wyn. eal.
38 longe.   39 somod. ætgædre.   40 anhogan.   41 þinceð. mon-.
43 honda.   44 in. -stolas.   46 gesihð. biforan. wegas.   48 hagle.
49 benne.   50 geniwad.

þonne māga ġemynd mōd ġeondhweorfeþ;
grēteþ glēo-stafum, ġeorne ġeondscēawaþ
secga ġeseldan. Swimmaþ eft on-weġ.
Flēotendra ferhþ nā þǣr fela bringeþ
55   cūðra cwide-ġiedda. Cearu biþ ġenīewod
þam-þe sendan sceal swīðe ġeneahhe
ofer waðuma ġebind wēriġne sefan."

"For-þon iċ ġeþenċan ne mæġ ġeond þās weorold
for-hwon mōd-sefa mīn ne ġesweorce
60   þonne iċ eorla līf eall ġeondþenċe,
hū hīe fǣrlīċe flett ofġēafon,
mōdġe magu-þeġnas. Swā þes middan-ġeard
ealra dōgra ġehwǣm drēoseþ and fealleþ;
for-þon ne mæġ weorðan wīs wer, ǣr hē āge
65   wintra dǣl on weorold-rīċe.— Wita sceal ġeþyldiġ,
nē sceal nā tō hāt-heort nē tō hræd-wyrde
nē tō wāc wīga nē tō wan-hyġdiġ
nē tō forht nē tō fæġen nē tō feoh-ġīfre
nē nǣfre ġielpes tō ġeorn ǣr hē ġeare cunne.
70   Beorn sceal ġebīdan, þonne hē bēot spriċeþ,
oþ-þæt collen-ferhþ cunne ġearwe
hwider hreðra ġehyġd hweorfan wille.
"Onġietan sceal glēaw hæle hū gǣstlīċ biþ
þonne eall þisse weorolde wela wēste standeþ,
75   swā nū missenlīċe ġeond þisne middan-ġeard
winde bewāwne weallas standaþ,
hrīme behrorene, hrīðġe þā eodoras.

Emendations: **53** eft] MS oft. **59** mod-sefa min ne] MS modsefan minne.
74 eall] MS ealle.

Variant spellings: **52** gliw-. **54** ferð. no. **55** cearo. geniwad.
57 waþema. **58** woruld. **59** forhwan. **60** eal. **61** hi. flet.
63 gehwam. **64** wearþan. **65** in. woruld. **66** no. **67** -hydig.
71 -ferð. **74** worulde. stondeð. **76** biwaune. stondaþ.
77 bihrorene. hryðge. ederas.

Wōriaþ þā wīn-salu,   wealdend licgaþ
drēame bedrorene,   duguþ eall ġecrang
80   wlanc be wealle.   Sume wīġ fornam,
ferede on forþ-weġ;   sumne fugol oþbær
ofer hēanne holm,   sumne se hāra wulf
Dēaðe ġedælde,   sumne drēoriġ-hlēor
on eorþ-scræfe   eorl ġehȳdde.

85   "Īeðde swā þisne eard-ġeard   ielda Scieppend,
oþ-þæt burg-wara   breahtma lēase,
eald enta ġeweorc   īdlu stōdon.
Sē þonne þisne weall-steall   wīse ġeþōhte
and þis deorce līf   dēope ġeondþenċeþ,
90   frōd on ferhþe,   feorr oft ġeman
wæl-sleahta worn   and þās word acwiþ:
'Hwær cōm mearh? Hwær cōm magu?   Hwær cōm
                                        māðum-ġiefa?
Hwær cōm symbla ġesetu?   Hwær sindon sele-drēamas?
Ēa-lā beorht bune!   Ēa-lā byrn-wiga!
95   Ēa-lā þēodnes þrymm!   Hū sēo þrāg ġewāt,
ġenāp under niht-helm,   swā hēo nā wære!
Standeþ nū on lāste   lēofre duguðe
weall wundrum hēah,   wyrm-līcum fāg.
Eorlas fornāmon   æsca þrȳðe,
100   wæpen wæl-ġīfru,   wyrd sēo mære,
and þās stān-hliðu   stormas cnyssaþ,
hrīþ hrēosende   hrūsan bindeþ,
wintres wōma,   þonne wann cymeþ,
nīpeþ niht-scua,   norðan onsendeþ

Emendations: 81 -weg] MS -wege.   89 deorce] MS deornce.
102 hrusan] MS hruse.

Variant spellings: 78 -salo. waldend.   79 bidrorene. eal. gecrong.
80 wlonc. bi. fornom.   81 in. fugel.   84 in.   85 yþde. ælda. scyppend.
88 weal-steal.   90 in. ferðe. feor. gemon.   92 cwom. mearg. cwom.
mago. cwom. maþþum-gyfa.   93 cwom.   95 þrym.   96 no.   97 Stondeð.
98 weal. fah.   99 fornoman. asca.   101 hleoþu.   103 won.

105   hrēo hæġl-fære,   hæleðum on andan.
        Eall is earfoþlīċ   eorðan rīċe,
        onwendeþ wyrda ġesceaft   weorold under heofonum.
        Hēr biþ feoh lǣne,   hēr biþ frēond lǣne,
        hēr biþ mann lǣne,   hēr biþ mæġ lǣne,
110   eall þis eorðan ġesteall   īdel weorðeþ.' "

        Swā cwæþ snottor on mōde,   ġesæt him sundor æt rūne.
        Til biþ sē-þe his trēowe ġehealdeþ,   nē sceal nǣfre his
                                                torn tō recene
        beorn of his brēostum acȳðan,   nefne hē ǣr þā bōte cunne
        eorl mid elne ġefremman.   Wēl biþ þam-þe him āre sēċeþ,
115   frōfre to Fæder on heofonum,   þǣr ūs eall sēo
                                                fæstnung standeþ.

        Variant spellings: 105 -fare.   107 weoruld.   109 mon.   110 eal.
        gesteal.   112 rycene.   113 nemþe.   115 eal.   stondeð.

The Seafarer

(*Exeter Book*, ff. 81ᵛ–83ʳ)

1st Seaf. "Mæġ iċ be mē selfum   sōþ-ġiedd wrecan,
            sīðas secgan,   hū iċ ġeswinċ-dagum
            earfoþ-hwīle   oft þrōwode,
            bitre brēost-ċeare   ġebiden hæbbe,
5   ġecunnod on ċēole   cear-selda fela,
            atol ȳða ġewealc,   þǣr meċ oft beġeat
            nearu niht-wacu   æt nacan stefnan,
            þonne hē be clifum cnossaþ.   Ċealde ġeþrungen
            wǣron mīne fēt,   forste ġebunden
10   ċealdum clammum,   þǣr þā ceara seofodon
            hāt' ymb heortan;   hungor innan slāt
            mere-wērġes mōd.   Þæt se mann ne wāt
            þe him on foldan   fæġrost limpeþ,
            hū iċ earm-ċeariġ   īs-ċealdne sǣ
15 †   winter wunode   wreċċan lāstum,
            wine-māgum bedroren,
            behangen hrīm-ġicelum;   hæġl scūrum flēag.
            Þǣr iċ ne ġehīerde   būtan hlimman sǣ,
            īs-ċealdne wǣġ.   Hwīlum ielfete sang

For the marginal directions and the punctuation see the notes. A dagger indicates a corrupt passage which the editor hesitates to emend. For suggestions see the notes.

Variant spellings in the MS: 1 sylfum. -gied. 3 þrowade.
5 gecunnad. in. 6 bigeat. 7 nearo. -waco. 8 calde. 10 caldum.
clommum. ceare. seofedun. 12 mon. 15 wunade. wrᴂccan.
16 -mᴂgum. bidroren. 17 bihongen. 18 gehyrde. 19 -caldne.
ylfete. song.

33

20   dyde iċ mē to gamene, ganotes hlēoðor
        and hwilpan swēġ fore hleahtor wera,
        mǣw singende fore medu-drince.
        Stormas þǣr stān-clifu bēoton, þǣr him stearn oncwæþ,
        īsiġ-feðra; full oft þæt earn beġeall,
25 †   ūriġ-feðra; nǣniġ hlēo-māga
        fēa-sceaftiġ ferhþ frēfran meahte.
        "For-þon him ġelīefeþ lȳt, sē-þe āg līfes wynn
        ġebiden on burgum, bealu-sīða hwōn,
        wlanc and wīn-gāl, hū iċ wēriġ oft
30   on brim-lāde bīdan scolde.
        Nāp niht-scua, norðan snīwde,
        hrīm hrūsan band, hæġl fēoll on eorðan,
        corna ċealdost."

2ND SEAF.   "For-þon cnyssaþ nū
        heortan ġeþōhtas þæt iċ hēan strēamas,
35   sealt-ȳða ġelāc self cunnie;
        manaþ mōdes lust mǣla ġehwelċe
        ferhþ to fēran, þæt iċ feorr heonan
        el-þēodiġra eard ġesēċe.
        For-þon nis þæs mōd-wlanc mann ofer eorðan,
40   nē his ġiefena þæs gōd, nē on ġeoguðe to þæs hwæt,
        nē on his dǣdum to þæs dēor, nē him his dryhten
                                        to þæs hold,
        þæt hē ā his sǣ-fōre sorge næbbe,
        to hwon hine Dryhten ġedōn wille.
        Nē biþ him to hearpan hyġe nē to hring-þeġe—

Emendation: **26** frefran] MS feran.

Variant spellings: **20** gomene. ganetes. **21** huilpan. **22** medo-.
23 beotan. **24** feðera. ful. bigeal. **25** -mæga. **26** ferð. **27** gelyfeð. ah.
wyn. **28** in. bealo-. **29** wlonc. **30** in. sceolde. **32** bond. feol.
33 caldast. **35** sylf. cunnige. **36** monað. gehwylce. **37** ferð.
feor. **39** -wlonc. mon. **40** gifena. in. **41** in.

45 nē to wīfe wynn   nē to weorolde hyht—
nē ymbe āwiht elles   nefne ymb ȳða ġewealc;
ac ā hafaþ langunge   sē-þe on lagu fundaþ.

"Bearwas blōstmum nimaþ,   byriġ fæġriaþ,
wangas wlitiġiaþ;   weorold ōnetteþ;
50 ealle þā ġemaniaþ   mōdes fūsne
sefan to sīðe   þam-þe swā þenċeþ
on flōd-wegas   feorr ġewītan.

Swelċe ġēac manaþ   ġeōmran reorde;
singeþ sumores weard,   sorge bēodeþ
55 bitre on brēost-hord.   Þæt se beorn ne wāt,
sēft-ēadiġ secg,   hwæt þā sume drēogaþ
þe þā wræc-lāstas   wīdost lecgaþ.

"For-þon nū mīn hyġe hweorfeþ   ofer hreðer-locan,
mīn mōd-sefa   mid mere-flōde,
60 ofer hwæles ēðel   hweorfeþ wīde,
eorðan sċēatas,   cymeþ eft to mē
ġīfre and grǣdiġ;   ġielleþ ān-floga,
hweteþ on hwæl-weġ   hreðer unwearnum
ofer holma ġelagu;—   for-þon mē hātran sind
65 Dryhtnes drēamas   þonne þis dēade līf
lǣne on lande.

"Iċ ġelīefe nā
þæt him eorþ-welan   ēċe standaþ.
Simble þrēora sum   þeġna ġehwelċum
ǣr his tīd-dæġe   to twēon weorðeþ:
70 ādl oþþe ieldu   oþþe ecg-hete
fǣgum framweardum   feorh oþ-þringeþ.

Emendations: **52** gewitan] MS gewitað.   **56** seft-eadig] MS eft eadig.   **63** hwæl-weg] MS wælweg.   **67** standaþ] MS stondeð.
68 þegna gehwelcum] MS þinga gehwylce.   **69** tid-dæge] MS tide ge.

Variant spellings: **45** wyn. worulde.   **46** owiht.   **47** longunge.
49 wongas. wlitigað. woruld.   **50** gemoniað.   **52** feor.   **53** swylce.
monað.   **54** sumeres.   **55** bitter (*perhaps an elided form of* bittere). in.
66 londe. gelyfe. no.   **68** simle.   **70** yldo.   **71** from-.

For-þon biþ eorla ġehwǣm   æfter-cweðendra,
lof libbendra   lāst-worda betst.

Þæt hē ġewyrċe,   ǣr hē on-weġ scyle,
75   fremum on foldan   wiþ fēonda nīþ,
dēorum dǣdum   dēofle toġēanes,
þæt hine ielda bearn   æfter herien,
and his lof siþþan   libbe mid englum
āwa to ealdre,   ēċan līfes blǣd,
80   drēam mid duguðum.

                    "Dagas sind ġewitene,
ealle anmēdlan   eorðan rīċes;
nearon nū cyningas   nē cāseras
nē gold-ġiefan   swelċe ġeō wǣron,
þonne hīe mǣst mid him   mǣrða ġefremedon
85   and on dryhtlīċestum   dōme lifdon.

Ġedroren is þēos duguþ eall,   drēamas sind ġewitene;
wuniaþ þā wācran   and þās weorold healdaþ,
brūcaþ þurh bisġu.   Blǣd is ġehnǣġed,
eorðan indryhtu   ealdaþ and sēaraþ,
90   swā nū manna ġehwelċ   ġeond middan-ġeard.

Ieldu him on fareþ,   ansīen blācaþ,
gamol-feax gnornaþ,   wāt his ġeō-wine,
æðelinga bearn   eorðan forġiefene.

Ne mæġ him þonne se flǣsc-hama,   þonne him
                        þæt feorh losaþ,
95   nē swēte forswelgan   nē sār ġefēlan
nē hand onhrēran   nē mid hyġe þenċan.

Þēah-þe græf wille   golde strēgan
brōðor his ġeborenum,   byrġan be dēadum

Emendations: **72** biþ] MS þæt.   **75** fremum] MS fremman.   **79** blæd]
MS blæð.   **82** nearon] MS næron.

Variant spellings: **72** gehwam.   **73** lifgendra.   **77** ælda. hergen.
78 lifge.   **80** dugeþum.   **81** onmedlan.   **83** swylce. iu.   **84** hi.
86 eal.   **87** woruld.   **88** bisgo.   **89** indryhto.   **90** monna. gehwylc.
91 yldo. onsyn.   **92** gomel-. iuwine.   **94** -homa. feorg.   **96** hond.

māðmum mislīcum,   þæt hine mid nyle;
100   ne mæġ þǣre sāwle   þe biþ synna full
gold to ġēoce   for Godes eġesan,
þonne hē hit ǣr hȳdeþ   þenden hē hēr leofaþ."

EPIL.   Miċel biþ sē Metodes eġesa,   for þon hīe sēo
molde onċierreþ;
sē ġestaðolode   stīðe grundas,
105   eorðan sċēatas   and upp-rodor.
Dol biþ sē-þe him his Dryhten ne ondrǣdeþ: cymeþ
him se dēaþ unþinġed.
Ēadiġ biþ sē-þe ēaþ-mōd leofaþ;
cymeþ him sēo ār of heofonum.
Metod him þæt mōd ġestaðolaþ,   for-þon hē on his
meahte ġelīefeþ.
Stīeran man sceal strangum mōde,   and þæt on
staðolum healdan,
110   and ġewiss wǣrum,   wīsum clǣne.
Scyle manna ġehwelċ   mid ġemete healdan
lufan wiþ lēofne   and wiþ lāðne bealu,
†   þēah-þe hē ne wille w——— fulne
oþþe on bǣle   forbærnedne
115   his ġeworhtne wine: wyrd biþ swīðre,
Metod mihtiġra,   þonne ǣnġes mannes ġehyġd.
Wuton wē hycgan   hwǣr wē hām āgen,
and þonne ġeþenċan   hū wē þider cumen;
and wē þonne ēac tilien   þæt wē tō mōten

Emendations: **99** nyle] MS wille.   **109** man] MS mod.   **112** lufan]
not in MS.   **113** ne] MS hine.   w——— (*some noun beginning with* w,
in the genitive)] MS fyres.   **115** swiðre] MS swire.   **117** hwær we]
MS. hwær se.

Variant spellings: **100** ful.   **101** egsan.   **103** meotudes.   egsa.   hi.
oncyrreð.   **104** gestaþelade.   **105** up-.   **108** meotod.   gestaþelað.
in.   gelyfeð.   **109** strongum.   staþelum.   **110** gewis.   werum.
111 monna.   gehwylc.   **112** bealo.   **116** meotud.   meahtigra.   monnes.
117 Uton.

120   on þā ēċan   ēadiġnesse
þǣr is līf ġelang   on lufan Dryhtnes,
hyht on heofonum.   Þæs sīe þam Halgan þanc,
þæt hē ūsiċ ġeweorðode,   wuldres Ealdor,
ēċe Dryhten,   on ealle tīd.

Amen.

Variant spellings: **120** in. **121** gelong. in. **122** in. sy. þonc.
123 geweorþade. **124** in.

Deor

(*Exeter Book*, f. 100^{r.v})

Wēland him be wearnum   wræces cunnode,
anhyġdiġ eorl,   earfoðu drēag,
hæfde him to ġesīðe   sorge and langoþ,
winter-ċealde wræce,   wēan oft onfand
5   siþþan hine Nīþhād on   nīeda leġde,
swancre sinu-benda,   on sēlran mann.
    Þæs oferēode;   þisses swā mæġ.

Beaduhilde ne wæs   hire brōðra dēaþ
on sefan swā sār   swā hire selfre þing,
10   þæt hēo ġearulīċe   onġieten hæfde
þæt hēo ēacen wæs;   æfre ne meahte
þrīste ġeþenċan   hū ymb þæt scolde.
    Þæs oferēode;   þisses swā mæġ.

Wē þæt Mæþhilde   māna ġefrugnon
15   wurdon grund-lēase,   Ġēates frīġe,
þæt hīe sēo sorg-lufu   slæp' ealle benam.
    Þæs oferēode;   þisses swā mæġ.

Þēodrīċ āhte   þrītiġ wintra
Mæringa burg;   þæt wæs manigum cūþ.

Emendations: 1 wearnum] MS wurman.   14 mana] MS monge.

Variant spellings in the MS: 1 Welund. cunnade.   2 anhydig.
earfoþa.   3 gesiþþe. longaþ.   4 onfond.   5 nede.   6 swoncre.
seonobende. syllan. monn.   8 Beado-. hyre.   9 hyre. sylfre.
10 gearo-.   12 sceolde.   16 hi. slæp. binom.   19 monegum.

20   Þæs oferēode;   þisses swā mæġ.

Wē ġe-āscodon   Eormanrīċes
wylfenne ġeþōht;   āhte wīde folc
Gotena rīċes;   þæt wæs grimm cyning.
Sæt secg maniġ   sorgum ġebunden,
25   wēan on wēnum,   wȳscte ġeneahhe
þæt þæs cyne-rīċes   ofercumen wǣre.
Þæs oferēode;   þisses swā mæġ.

Siteþ sorg-ċeariġ,   sǣlum bedǣled,
on sefan sweorceþ,   selfum þynċeþ
30   þæt sīe ende-lēas   earfoða dǣl,
mæġ þonne ġeþenċan   þæt ġeond þās weorold
wītiġ Dryhten   wendeþ ġeneahhe,
eorle manigum   āre ġescēawaþ,
wislīcne blǣd,   sumum wēana dǣl.

35   Þæt iċ be mē selfum   secgan wille,
þæt iċ hwīle wæs   Hedeninga scop,
dryhtne dīere;   mē wæs Dēor nama.
Āhte iċ fela wintra   folgoþ tilne,
holdne hlāford,   oþ-þæt Heorrenda nū,
40   lēoþ-cræftiġ mann,   land-riht ġeþeah
þæt mē eorla hlēo   ǣr ġesealde.
Þæs oferēode;   þisses swā mæġ.

Emendations: **25** wenum] MS wenan *(leveled ending or error)*.
30 earfoða] MS earfoda.

Variant spellings: **21** geascodan.   **23** grim.   **24** monig.   **28** bidæled.
29 sylfum. þinceð.   **30** sy.   **31** woruld.   **33·** monegum.   **35** bi.
sylfum.   **36** heodeninga.   **37** dyre. noma.   **38** folgað.   **40** monn.
londryht. geþah.

COMMENTARY

Old English poetry is descended from a preliterary stock once common to the Germanic tribes of the European continent. Its basic alliterative verse form appears with minor modifications in the oldest poetical remains of other Germanic peoples, High German and Saxon on the one hand, Scandinavian (chiefly Icelandic) on the other. Certain features of its diction, even verse formulas, besides many of its themes and stories, are similarly shared and betray a common inheritance supplemented now and then by early borrowing. In England itself the earliest poetry of the Anglo-Saxon settlers was necessarily composed orally, like that of their ancestors; and Bede's story of Cædmon indicates that even in his time it was often if not always sung or chanted to the accompaniment of the traditional Germanic instrument, the harp. It is probable that oral composition was practiced throughout the Anglo-Saxon period in spite of the introduction of writing; for writing was an art restricted to a relatively small portion of the population. How much of the output of unlettered singers may have found its way into books by dictation or by memorial reconstruction we have no reliable means of discovering; but it is evident from the style of the surviving poetry, with its use of a common verse form and its ready acceptance of a host of verse formulas, that the art of the oral practitioners has left its mark on even the most learned of the literary poets.

Writing as a literary art, in contrast to the old half-magical runic writing—confined to brief inscriptions—of the primitive Germanic peoples, was introduced among the Anglo-Saxons in the course of the seventh century by missionaries from the Mediterranean world and from Ireland. Englishmen were engaged in literary pursuits, writing in Latin or English, prose or verse, from about the middle of the seventh century onwards, so that we have some four centuries to reckon with before the Norman Conquest brought about the subversion of the old aristocracy and the beginnings of a new era. Culturally these were centuries marked by astonishing intellectual advances and sudden retrogressions, by sharp contrasts between the learned few, chiefly though not exclusively clerics, and the rest of society, but also in some quarters by a fruitful blending and assimilation. Old English poetry shows at times the collision, but often the harmonious fusion, of Christianity and a submerged paganism, Mediterranean civilization and a more primitive but not always inferior Germanic heritage.

Some thirty thousand lines of Old English poetry have come down to us out of an incalculably larger quantity.[1] Much of the best of it belongs, so far as we can tell, to the eighth and ninth centuries, but its broad characteristics are little changed from beginning to end; and the older works were still prized, as our manuscripts show, on the eve of the Conquest. The longest and finest of all the surviving poems is the three-thousand-line *Beowulf*, but there are many smaller pieces of distinction, among which the seven in this volume hold a high place. They very nearly span the four literary centuries. Cædmon's Hymn should have been composed about 665; *The Battle of Maldon*, shortly after 991. The others, some of which can be dated only within wide limits, fall between these extremes.

Among the numerous histories of Old English literature, the most recent and one of the most helpful is Stanley B. Greenfield's *A Critical History of Old English Literature* (New York University Press, 1965). For the poetry alone, a stimulating guide is Charles W. Kennedy's *The Earliest English Poetry* (New York: Oxford University Press, 1943). The great bulk and variety of writings that survive from the period, in both prose and verse, make it difficult for the student to get his bearings while he is still struggling with the language. A work of the first importance

---

[1] The standard collective edition is *The Anglo-Saxon Poetic Records* in six volumes, each with its own special title, edited by G. P. Krapp and E. V. K. Dobbie (New York: Columbia University Press, 1931–1953).

for both beginners and advanced students is *English Historical Documents*, Volume I, *ca.* 500–1042, edited by Dorothy Whitelock (London: Eyre and Spottiswood, 1955). This contains a very broad selection of documents, from laws and charters to letters, histories, sermons, and poems, admirably translated into modern English from Latin, Old English, and occasionally Old Norse. The introductions, notes, and bibliographies are of the highest quality. There could be no better guide to the general cultural background of Old English poetry.

Cædmon's Hymn

This little hymn has a peculiar importance among the relatively abundant relics of Old English poetry, an importance by no means limited to its modest charm or its supposedly miraculous origin. It has come down to us as the maiden effort of the first English poet to treat the major themes of the Christian religion, and although he is described as the author of a great many poems, this is the only surviving composition that can with any degree of assurance be attributed to him. Even the copies of it are notable, for the two oldest are our earliest manuscript records of Old English poetry. The hymn itself has a further interest: as the work of a man who had never learned to read and write, it affords a brief yet precious example of that orally composed poetry, largely unrecorded, by which the written poems were preceded and in all probability surrounded.

All our ancient copies of the hymn have been preserved in the manuscripts of Bede's *Ecclesiastical History of the English Nation*, either in its original Latin form [1] or in the Old English

1 *Historia Ecclesiastica Gentis Anglorum*, best edited by Charles Plummer, *Venerabilis Bedae Opera Historica*, 2 vols. (Oxford: The Clarendon Press, 1896).

version produced more than a century later; [2] and our knowledge of Cædmon himself depends entirely on a single chapter of that work. Bede completed the history about 731, some four years before his death. Cædmon had died long before, probably while Bede was still a boy, and there is nothing in Bede's account to suggest that the two had ever met; but they were both Northumbrians, and Cædmon's monastery at *Streoneshealh* (the modern Whitby) was only sixty or seventy miles to the south of Bede's at Jarrow. Bede, who was assiduous in gathering information for the history and received some of it from much more distant regions, would have had ready access to the records of Cædmon's monastery, and had probably talked with persons who had been well acquainted with the poet.

According to Bede, the beginning of Cædmon's poetical career and the greater part at least of his subsequent achievement belonged to the period between 657 and 680, when Hild, having built the monastery, governed it as abbess. This remarkable woman, whom Bede celebrates in the previous chapter of the history, was a grand-niece of Edwin, the first Christian king of Northumbria. Having taken the veil in middle life and acquired some experience as abbess at another foundation, she ruled at Streoneshealh with wisdom and vigor. The monastery, which was of the double type not uncommon at this period, with separate houses for men and women, soon became renowned for learning as well as devotion. It was chosen as the meeting place of the great synod of 663, where Roman authority prevailed over Irish. Several of its monks were afterwards bishops; but Cædmon, a simple herdsman on the monastic estate at the time of the miracle, was to become the most distinguished of all the

---

[2] Edited with modern English translation by Thomas Miller, *The Old English Version of Bede's Ecclesiastical History of the English People* (Early English Text Society, London, 1890–1899); reprinted for the society by the Oxford University Press, London, 1959 (Part I, text and translation) and 1963 (Part II, collation of the MSS.). This version has sometimes been attributed, though mistakenly, to King Alfred, and was probably produced in or about his time if not at his instigation.

brotherhood. Bede's account of him is too rich and too skillfully wrought to be summarized without loss. The greater part of it runs as follows: [3]

> In the monastery of this abbess there was a certain brother made notable by a grace of God specially given, for that he was wont to make songs fit for religion and godliness; insomuch that, whatsoever of the divine writings he learned by them that expounded them, he set it forth after a little time with poetical language, put together with very great sweetness and pricking of the heart, in his own, that is to say, the English tongue. With whose songs the minds of many men were oft inflamed to the contempt of the world and desire of the heavenly life. And indeed other too among the English people after him assayed to make religious poems; but no man could match his cunning. For he himself learned the art of singing without being taught of men nor of men's help; [4] but he received the gift of singing freely by the aid of God. And therefore he could never make any fond or vain poem, but only such as belong to religion befitted his religious mouth. For as long as he was settled in secular life, until he was well stricken in age, [5] he had at no time learned any songs. And so it was that at the table, [6] when the company was set to be merry and had agreed that each man should sing in his course, he, when he saw the harp to be coming near him, would rise up at midst of supper and going out get him back to his own house.
>
> And as he did so on a certain time, and leaving the house of feasting had gone out to the stable of the beasts which had been appointed him to look to that night, and there at the fitting hour had bestowed his limbs to rest, there stood by him

[3] Book IV, chapter 24 of the history. By kind permission of the Harvard University Press, I quote from the translation by R. E. King in the Loeb Library edition, *Baedae Opera Historica*, 2 vols. (Cambridge, Mass., Harvard University Press, and London, William Heinemann Ltd., 1930; reprinted 1954, 1962), II, 141 ff. King's translation is based on that of Thomas Stapleton, made in 1565.

[4] This echoes St. Paul's reference to his calling as an apostle in Galatians 1:1.

[5] The Latin, *usque ad tempora provectioris aetatis*, might suggest any time past the prime of life, perhaps no more than forty, though both the Old English and the modern translators seem to think of a greater age.

[6] Bede's expression, *in convivio*, is rendered as *on beorscipe*, "at a beer-drinking" in the Old English version.

a certain man in a dream and bade him God speed, and calling
him by his name said to him: "Caedmon, sing me something!"
Whereupon he answering said: "I know not how to sing; for
that too is the matter why I came out from the table to this
place apart, because I could not sing." "But yet," quoth he,
again that spake with him, "thou hast to sing to me." "What,"
quoth he, "should I sing?" Whereupon the other said: "Sing
the beginning of the creatures!" At which answer he began
forthwith to sing in praise of God the Creator verses which he
had never heard before, of which the sense is this: "Now ought
we to praise the Maker of the heavenly kingdom, the power of
the Creator and His counsel, the acts of the Father of glory;
how He, being God eternal, was the author of all miracles;
Which first created unto the children of men heaven for the
top of their dwelling-place, and thereafter the almighty Keeper
of mankind created the earth." [7] This is the sense but not the
selfsame order of the words which he sang in his sleep: for
songs, be they never so well made, cannot be turned of one
tongue into another, word for word, without loss to their grace
and worthiness.

Now on rising from slumber he remembered still all the
things that he had sung in his sleep, and did by and by join
thereto in the same measure more words of the song worthy of
God. And coming on the morrow to the town reeve under
whom he was, he showed unto him what gift he had received;
and being brought to the abbess, he was commanded in the
presence of many learned men to tell his dream and rehearse
the song, that it might by the judgment of them all be tried
what or whence the thing was which he reported. And it seemed
to them all, that a heavenly grace was granted him of the Lord.
And they recited unto him the process of a holy story or lesson,
bidding him, if he could, to turn the same into meter and verse.
Whereupon he undertaking so to do went his way, and on the
morrow came again and brought the same which they had re-
quired of him, made in very good verse. Wherefore by and by
the abbess embracing the grace of God in the man, instructed
him to forsake the secular habit and take upon him the
monastical vow, and when he had so done she placed him in
the company of the brethren with all them that were with her,

[7] It is important here to have Bede's exact words: "Nunc laudare debemus
auctorem regni caelestis, potentiam Creatoris, et consilium illius, facta Patris
gloriae; quomodo ille, cum sit aeternus Deus, omnium miraculorum auctor
exstitit; qui primo filiis hominum caelum pro culmine tecti, dehinc terram
custos humani generis omnipotens creavit."

and gave commandment for him to be instructed in the regular course of holy history. But he by thinking again with himself upon all that he could hear and learn, and chewing thereon as a clean beast cheweth the cud, would turn it into very sweet song; and by melodiously singing the same again would make his teachers to become in their turn his hearers. [8]

Now he sang of the creation of the world, and beginnings of mankind, and all the glory of Genesis, of the going of Israel out of Egypt, and their entering in the land of promise, and of very many other histories of Holy Scripture, of the incarnation of the Lord, of His passion, resurrection and ascension into heaven, of the coming of the Holy Ghost, and the teaching of the apostles. Also he would make many songs of the dread of judgment to come, of the terror of the pains of hell, and of the sweetness of the kingdom of heaven; moreover, many other songs of the divine benefits and judgments, in all which his endeavor was to pull men away from the love of wickedness and stir them up to the love and readiness to do well. For he was a man very devout and humbly obedient to the discipline of the rules; but very zealous and fervently inflamed against them that would do otherwise: wherefore too he closed his life with a goodly end. [9]

Although Bede did not include the hymn itself in his account of Cædmon, the scribes of the original Latin version of his history frequently added it marginally, and the author of the Old English version substituted it for the Latin paraphrase. In this way all seventeen of our surviving copies of the hymn came into being. Since there are substantive variations in these copies, there have been differences of opinion about the best readings, for it is conceivable that certain variations are attributable to Cædmon himself or to those closest to him. It has seemed best to select the oldest Northumbrian version for our text, since this is the one with which Bede's paraphrase most nearly agrees, and to

[8] The Old English translator says that they wrote at his dictation. Was this simply the translator's notion of the proper way to learn, or was he familiar with written poems that were thought to be Cædmon's? Bede's description suggests the possibility that many of the poems were recorded by dictation, but we cannot prove it by the surviving records.

[9] The remainder of Bede's chapter tells an affecting story of Cædmon's last hours. Whether he died before or after Hild is not known.

present it first with its original Northumbrian spellings as they appear in the two oldest copies, then in the normalized West Saxon spellings adopted for the other poems in this edition. A sampling of the actual West Saxon versions is given at the foot of the page below the normalized text. [10]

The manuscripts containing the two oldest copies are essentially of Bede's own time. The Moore manuscript, dated 737, contains the Northumbrian version at the top of its last page rather than where one would expect it, in the margin near Bede's paraphrase. It is followed by the identifying statement, *primo cantauit caedmon istud carmen*, and by three glosses, alphabetically arranged, of Latin words that appear in the history. Apparently the scribe of the manuscript was gathering together at this spot certain items from the margins of his exemplar which he had passed over while he was copying the text. In the Leningrad manuscript, of which the main text may be some years earlier than the chronological notations dated 746, the Northumbrian version of the hymn is at the foot of the page that contains Bede's paraphrase of it. [11]

Bede's well-established respect for documentary evidence, together with the inconsistently archaic spelling in these copies (especially the copy in the Moore MS.), suggests that he had in

[10] The fullest study of the text and its manuscripts is by E. V. K. Dobbie, *The Manuscripts of Cædmon's Hymn and Bede's Death Song* (New York: Columbia University Press, 1937). Dobbie's later edition of it in *The Anglo-Saxon Minor Poems (Anglo-Saxon Poetic Records*, VI), Columbia University Press, 1942, pp. 105 and 106, presents the Northumbrian and West Saxon versions with very full collations of other manuscripts. The Northumbrian text, with discussion of its background, is edited by A. H. Smith, *Three Northumbrian Poems: Cædmon's Hymn, Bede's Death Song and the Leiden Riddle* (London: Methuen's Old English Library, 1933).

[11] Both these manuscripts are now available in facsimile, with valuable introductions, in the series *Early English Manuscripts in Facsimile*, under the general editorship of Bertram Colgrave and his successor Peter Clemoes, published by Rosenkilde and Bagger, Copenhagen: *The Moore Bede*, with preface by P. Hunter Blair and a contribution by R. A. B. Mynors, 1959; *The Leningrad Bede*, edited by O. Arngart, 1952.

his possession a considerably older copy from which these two were made. Since Bede makes it plain that Cædmon was unable to read and write when he entered the monastery, and gives no indication that he learned to do so later, we may assume that the hymn was first recorded by someone else, quite possibly during Cædmon's lifetime if not on the occasion of the alleged miracle.

In spite of Cædmon's supposed incompetence as a singer before the moment when this hymn came into being, it exhibits the characteristic meter and style of Old English poetry under skillful control. The individual half-lines or verses have the typical range in number of syllables and stress patterns, the alliteration linking each pair of verses is placed according to the rules—no easy task for the novice—and the sequence of verses has, for so short and simple a piece, a surprisingly varied yet expressive movement. One would not expect, and does not find, the rhythmical elaborations of the finest passages in the longer poems, for these require more room and more complicated matter; but within its limits this is an accomplished piece of versification. Conspicuous also is the familiar stylistic device of variation, the deliberate dwelling on different aspects of an important subject by partially synonymous repetition. In these nine lines there are seven different epithets for God, only one of them repeated. Among these epithets, moreover, we recognize a number that appear in other poems. If they were not already verse formulas of the type essential to the oral composition of long poems and by no means distasteful to the literary poets of the period, they were soon to become so, perhaps as much by Cædmon's subsequent repetition of them as by the currency of the hymn. Documentary evidence for the formulas and formulaic expressions in the hymn has been presented very fully by F. P. Magoun, Jr., "Bede's Story of Cædman: The Case History of an Anglo-Saxon Oral Singer," *Speculum*, XXX (1955), 49–63, an article which raises questions of great interest about oral singers, and needs

pondering. Tentative discussion of these and other points will be
found in the somewhat earlier Gollancz Memorial Lecture by C.
L. Wrenn, "The Poetry of Cædmon," *Proceedings of the British
Academy*, XXXII (1946), 277–296. Magoun's suggestion that
some of the expressions in the hymn had already been coined for
Cædmon by earlier religious poets has been vigorously opposed
by Kemp Malone, "Cædmon and English Poetry," *Modern Lan-
guage Notes*, LXXVI (1961), 193–195.

In one respect the structure of the hymn is unusual. In most
Old English poems the pairs of verses constituting what we print
as lines are loosely organized in verse paragraphs of uneven
length. Here we find a tendency toward stanzaic structure. The
first four lines, celebrating God's divine powers and the unspeci-
fied wonders of the Creation, introduce him as the guardian of
the heavenly kingdom. The next four direct attention to his care
for the human race and call him the guardian of mankind. The
two sets of four are marked and balanced by the one repeated
epithet, *ēce Dryhten,* in lines 4 and 8. The ninth line partly off-
sets this symmetry, because it is technically a mere variation of
the statement in lines 7 and 8 and to this extent differentiates the
second part from the first. But the closing epithet, *Frēa ælmihtig,*
harks back to the magnificence of God as he is described in the
first section. Hence this final line sums up the essential meaning
of the whole poem. Bede's prose paraphrase, by deliberately
avoiding the repetition and shortening the second section, sacri-
fices all such structural interest.

Although the formal elements of the hymn, like its language,
are of native origin and representative of an age-old tradition, its
sentiment is obviously Biblical. Attention has recently been
called to its close dependence on the Psalms, not only for the very
notion of praising God but for the specific powers and functions
assigned to him as creator and governor of heaven and earth,
magnificent in the heavens yet mindful of the children of men.
The very expression "children of men," the *ielda bearnum* of
line 5, occurs in an appropriate context in Psalm 115:15–16: "Ye

are blessed of the Lord which made heaven and earth. The heaven, even the heavens, are the Lord's: but the earth hath he given to the children of men." (Vulgate, 113:23–24: *Benedicti vos a Domino, qui fecit cælum et terram. Cælum cæli Domino: terram autem dedit filiis hominum.*) [12] The varied epithets for God probably owe something, as a stylistic device, to royal panegyrics and even, perhaps, to the praise of pagan gods; but their substance is fully justified by the Psalms, and the naming itself, as has often been observed, is enjoined in one of the most famous of the prophetic passages, Isaiah 9:6: "For unto us a child is born: . . . and his name shall be called Wonderful, Counsellor, The mighty God, The everlasting Father, The Prince of Peace."

It is perhaps idle to speculate on the origins of a miracle. Dream-visions have been credited to other poets, from Hesiod on, to account for their inspiration, and legends quickly acquire ideal shapes that baffle all attempts to isolate some kernel of fact. Yet it may not be irrelevant to consider the impact, on a simple man of strong feelings and powerful imagination, of a new religion planted so impressively in the very soil to which he had been attached for a great part of his life. The building of Hild's monastery, the sudden aggregation of monks and nuns, the mysterious liturgy, possibly (if it came before the dream) the great synod attended by the king himself as well as the ecclesiastical dignitaries—all these things, given some curiosity on Cædmon's part and some reflection on what he learned, could have played a part in preparing him to receive that seemingly instantaneous gift of song.

Notes

2. *meahta*, "powers." The distinctively plural ending -*a* of the feminine ō-stem nouns has been chosen for the normalized text in view of the *maecti* of the Moore MS. and the *mehti* of the

[12] See N. F. Blake, "Cædmon's Hymn," *Notes and Queries*, CCVII (1962), 243–246.

Leningrad MS. The word *meaht* or *miht* was originally a femi-
nine *i*-stem with no ending in the accusative singular and *-i* in
the accusative plural, but in West Saxon it came to be declined
like the *ō*-stems with *-e* in the accusative singular and *-a* in the
accusative plural. The spelling *meahte* in the West Saxon Tanner
MS. may represent either the old plural or the new singular.
Bede's choice of the singular *potentiam* in his paraphrase may
be due to his sense of Latin usage.

3, 4. *swā hē wundra ġehwæs, /ēċe Dryhten, ōr astealde.* The
expression *wundra gehwæs*, "of each of wonders," goes together
as if it were a compound, and the genitive *ġehwæs* depends on *ōr*,
the direct object of *astealde*: "as he, eternal Lord, established the
beginning of every wondrous thing."

7. By putting the object, *middanġeard*, ahead of the subject,
Weard, the poet not only solves a metrical problem but adds a
syntactical contrast to his parallel clauses.

9. The verb *tēode* is to be understood as repeated from the
previous line.

The Battle of Brunanburh

The victory of the English forces at Brunanburh under the com-
mand of Athelstan and his brother Edmund was the military
climax of a movement by which Alfred the Great and his imme-
diate successors, having first freed their hereditary West Saxon
kingdom from the threat of a Danish conquest, gradually gained
power over the whole of England and made themselves secure
against their enemies abroad.[1] The poem describing the battle

---

[1] The historic significance of the battle is carefully assessed by Sir Frank
Stenton, *Anglo-Saxon England*, 2nd ed. (Oxford: The Clarendon Press, 1947).
See especially chapter X and, on the battle itself, pp. 338–339.

was early put on record as chief witness to the event. Accordingly it has survived in four manuscripts of the *Anglo-Saxon Chronicle*, appearing in each of them as the sole entry for the year 937.[2]

In spite of this association, the exact time and circumstances of the composition of the poem are uncertain. In our earliest manuscript (A), it is included in a block of texts that were not transcribed till about 955. We cannot tell how much earlier it was entered in the master copy from which A is derived, or how long before that it was composed. Neither do we know whether the author intended it for a place in the *Chronicle*. Its length and elaboration, no less than its poetic form, distinguish it sharply from the otherwise meagre and perfunctory annals of Athelstan's reign. Its ardor suggests that the battle had occurred very recently; its self-sufficiency, that it was designed as an independent piece; yet its perspective and its concerns are not far removed from those that govern the *Chronicle* as it had taken shape under Alfred and Edward.

Although this is perhaps the most familiar of all Old English poems through Tennyson's translation—a brilliant and thoroughly Tennysonian performance for good and for ill—it is not altogether easy to evaluate in its tenth-century form and setting. Critics have been able to show, by comparing it with earlier Old

---

[2] The manuscripts are listed above, in the headnote below the text of the poem. The readings of a fifth manuscript, destroyed by fire in 1731, have been reconstructed from earlier transcriptions by Campbell in Appendix I of the edition mentioned below, but have no independent value as witnesses to the text of the poem, for the manuscript was a direct copy of A. MS. A. is available in facsimile: *The Parker Chronicle and Laws*, edited by Robin Flower and Hugh Smith (London: Oxford University Press, 1941). The various versions of the *Chronicle* are printed, with translation in a second volume, by B. Thorpe, *The Anglo-Saxon Chronicle*, Rolls Series (London, 1861). Of great importance for its annotation is Charles Plummer's edition, *Two of the Saxon Chronicles Parallel*, 2 vols. (Oxford: The Clarendon Press, 1892 and 1899; reprinted 1952 with two notes by D. Whitelock). The clearest and most up-to-date presentation of the work in its various versions is in *The Anglo-Saxon Chronicle, A Revised Translation*, edited by Dorothy Whitelock with David C. Douglas and Susie I. Tucker (London: Eyre and Spottiswoode, 1961).

English poetry, that it is highly conventional, even archaic, in meter and diction. What is likely to escape us is its no less remarkable originality in design and vision. Nothing quite like it in genre has survived from earlier periods, nor are there close parallels in the poetry of other Germanic peoples. It does indeed have partial parallels, and it probably had antecedents, insofar as it can be classified as a royal panegyric; but it is much more than a panegyric by reason of its strong national feeling. This feeling depends in part, doubtless, on the long antecedent years of humiliation by Scandinavian ravagers and invaders and in part on the consolidation of England that had been achieved under West Saxon leadership since the time of Alfred. Likewise original, though now it seems a matter of course, is the author's historical perspective, not quite the same thing as the knowledge of heroic tradition of which the Norse panegyrists made use. He has been reading Bede and the *Chronicle* and (to judge by his connoisseurship in the diction and phraseology of battle poetry) several of the older poems in manuscript, as well as keeping his ears open. He places the battle historically within a firmer frame of reference than an unbookish author might be expected to supply, and even in treating the conflict itself maintains a distant view, surveying the scene as from a height and noting armies and battalions rather than individuals. He had some precedent for this in the battle scenes of Cynewulf and the Biblical poets, but a more traditional method of describing a battle in poetry is to be seen in *The Battle of Maldon*, where the originality, equally notable and doubtless of a higher poetic order, lies in a different sphere.

A thorough edition of the poem from all the manuscripts, with full historical introduction and notes, has been produced by Alistair Campbell, London, Heinemann, 1938. See also the edition by E. V. K. Dobbie, *The Anglo-Saxon Minor Poems* ("Anglo-Saxon Poetic Records," VI), Columbia University Press, 1942, pp. 16–20. Dobbie's full presentation of the text is followed by that of the other conventionally composed poems of the *Chronicle*, which celebrate later events and are poetically of less importance. I have depended on these editions for my report, slightly abridged, of the manuscript readings, except for those of MS. A, which are taken from the facsimile.

The main facts about the battle as presented in the poem are confirmed by a number of later accounts, partially or wholly independent. Among those cited in Campbell's edition are Irish and Scottish annals, a Norse saga, and Latin histories produced in England. Yet the location of Brunanburh is still uncertain. Of the various sites proposed, those that seem most probable lie near the west coast of England between Chester and southern Scotland. According to the poem, the opposing army consisted of two main forces: Scots under their king *Constantinus* (Constantine III, king of the combined Picts and Scots), and Norse vikings, the *scip-flotan* of line 11, who had come by sea from Ireland under the command of a certain *Anlaf*. Other reports make it clear that this Anlaf, a son of Guthfrith,[3] ruled a viking settlement in and around Dublin. His uncle Sihtric had held sway in York, but Guthfrith, claiming the succession after Sihtric's death, had been driven out of England by Athelstan and had ruled for a few years in Ireland before he died and left his kingdom there to Anlaf. The Scottish forces were apparently supported by their neighbors and allies, the Welsh of Strathclyde, who held the coastal region west of Northumbria.

Brief treatments of some of the puzzling details, such as the problematical *dennode* of line 12 and the body of water called *Dinges mere* in line 54, will be found in the glossary and the index of proper names, where also are identifications of the chief persons. For full discussion of such matters the reader must be guided by the notes and bibliographies of Campbell and Dobbie.

---

[3] This Anlaf, the later form of whose name is *Olaf*, appears in a seventeenth-century English version of some Irish annals (quoted by Campbell, p. 159) as *Awley McGodfrey*.

Notes

1. The word *Hēr*, "Here," introduces each annal in the *Anglo-Saxon Chronicle* directly after the number of the year. Hence it takes on the temporal meaning, "In this year." It is probably not a genuine part of the poem, which makes perfect sense and correct meter without it. The later poems of the *Chronicle* also begin with *Hēr*, and in one of them, *The Coronation of Edgar*, it is clearly required by the meter. Perhaps some or all of these later poems were written specifically for the *Chronicle*, as *The Battle of Brunanburh* in all likelihood was not.

6. The expression *hamora lāfum*, "with swords," literally "with leavings of hammers," is a familiar poetic periphrasis of a type cultivated by the ancient Germanic poets and especially popular in Norse poetry, where it received the name "kenning," from the verb *kenna*, "to call, name." The term is often applied to any periphrasis consisting of two or more words or a compound even if the meaning is obvious, but there is frequently something metaphorical or recondite about a kenning. Here, although a sword is in fact left on the anvil after a smith's hammer has forged it, there is probably a latent comparison to a human warrior as the survivor of a battle. In line 54 we find the expression *daroða lāf*, "what was left by the spears," applied to the bedraggled remnant of Anlaf's army.

7–9. *swā . . . ealgoden*, "as befitted the nobility they got from their ancestors, that they should often defend the land in battle against every foe." Instead of the distinctively subjunctive ending *-en* of the normalized *ealgoden* the manuscripts have *-on* or *-an*, which at this period can be either indicative or subjunctive. Campbell recommends the subjunctive, which yields a more plausible meaning and firmer syntax.

22. *on lāst leġdon lāðum þēodum*, "pursued the hostile peoples." Since *lecgan*, "to lay," is normally transitive, the ex-

pression *on lāst leġdon* is evidently elliptical: probably, as Camp-
bell has suggested, for *on lāst leġdon lāstas*, "they laid tracks on
the track." It is probably too early for Shakespeare's idiom, "Lay
on, Macduff," which implies "lay blows on, strike vigorously";
but this would surely be appropriate. The phrase *lāðum þēodum*
goes with *on lāst*, "on the track of the hostile peoples," the dative
being used with possessive force instead of the genitive, a usage
that is customary with nouns closely associated with parts of
the body, as *lāst*, "footprint, track," is evidently felt to be.

51. The demonstrative *þæs* is here used as a relative, "which,"
agreeing with the last of its series of antecedents, each of which
is in the genitive singular, and serving also as object of
plegodon, which normally takes the accusative (Campbell's ex-
planation). MS. D has substituted the more usual compound
relative, *þæs þe,* where *þæs* agrees with the antecedent and the
indeclinable *þe* serves as object of the verb.

54. *drēoriġ.* Campbell maintains that the meaning "bloody"
attributed to this word in addition to "dejected" cannot be sub-
stantiated from its use in Old English poems; but since *drēor,* as
he admits, means "blood," it is difficult to see how *drēoriġ* can
fail to suggest "bloody" in the context of a battle. That is not
its most frequent meaning, however, and it need not be domin-
ant even here.

60–65. In this enumeration of the creatures that prey on corpses
after a battle—a familiar motif in Old English poetry—one
may choose to combine the words in several ways. I prefer to
take *sealwiġ-pādan* as a noun, "dark-coated ones," applicable to
all the creatures that are then enumerated, each being credited
with a slightly different shade of the common darkness: "the
black raven with horny beak, and the dusky-coated one, the eagle
white from behind—greedy war hawk—and that grey beast, the
wolf in the forest." Campbell suggests that *gūþ-hafoc* is not the
name of some unknown kind of hawk but a kenning for the

white-tailed eagle previously mentioned. Raven, eagle, and wolf are the usual trio. It is true that the *earn* is separated from the *gūþ-hafoc* by the verse *ǣses brūcan*, but this is only a variation of *hrǣw bryttian* above and may well be followed by a variation of *earn æftan hwīt*. The uninflected *hwīt* is metrically necessary and may, as Campbell suggests, be excused if the verse is felt to be parenthetical.

65b–68a. "No greater number of people was ever yet slain in this island before this by sword's edges." Campbell points out that *wæl*, in its frequent sense "number of slain," governs the genitive *folces*, and that *wearþ* goes with *ġefielled* to form the preterite passive of *ġefiellan*.

68b. Here *þæs-þe* is used as a conjunction, "according to what, as." This use is found in other poems, for instance in *Beowulf* 1341, *þæs þe þincean mæg þegne monegum*, "as it may seem to many a thane."

The Dream of the Rood

This, the earliest extant example of a dream-vision poem to emerge from Western Europe, has been elaborately edited by A. S. Cook, Oxford, 1905, and later (with greater authority in some matters) by Bruce Dickins and Alan S. C. Ross, Methuen's Old English Library, 1934; fourth edition, 1954, reprinted with further additions and corrections, 1963. The manuscript is available in facsimile, *Il Codice Vercellese*, ed. Max Förster, Rome, 1913; the poem stands on ff. 104ᵛ–106ʳ, being the fifth of six religious poems interspersed in the volume among twenty-three homilies.

That the poem was first composed before A.D. 750 (even, as some think, before 700) is attested by the presence of the central part of the rood's speech, somewhat abridged and in some places obliterated, in the runic inscription on the monumental cross at Ruthwell in Dumfriesshire, southwestern Scotland. Dickins and Ross believe that the character of the runes points to a date not later than about 750. On the monument itself, see especially G. Baldwin Brown, *The Arts in Early England,* Vol. V, London, 1921, pp. 102–317; Fritz Saxl, "The Ruthwell Cross," *Journal of the Warburg and Courtauld Institutes,* VI (1943), 1–19; Meyer Shapiro, "The Religious Meaning of the Ruthwell Cross," *Art Bulletin,* XXVI (1944), 232–245; and Eric Mercer, "The Ruthwell and Bewcastle Crosses," *Antiquity,* XXXVIII (1964), 268–276. The runic inscription and a transliteration of it are included in Dickins and Ross, and again in Dobbie, *Anglo-Saxon Minor Poems,* pp. 114–115. The poem may have been considerably revised, especially at beginning and end, before making its appearance in the Vercelli Book late in the tenth century; but of such revision, apart from mere modernization of forms and spellings, there is no substantial evidence.

The emergence of a dream-vision poem in the latter part of the seventh century or the beginning of the eighth harmonizes very well with the story behind Cædmon's hymn and with the religious visions attributed to a number of Irish and English persons, several of which are reported with delight and sympathy by Bede. What is remarkable about this vision is, on the one hand, the depth and subtlety of its understanding; on the other, the art and imagination with which the speeches of dreamer and cross are invented, complexities of meaning and emotion are conveyed, order is maintained, and a significant progression is unfolded from beginning to end.

The presentation of the cross as a person able to address the dreamer—a device that gives the poet opportunity for his highly original account of the crucifixion—may owe less to the talking trees of classical poetry than to the technique illustrated in many of the riddles of the Exeter Book, a few of which go back to

Latin originals composed by Aldhelm before the end of the seventh century. Aldhelm learned something from the Latin riddles of Symphosius, but he was probably familiar with a native tradition of riddles as well. It should be added, however, that there was a much broader basis for the device in classical and post-classical Latin poetry and rhetoric. This is admirably set forth by Margaret Schlauch, "The 'Dream of the Rood' as Prosopopoeia," *Essays and Studies in Honor of Carleton Brown* (New York University Press, 1940), pp. 23–34.

Equally important in the background of the poem is the devotional and doctrinal literature accorded to the cross. Its discovery by St. Helena, the mother of Constantine the Great, was celebrated in the feast of the Invention of the Cross on the third of May. Two Latin hymns on the cross, composed by Venantius Fortunatus, an Italian who spent most of his life in Merovingian Gaul, became bishop of Poitiers in 599, and died about 610, show an equal fervor and some of the same concepts. They are reprinted conveniently in the *Oxford Book of Medieval Latin Verse*, ed. F. J. E. Raby (Oxford: The Clarendon Press, 1959), pp. 74–75. On such matters as these see, besides the editions mentioned, Howard R. Patch, "Liturgical Influence in *The Dream of the Rood*," *PMLA*, XXXIV (1919), 233–257. The theological background is significantly illuminated by Rosemary Woolf, "Doctrinal Influences on *The Dream of the Rood*," *Medium Ævum*, XXVII (1958), 137–153.

A brief but discerning critical study of the poem, with incidental comparisons to some Middle English treatments of the theme, has been published by J. A. Burrow, "An Approach to the *Dream of the Rood*," *Neophilologus*, XLIII (1959), 123–133.

Notes

4. *seldlīcre*, "exceedingly rare," an absolute use of the comparative somewhat like what we find in Latin. Compare the old expression, "passing rare."

5. *on lyft lǣdan*, "extending into the air; rising aloft." It is tempting to think there may have been some confusion with the rare verb *lēodan*, "spring up," since this would be appropriate to a tree, but since *lǣdan* can readily mean "extend" there is no occasion to emend.

8. *æt foldan scēatum*, "at the surface of the earth"—that is, at the base of the cross—a natural conception if the poet was thinking in part of ornamental crosses he had seen. Dickins and Ross quote Patch's very different notion: "*Foldan sceatas* are the corners of the earth, to which the cross reaches as it spreads over the sky," and compare the tree in Nebuchadnezzar's vision as described in the Old English poem, *Daniel*, 497–503. This interpretation of *scēatas* is entirely legitimate, but the meaning "surface" fits better at 37 and is imperative at 43; and the image proposed by Patch seems confused and improbable even for a dream. Cook, following Sweet, gave "surface" as the meaning throughout the poem.

9. *engel-dryhta fela*, "many hosts of angels." I first proposed this emendation in *The Rhythm of Beowulf*, New Haven: Yale University Press, 1942, p. 101. The reading of the manuscript, *engel dryhtnes ealle*, does not make sense and violates the syllabic and alliterative scheme characteristic of hypermetric verses in this poem and elsewhere. Two other proposed emendations, *englas Dryhtnes* (Sievers) and *engeldryhte* (Dickins and Ross), give acceptable sense and sound meter, but they do not account for the presence of *ealle* in the manuscript. It was my notion in proposing *engeldryhta fela* that the sequence *dryhta feala* (a common spelling of *fela*), if the words were written rather close together, might look enough like *dryhtnes ealle* to produce the error. In the insular script *f* and *s* have forms that are easily confused. The compound *engel-dryht* does not, to be sure, occur elsewhere and its genitive plural form strains the verse-type (a hypermetric verse with a close resembling type E in the Sievers scheme) unless we treat *engel*, as I think we may, as nearly equivalent to one syllable on the analogy of historically mono-

syllabic words like *tācn* and *ādl*. It is of no great moment which of the three emendations one chooses, but the one here adopted forms a more grandiose image, which seems appropriate.

10. *fæġere þurh forþ-ġesceaft*, "fair by their pre-ordained condition," or more freely, "fair by eternal decree," with reference to the angels who were destined not to fall but to maintain their original brightness. The word *forþ-ġesceaft* occurs in five other poems (never in prose) with two apparently diverse meanings: the nature of things or the created world on the one hand, future destiny or the future state or condition on the other. These meanings can be reconciled by taking *ġesceaft* in the basic sense, "that which has been created or ordained," and *forþ*, "forth, onward," as indicating its perpetuation if it is already present or its prospective existence if it is not. Thus the combination means "that which has been created or ordained to be," either for all time (the nature of things, the created world, or some preordained condition) or in the future. This explanation slightly modifies the interpretations of Cook and of Dickins and Ross without changing the basic concept. A minor problem is the gender of the nominative plural adjective *fæġere*, which obviously refers to the angels or the angelic hosts, and modifies the subject of *behēoldon* in the previous line, either *fela* according to the chosen reading or *engeldryhte* or *englas* according to the readings mentioned above. If it modifies *englas* it is masculine, as we expect; but if *engeldryhte* or *fela*, it is feminine, with the generalized ending *-e* that prevails in most of the manuscripts; for the indeclinable *fela* becomes implicitly feminine in agreement with *dryhta*. It is plural as subject of the verb. A similar construction, where *fela* is treated as nominative plural masculine, occurs in the Old English *Genesis*, 2335–2336, *bregowearda fela rōfe arīsað*, "many valiant princes will arise."

15. *wǣdum ġeweorðod*, literally "worthily adorned with garments," but perhaps the phrase means no more than "splendidly

appareled." Cook suggested that the *wǣdum* were some kind of streamers such as those with which processional crosses were decorated, and this seems possible. Yet when *wǣdum* is repeated at 22, it seems primarily to refer to the contrasted costumes, gold and jewels on the one hand, blood on the other. In that context streamers are either superfluous or positively distracting.

19. *earmra ǣr-ġewinn*, literally "the former agony of wretched (ones)." The dreamer associates the blood not only with Christ but, typically, with the many wretches who have endured this form of punishment. Note that the cross itself, at line 31, says it was commanded by its makers to lift up their criminals (plural *weargas*), though it actually served for Christ alone. It is true that the dreamer has already identified the cross as the Lord's (*Wealdendes trēo*, 17), and that the blood issuing from its right side is calculated to recall the wound inflicted by the centurion, as the next note explains more fully; but the vague generality of the plural *earmra* is appropriate not merely to dream psychology but to the implicit doctrine of the poem. The cross is later to say (lines 83 ff.) that the Son of God has transformed it by his suffering from the hardest of punishments to a glorious instrument of salvation. It is unique, but it typifies all crosses. Similarly, the suffering endured by Christ in his human nature is unique, but it may typify the suffering of the sinful wretches for whose punishment crosses were devised. The alternative interpretation advocated by Cook, that *earmra ǣr-ġewinn* refers to the former strife against Christ of the wretches who were responsible for the crucifixion, seems less in accord with the train of thought in the passage and less closely related to the central themes of the poem. In line 65 the meaning of *ġewinn* is shifted and enlarged, but still closely related to that which is here recommended.

20. The cross bleeds *on þā swīðran healfe*, "on the right side," because, according to post-Biblical tradition, it was Christ's right side that was opened by the centurion's lance (John 19:34). This

tradition is mentioned by the modern authorities cited in Cook's note, and also by Bede in his treatise on the temple of Solomon. He interprets a certain door on the right of the temple (I Kings 6:8) as a type of the wound in Christ's side, "because," he says, "holy Church believes it was his right side that was opened by the soldier." (*De Templo Salomonis Liber*, chap. viii, in *Patrologia Latina*, ed. J. P. Migne, XCI, 753.)

22. *blēoum*. The uncontracted form is metrically desirable.

31, 32. *þǣr*. Dickins and Ross urge very plausibly that the word here means "at that juncture; at that; on that occasion; then" (*Oxford English Dictionary, there* adv. 5, earliest quotation *c.* 1400). See the glossary, where these and other instances (at 30, 57, 60) are listed tentatively under the definition "thereupon, then."

39–49, 56–64. These are the lines partially preserved and somewhat abridged on the Ruthwell Cross. See Dickins and Ross or Dobbie. At 39–40 the corresponding passage on the Cross consists of a single pair of hypermetric verses, running as follows in normalized spelling:

Onġierede hine God ælmihtiġ   þā hē wolde on ġealgan ġestīgan.

The greater regularity of the form suggests that the inscription may at this point be giving us an earlier reading rather than an abridgment; but it is certainly inferior, for the *ġeong hæleþ* of the Vercelli Book text brings out much more imaginatively the heroic aspect of the action, an aspect which the poet is all along at pains to emphasize as proper to Christ in his divine nature. Cook cites classical parallels to the notion that Christ here strips himself as for battle, and Miss Woolf quotes Ambrose, who makes the stripping voluntary and heroic, saying, "Most rightly, when he was about to ascend the cross, he laid aside his royal garments." (*Pulchre ascensurus crucem regalia vestimenta deposuit.* Quoted by Miss Woolf, p. 146 of her article, from

Patrologia Latina, XV, 1830–1831). The next few words of the inscription, corresponding to lines 41–42 of our text, are partially defaced, but what remains looks like an unmetrical abridgment. All the other remnants of the inscription show verse-by-verse correspondence with our text, with only minor verbal variations.

55. *Wēop eall ġesceaft*, "all creation wept." The sympathy of inanimate nature, familiar in classical elegy, lies close at hand in Matthew's account of the crucifixion, and the theme was developed by some of the church fathers. There may, however, be a coalescence of two traditions. The weeping of all creatures, animate and inanimate, for the dead Balder seems by no means irrelevant. Unfortunately we cannot be certain that the myth was known in England at the time the poem was composed. See the note in Dickins and Ross.

63. *ġestōdon him æt līċes hēafdum*. The interpretation of *him* is somewhat problematical. One might take it as a possessive dative singular, proper to the simple phrase *him æt hēafdum* but rendered unnecessary by *his līċes*. If so we might either leave it untranslated or, to give it some slight recognition, say, "They stood by him at the head of his body." But *him* is more probably a "reflexive" or "ethical" dative plural, suggesting deliberate action on the part of the subject: "they took their stand" or "they came and stood." For what may be a comparable instance see the note on *Maldon* 300.

65. The word *ġewinn* here refers most directly and obviously to Christ's agony on the cross, but the military connotations of the word are also appropriate. In his divine nature Christ has waged war against the devil and all the forces of evil.

66. *banan*, probably the cross itself as the agent of death; the word *bana* is applied to one who has killed another even if unintentionally. Possibly, however, this is an error for, or a Late West Saxon levelled form of, the genitive plural *banena*, as Cook

and others have thought. The reference would then be to the
human agents of the crucifixion. It is slightly more difficult,
however, to accept their presence at this juncture than to suppose
that the cross is alluding once more to its own unwilling parti-
cipation in the affair.

69. *mǣte weorode*, literally "with limited company," meaning
"alone"; a characteristic example of ironic understatement. So
also in line 124.

71. *stefn*. Most editors, noting the lack of sense and alliteration,
have followed Kluge in inserting this word; but Kluge substituted
it for the *syððan* of the manuscript, as did Sweet and Craigie after
him; whereas Cook, Krapp, and Dickins and Ross retain *syððan*
and add *stefn* after it. The sense thus produced is good, but the
meter is defective, for *syððan* becomes "anacrusis" before a verse
of the type Sievers called D, which ordinarily does not admit even
one such preliminary syllable in the second half-line. Since there
is no real need for the conjunction here it seems better to follow
Kluge.

76–77. The reference here to St. Helena's discovery of the cross
and its adornment under her direction is surprisingly brief, and
since the meter is defective we may suppose that several verses
have been accidently omitted by a scribe.

79. *bealu-wara weorc*, "the work (or deeds) of dwellers in in-
iquity (wicked men)." If we take the expression so, as Dickins
and Ross recommend, it would seem that *sārra sorga* in the next
line must depend directly on *ġebiden hæbbe*, even though this
means that the verb (usually governing the accusative) must
govern two different cases in sequence. One might possibly ex-
cuse this on the ground that *sārra sorga* is almost partitive in
feeling, " (a number of) sore sorrows"—compare the French use
of *des*. Alternatively we might take *bealuwara* as a miswriting of
bealuwa or *bealwa*, genitive plural of *bealu* and directly parallel

to *sorga*, both nouns depending on *weorc*, which would then mean "pain" or "working, effect." Cook argues persuasively for this emendation on the strength of meter as well as meaning, and it is with considerable doubt that I have allowed the manuscript reading to stand.

93. The meaning of *for ealle menn* is best taken, perhaps, as "for the sake of all men." In choosing Mary for his mother God honored her above all womankind, and he did this for the sake of all men, in that his ultimate purpose was their redemption.

112. The word *sīe* has the metrical value here (as in some other poems, especially the older ones) of two syllables, and may be pronounced accordingly (*sī-e*).

125. *on forþ-weġ*. The accusative form is substituted for the dative here and at *Wanderer* 81 on the analogy of several parallels: *on forþ-weg* at *Beowulf* 2625, *Exodus* 129, *Menologium* 218, *Guthlac* 801 and 945; *on forþ-wegas* at *Exodus* 32, 350, and [*on*] *forþ-wegas* at *Genesis* 2814. In all these instances, as here, motion is implicit, and *on* (or Anglian *in* in *The Wanderer*) would be expected to govern the accusative. Here and at *Wanderer* 81, substitution of the accusative gives a sound verse of type A instead of a very unusual instance of A with final resolution or expanded D. This is a small matter, however, and it is possible that poets differed.

146. *guman*. Dickins and Ross defend this as a generic singular, "man" in the sense "mankind," genitive "man's," and I have let it stand on that assumption, though Cook's emendation to *gumena*, genitive plural, may be right. C. L. Wrenn, wishing to interpret *wyrsan* at *Beowulf* 525 as genitive plural of the comparative, as had been suggested earlier, cites both *guman* here and *banan* at 66 as examples of a Late West Saxon genitive plural in *-an*. If this is the right explanation we ought to normalize the words as *gumena* and *banena*, since these are not Late

West Saxon poems; but neither *wyrsan* in *Beowulf* (as Klaeber explains in his note) nor these words in the *Rood* are necessarily to be interpreted as, or emended to, genitive plurals. Late West Saxon *-an* for *-ena*, if it exists, is very rare.

148–151a. The allusion in these lines is to the harrowing of hell: Christ's descent into hell, his effortless victory over Satan, and his redemption (in some versions of the story from limbo, but here from hellfire itself) of all the virtuous men of old, from Adam onward. The adverb *þǣr* in 149 points to hell, as implied by *bryne* and the context as a whole. Dickins and Ross put a period after *spēdiġ*, 151, in order to make *þam sīþ-fæte*, 150, "that expedition," refer exclusively to the harrowing; but I have reverted to Cook's punctuation because it seems essential to maintain a parallel between the two clauses introduced by *þā* in 151b and 155b. With this punctuation, *þam sīþ-fæte* must refer not simply to the harrowing but also to the subsequent entry into heaven, even though this was delayed for forty days until the Ascension. Both Bede's hymn on the Ascension and the poem on the subject by Cynewulf associate the harrowing with the Ascension in the same way. The procession that advances toward the gates of heaven includes an escort of angels and a vast throng of the redeemed led by Christ. For hymn and poem see *The Christ of Cynewulf*, ed. A. S. Cook (Boston: Ginn and Co., 1900; reprinted from the second impression of 1909 by Archon Books, 1964, with a new preface by J. C. Pope), pp. 22–23 and 116–118.

The Battle of Maldon

In the *Anglo-Saxon Chronicle* for 991 the battle of Maldon figures as a comparatively small though ill-starred engagement between Byrhtnoþ, ealdorman of Essex, at the head of the local

levy, and a band of vikings, part of a large Scandinavian—
mainly Norwegian—army under the general direction of Anlaf
(Olaf) Tryggvason, who later became king of Norway. The series
of harryings and invasions that began in 991, after half a century
of comparative tranquillity, continued with occasional inter-
mission under several different Scandinavian leaders, some
Norwegian, some Danish, until Cnut the Dane became king of
England in 1016. The poem presents this battle in far greater
detail than we find in any other account of it, but not in histori-
cal perspective; rather as a self-contained little tragedy, a revela-
tion of men's strength and weakness under duress. Thus it resem-
bles such legendary encounters as we read of in the fragmentary
Old English lay, *The Fight at Finnsburg*, or, on a much greater
scale, the unavailing last stand of the Burgundians in the hall of
Attila the Hun. But it is the poet's distinction to have made us
feel the contrast between those carefully shaped, heroic old
stories and this vividly actual battle, enacted by everyday men,
many of them untrained for war, many of them but dimly aware
of the seriousness of the occasion, who nevertheless find them-
selves put to a test as absolute as any that the heroes of legend
encountered. In his poetic style, as in his basic conception, he
holds the ideal and the actual in balance, letting us see the im-
perfect, sometimes haphazard quality that belongs to most events
as we experience them, and nevertheless the emergence of a
pattern, the partial reenactment of something long familiar to the
imagination but larger than life. The result is a document a
good deal less reliable for its fact than a sober newspaper report,
as we have properly enough been warned in a recent article; [1]
but there would have been no occasion for the warning if the
poet had not deliberately, for his greater purpose, tempted us
into overliteral responses by making important use of fact. We
must suppose that the general setting, still more the named per-

[1] J. B. Bessinger, Jr., "*Maldon* and the *Óláfsdrápa*: an Historical Caveat,"
Comparative Literature XIV (1962), 23–35.

sons, great and small, are altogether actual, for without this kind of local fidelity the poet could not have persuaded his contemporaries to take him seriously. Indeed his own inspiration clearly depended in great measure on his belief in these men and their sudden emergence from nonentity into tragic splendor. What he has given us, however, is not the petty external truth of chronicle, but the higher truth that Aristotle discerned in the best fiction, a truth which is hardly to be attained without some perception of a significant relation between fiction and reality. For an excellent study of this aspect of the poem as revealed by its style, see E. B. Irving, Jr., "The Heroic Style in *The Battle of Maldon*," *Studies in Philology*, LVIII (1961), 457–467.

It has always been difficult to assess the exact blend of feelings with which the poet regards the leader, Byrhtnoþ; for although at most points his admiration is unequivocal, he makes Byrhtnoþ fully responsible for the decision that constitutes the turning-point of the action and costs both his own life and the lives of his loyal retainers. It is possible to argue that the historical Byrhtnoþ had very good reason to accept the challenge of the vikings, for he may have thought there was no other way to prevent them from evading the battle and attacking some other undefended part of the coast; [2] but the poet does not consider this aspect of the problem. For him, the decision is simply catastrophic in the light of its tragic consequences, and the motives that provoke it reside in the character of Byrhtnoþ and the cunning with which the vikings take advantage of it. It is partly his integrity they count on, the certainty that he will not break his word when he gives them leave to cross the ford; but it is also his pride, his readiness to take a dare. The poet seems very clearly to recognize this trait in the phrase *for his ofermōde* in line 89. I have allowed Gordon's definition of *ofermōd*, "great pride, overconfidence," to stand in the glossary because I think that whatever moral blame

[2] See W. A. Samouce, "General Byrhtnoth," *Journal of English and Germanic Philology*, LXII (1963), 129–135.

the poet attaches to Byrhtnoþ is not very severe and is mingled with admiration for a magnanimity that is almost inseparable from this imperfection. Yet no doubt it is an imperfection. The case against a too complacent acceptance of Byrhtnoþ as hero has been put by Tolkien in a brief but penetrating essay which reveals his abiding sympathy for the heroism of the little man.[3]

For a grasp of the action it is useful to accept the hypothesis first advanced by E. D. Laborde, *English Historical Review*, XL (1925), 161–162, that the vikings had sailed up the estuary of the river Blackwater, then called the Pante, in Essex, to a small island called Northey near the village of Maldon, evidently planning to use the island as their base for raids on the neighboring countryside. This island was cut off from the mainland at high tide, but at low tide a ford gave access to the shore on the Maldon side of the river. When the poet says at line 97 that the vikings bore their shields *west ofer Pantan* he is approximately correct: the exact direction is said to be southwest.

For the setting, the identification of persons, the general historical background, and many particular notes, an indispensable guide is the edition by E. V. Gordon, Methuen's Old English Library, 1937; second edition, 1949. The general appraisal of the poem in the introduction is likewise of value. For the text alone and some helpful notes, the edition by Dobbie, *Anglo-Saxon Minor Poems*, 7–16, should also be consulted. In my presentation of the fragmentary text, based on John Elphinston's transcription of the burnt Old English manuscript, I have depended entirely on Gordon's and Dobbie's reports. My glossary of proper names gives only a digest of the much richer informa-

---

[3] J. R. R. Tolkien, "The Homecoming of Beorhtnoth Beorhthelm's Son," *English Association Essays and Studies*, New Series VI (1953), 1–18. The central part of this is an imaginary dialogue on the field of Maldon after the battle. The essay on *ofermod* is at the end, pp. 13–18. See also a more limited comment in support of Tolkien by F. S. Battaglia, "Notes on *Maldon*: Toward a definition of *ofermod*," *English Language Notes*, II (1965), 247–249.

tion in Gordon's edition, and at several points I have referred to
his notes in support or illustration of definitions in the main
glossary.

Notes

4. *hycgan to handum,* "be intent on (the work of) hands"—
that is, "on deeds of arms" (Gordon).

5. The pronoun *þæt* is the object of *onfunde,* anticipating the
clause in line 6. It need not be translated. The same construction
appears in lines 36, 84, and 246.

23. *þǣr him lēofost wæs,* literally, "where it was most pleasing
to him"—that is, "where he was most pleased to be" (Gordon).

34. *ġif ġē spēdaþ to þām,* " 'if you are prosperous to that ex-
tent,' i.e. if you are wealthy enough to meet our demand."
(Gordon's tentative explanation; the idiom is not found else-
where.)

45. *sǣ-lida.* If this word is correct, the alliteration of the second
half-line is irregular, falling on *sæġeþ,* which should yield prece-
dence to *folc.* The line runs too smoothly to invite rearrange-
ment, but it seems possible that *sǣ-lida* is a scribal substitution
for a less familiar compound with the same meaning, such as
flot-lida, which would alliterate in orthodox fashion with *folc.*
There are several departures in this poem from the strict metrical
practice of earlier poets, but this particular departure looks more
radical than most.

48. *here-ġeatwe.* Most editors have retained the manuscript
reading, *-geatu,* interpreting it as accusative singular even though
other feminine *wō*-stem nouns have accusative singular *-we.*
Retention of *-geatu* in an unnormalized text is defensible, espe-
cially since the recorded instances of the compound show some-

what irregular endings and a tendency to use the plural rather than the singular; but since I am normalizing I have followed Kluge's *Lesebuch* (to which Dobbie draws attention) in reading *-geatwe*. The general meaning "war-equipment" makes good sense, as Dobbie maintains, but I agree with Gordon in accepting the richer meaning "heriot," first proposed by C. Brett, *Modern Language Review*, XXII, 260. See the glossary.

51. *unforcūþ eorl*. Gordon points out that the phrase is traditional, occurring in reverse order at *Andreas* 475 and again at 1263, both times with reference to Andrew himself. Gordon thinks the meaning of the adjective in *Andreas* is primarily "dauntless" with some connotation of nobility, but the most recent editor of that poem, K. R. Brooks, contents himself with the more literal interpretation, "not notorious; of unstained reputation"; and this seems nearer the mark in *Maldon* also. The negative expression allows Byrhtnoþ to say in effect that he has not yet suffered disgrace and does not intend to suffer it now, without claiming to be a paragon of nobility or courage.

75. *sē wæs hāten Wulfstān*. This parenthesis has a prosaic look, though it may be intentional. The orthodox verse-formula here would be simply *Wulfstān hāten*, with alliteration where it belongs, on the first lift.

115. *sweostor sunu*. A sister's son was traditionally dear among the Germanic peoples. Gordon quotes Tacitus in illustration of the antiquity of the sentiment. The poet shows his consciousness of the tradition as well as his sense of design by opening his account of the slain with the death of the sister's son and the quick reprisal for it.

136–137. As Gordon points out, Byrhtnoþ breaks the spear-shaft by thrusting the edge of his shield against it, and this action imparts a strain to the fragment carrying the spearhead—springs it—so that it quivers and flies out of the wound. Note the play on transitive *sprengde* and intransitive *sprang*. The subject of *sprengde* can be either Byrhtnoþ or the shaft, which in bursting imparts a spring to the fragment.

143. *ōðerne*, "another (viking)."

170 ff. I have adopted Dobbie's punctuation for 170 and 171, which enables us to hold together lines 166–171 as a progression from Byrhtnoþ's dropping of his sword to his sinking to the ground. The half-line at 172 introducing the prayer is clearly in need of a mate, either before or after it, and there may have been a greater loss; but in any event the prayer should be set apart from the exhortation to the retainers in 168–170, which is uttered by Byrhtnoþ as he makes a last effort not to fall.

183. Like Gordon and Dobbie I have allowed this obviously faulty line to stand because I do not know how to correct it.

212. *ġemunaþ þāra mǣla*. Dobbie emends differently. Keeping *þa mæla* of the manuscript as a correct accusative plural of *mǣl*, "speech," on the assumption that this word (not elsewhere recorded) is feminine, he emends *ge munu* to *gemunan*, calling this a first person plural imperative (which I should prefer to call a hortatory subjunctive), on the analogy of *Christ and Satan* 207. He maintains that the loss of *n* is more likely than the loss of *þ*. But since the next word begins with *þ* the odds would appear to be at least even. Furthermore the *gemunan* of *Christ and Satan* 207 is made clear by the explicit *gemunan we* in 202 at the head of the series of subjunctives. On the whole, therefore, Grein's form, *gemunaþ*, seems better. The choice between *þä* (supported by the manuscript) and *þāra* (the emendation adopted by Sweet, Wyatt, and Gordon) is not so clear. The gender of *mǣl* may be feminine, as Dobbie assumes, following the deduction made by Bosworth-Toller and Holthausen, among others, from this particular passage. But the Old Norse *mál*, "speech," is neuter, and so is Old English *mæðel*, which is simply

an alternative form of the same word *mǣl*. Again, though *gemunan* often takes the accusative, and does so in this poem at 196, examples with the genitive in Bosworth-Toller include several that have to do with being mindful of words or speeches. Perhaps the choice between genitive and accusative depended somewhat on the shade of meaning and the object governed. If *mǣla* is genitive, its gender can as well be neuter as feminine. Consequently I have rather hesitantly retained the emendation favored by Gordon.

224. *hē wæs ǣġðer mīn mǣġ and mīn hlāford*. It is tempting to read this line in total disregard of the customary verse-rhythm, with the following major stresses:

hē wæs ǽġðer mīn mǽġ and mīn hláford

That is the ordinary way to say it. But by sticking to the rhythm indicated by the metrical form, with its alliteration on *m* and its apparent adherence to the familiar verse-types classified as A3 and C by Sievers, we get an unexpected but significant shade of meaning. In the following notation I use ′ for primary accent, ‵ for secondary, and I double these marks, ″ and ‶ , for the syllables that are most prominent by the combined testimony of meter and meaning. Vertical bars indicate the limits of the approximately isochronous measures:

hé wæs ǽġðer mͮín mǽġ and mͮín hlͣáford

The double primary accent on *mǣġ* modifies the customary rhythm slightly in order to bring out the parallelism of *mǣġ* and *hlāford*, and this can be further emphasized by a slight pause at the cæsura; but the really surprising feature of this reading is the emphasis on *mīn*, and if we take careful note of Ælfwine's whole speech and remember that the poet has chosen him as the first speaker, we shall see that this is a calculated emphasis. Ælfwine's affliction is the greatest possible, as he has said, because for him (but not for everyone among the retainers) the loss is double. Presumably he is the closest of Byrhtnoþ's kinsmen, now that Wulfmær, the sister's son mentioned in line 113, is dead. Since no subsequent speaker claims kinship we may assume that most of the other members of the group, if not all, are unrelated. Because Ælfwine is aware of this difference, he sets the example of sacrifice and puts a certain emphasis on *mīn*. We do not need to exaggerate this emphasis to the point of turning the gesture into an uncalled-for assertion of superiority to his less well-connected associates, some of whom may in fact be equally noble. The distinction is one of kinship, not rank, and the privilege it carries is simply the obligation to die first. As one man after another follows his example, the poet shows us in everyone, high and low, an equal nobility of spirit.

230 ff. Offa's approval of Ælfwine's exhortation, his use of the first person plural, his explanation of the disastrous mistake made by some who had followed Godric in flight, and the fact that unlike the other speakers he does not immediately go forth to die—all point to the assumption that he was second in command to Byrhtnoþ and has now assumed the leadership.

283. The meaning of *cellod* remains unknown.

284. It has not, I think, been observed by previous editors that something is missing before this line. The antecedent implied by *þone* in 286 does not appear, and if we look more narrowly at the passage with this hint to guide us we see that the account of Offa's death is incomplete. There should have been mention of a viking's assault upon Offa, for it is the *lærig* of Offa's shield that bursts and his corselet that sings a terrible song. He has been fatally wounded, and though he manages to kill his assailant, he falls in the very act of doing so and is cut to pieces at once by other vikings.

300. For a desperate attempt to resolve the confusion of names

here, see the glossary of proper names under *Wīstan* and *Wīghelm*. The reflexive datives *him* in this line and *mē* in 318 mark a distinction of meaning for the verb *licgan*. At all other places in the poem it refers to someone who is already lying prostrate or to an enemy who is caused to lie dead. At the two places mentioned, the person who is the subject of the verb is felt to be sacrificing himself voluntarily and so to be deliberately assuming a prostrate position. The sense indicated by the pronoun can be conveyed by translating the verb as "lie down". See the note on *The Dream of the Rood* 63 for a possible though less interesting parallel.

The Wanderer

The quotation marks in this edition are so placed as to imply that the poem consists principally of two complementary speeches, the first (1–5 and 8–57) uttered by the *eardstapa* or wanderer of line 6, the second (58–110) by the philosophical person who is described as *snottor on mōde* in line 111, and that the poet, as master of ceremonies, after identifying the second speaker, supplies a bit of sage advice by way of epilogue (112–115). The main body of the poem (8–110, with or without 1–5) has ordinarily been regarded as a monologue spoken by the *eardstapa*, who after speaking of his own experiences and the sufferings of others like himself philosophizes more broadly and thus earns the descriptive epithet of line 111. This is a perfectly possible way to read the poem, and anyone who wishes to read it so still can readily do so by ignoring the closing quotation mark after line 57. I prefer to think that the *eardstapa* and the *snottor on mōde* are different chiefly because the characterization becomes much sharper if the poem is read in that way; but its total meaning as a sequence of ideas and emotions is very little altered. I have given a full exposition of my reading in an essay, "Dramatic Voices in *The Wanderer* and *The Seafarer*," in *Franciplegius: Medieval and Linguistic Studies in honor of Francis Peabody Magoun, Jr.*, edited by J. B. Bessinger, Jr. and Robert P. Creed, New York University Press, 1965, pp. 164–193. This same essay will serve as a guide to a number of articles published since the edition by Krapp and Dobbie in *The Exeter Book* ("Anglo-Saxon Poetic Records," III), Columbia University Press, 1936. For a good presentation of the poem as essentially a monologue, see S. B. Greenfield, "*The Wanderer*: A Reconsideration of Theme and Structure," *Journal of English and Germanic Philology*, L (1951), 451–465. Working on the same assumption, J. L. Rosier has made an interesting study of the imagery in "The Literal-Figurative Identity of *The Wanderer*," *PMLA*, LXXIX (1964), 366–369. An important new edition, separately edited by R. F. Leslie with introduction, notes, and glossary, has been published by the University Press, Manchester, England, 1966. Unfortunately it appeared too late to be of service here.

The poem has many elements of elegiac lament interspersed with philosophic meditation, and can be seen, in the last analysis, as somewhat akin to the type of consolation developed on the grand scale in the *Consolatio Philosophiae* of Boethius, one feature of such consolations being the effort to alleviate a personal sorrow by recognition of the instability of all earthly values and the necessity of seeking for lasting satisfactions in another realm. Two critics comment pertinently on this aspect of the poem: R. M. Lumiansky, "The Dramatic Structure of the Old English *Wanderer*," *Neophilologus*, XXXIV (1950), 104–112, and J. E. Cross, "On the Genre of *The Wanderer*," *Neophilologus* XLV (1961), 63–75. Yet it seems clear that the poet was a good deal less interested in the possible medicinal virtue of his discourse than in the imaginative realization of loss and loneliness in this unstable world.

Almost equally interesting, and more sharply evident if there are two speakers, is the interplay of traditional attitudes of the heroic, pre-Christian tradition with the ideas and feelings made available by Christian, largely Mediterranean, learning. The author and his chief speaker or speakers are Christians in the conventional sense, but the poem is full of tensions of a sort that are still with us, if with some change of costume.

The Exeter Book, an anthology written in an unusually handsome script of about A.D. 975, containing the unique copies of this and the next two poems, is available in facsimile: *The Exeter Book of Old English Poetry*, with introductory chapters by R. W. Chambers, Max Förster, and Robin Flower. London, 1933.

Notes

1. *ān-haga*, "solitary one." This word is used to describe Beowulf when he has lost his uncle Hygelac and all his former comrades in the battle with the Franks and Frisians and is forced to swim home alone. Thus it has no necessary connection with the religious recluse, and is certainly not so used here.

7. On the puzzling grammatical form of *hryre*, see the glossary.

15. *wērig-mōd*. This has often been taken as two words, "a dejected spirit," but several editors from Sweet to Magoun have printed it as a compound adjective with the force of a noun, "a disheartened (man)." This reading sharpens the distinction between the clause to which it belongs and the varied clause in the next line with its impersonal *se hrēo hyġe*, where such a distinction may possibly be indicated by the use of *se*.

17. The masculine noun *hyġe*, which occurs in the preceding line, is apparently to be understood after *drēoriġne*.

23. *heolstre.* This reading, that of the manuscript, seems better than Bright's emendation to the nominative *heolstor*, since it makes the wanderer the subject. He himself has buried his lord. In 84–85 a similar situation is imagined.

25. *sōhte sele-drēoriġ sinces bryttan.* If, as previous editors have assumed, *sele* and *drēoriġ* are separate words, the line means "Dejected, I sought the hall of a giver of treasure." But this interpretation conflicts with the order of words and the meter. The order is awkward because *drēoriġ*, modifying the subject of the verb, is sandwiched between the object, *sele*, and *sinces bryttan*, which has to be taken as a genitive phrase limiting the object. To convey this intricate structure orally requires a peculiar emphasis on *drēoriġ* and a pause after it. Such a reading, difficult at best, runs counter to the metrical pattern, which subordinates *drēoriġ* to the bearers of the alliteration, *sōhte* and *sele*. The difficulty is overcome by reading *sele-drēoriġ*, "sad for want of a hall," and taking *sinces bryttan* as the object of *sōhte*: "sad for want of a hall, I sought a giver of treasure." [1] The compound here postulated occurs nowhere else. It exhibits a rare but not unexampled relation between its two members, being almost exactly paralleled by the modern "homesick" and by Old English *wine-ġeōmor*, "mournful for loss of friends," which occurs at Beowulf 2239. The idea of deprivation that must be supplied for the understanding of all these compounds is readily suggested by their second members. (The OED derives *homesick* from *homesickness*, apparently a translation of German *Heimweh*. The same German word appears to have given rise, as early as 1678, to neo-Latin *nostalgia*, formed from Greek elements.)

27. *mīne wisse*, "might know of my (people)." There are several parallels in Old English to this use of *mīn* without a

[1] This reading was first suggested by Walther Fischer, *Anglia*, LIX (1935), 300. It has now been adopted independently by R. F. Leslie in the edition cited above.

specified noun, of which the following occur in verse: *hēold mīn tela*, "I held well (what was) mine," *Beowulf* 2737; *ġif ic mōt for þē mīne wealdan*, "if I am permitted by you to rule (her who is) mine," *Genesis* 2253; *þæt þū mundbora mīnum wǣre*, "that you would be a protector to my (people, followers?)," *Descent into Hell* 75. One must take *wisse* as "might know of," not "might know, be acquainted with," which would presumably have been expressed by *cūðe*. The traditional emendation, *mīn myne wisse*, "might feel affection for me," is adapted from a passage of uncertain meaning, *Beowulf* 169, and seems unnecessary if *mīne wisse* is interpreted as here suggested.

37. The verb *wāt* is used elliptically, "knows (how)," to introduce the entire passage in lines 39–48, where the main clauses begin with *þynceþ*, 41, and *þonne*, 45. Translate: "Indeed he that must long be deprived of his beloved lord's counsel knows how, when sorrow and sleep joined together bind the wretched solitary, as they often do, it seems to him. . . . Then. . . ." What starts as a rather vague generalization becomes particularized as the passage advances. (See Leslie's note for a more elaborate discussion of the grammar.)

53. *secga ġeseldan*. Usually interpreted as "men's companions in the hall," where *secga* seems superfluous; but see glossary, and the article by Vivian Salmon, "*The Wanderer* and *The Seafarer*, and the Old English Conception of the Soul," *Modern Language Review*, LV (1960), 1–10.

53. *eft*. This traditional emendation is better than the MS *oft*, if I understand the passage as a whole, because it sticks to a single imagined situation instead of generalizing.

58 ff. If we suppose that a second speaker begins here, we can give extra force to *mīn* as implying "my mind too." Indeed if the wanderer is still speaking it may seem odd that he should talk of the darkening of his mind at this point, as if he had not al-

ready known darkness enough in his own experience. A new speaker can properly counterbalance the wanderer's experience with reflections on the general human condition, viewing what has seemed the special plight of a few exiles as a much more general affliction, and deriving his melancholy from contemplation rather than from any personal sorrow. The opening "Forþon" can be taken as something vaguely connective, "As to that," or just "Indeed."

80b. The *Sume* of the manuscript is probably correct, referring with understatement to *many* who fell in battle. The singulars that follow suggest the varying fate of individual corpses left on the battlefield: one is carried off by a bird of prey, another eaten by a wolf, a third buried by a sad-faced survivor.

81. *forþ-weġ.* On this minor emendation, see the note on *The Dream of the Rood* 125.

83. *Dēaðe ġedǣlde,* "shared with Death." This seems the most satisfactory interpretation, since the victim is already dead when the wolf devours him. The poet imagines Death and the wolf as rival scavengers, dividing the spoils.

88. *Sē* can best be taken as equivalent to *Sē-þe,* indefinite "he who; whoever."

92. *Hwǣr cōm,* "where is; what has become of?" On the theme expressed by this formula, see J. E. Cross, " 'Ubi Sunt' Passages in Old English," *Vetenskaps-Societetens i Lund, Årsbok 1956,* 23–44. The earliest known examples are in the Old Testament, but there, the note of regret is less conspicuous than that of scorn or warning.

The Seafarer

Like *The Wanderer,* this poem has been punctuated in accordance with a novel theory of its form, and here it has been necessary to add marginal identifications of the supposed speakers, since the poem is in direct dramatic discourse from beginning to end, lacking entirely the narrative interpolations that identify the speaker or speakers of *The Wanderer* at lines 6 and 111. In this respect *The Seafarer* resembles *The Dream of the Rood, Deor, The Wife's Lament, The Husband's Message, Wulf and Eadwacer*, and most of the Old English riddles; nor has its dramatic character ever been doubted. But ever since 1869, when Max Rieger put forward his theory that the poem is a dialogue between an old man and a youth, there has been disagreement about the number of speakers. Most scholars have preferred to believe that there is only one speaker, since they think the evidence for a second is slight or non-existent; and those who have accepted the idea of a second speaker have not agreed about the limits of his speeches, though they have always supposed, with Rieger, that his first speech begins at line 33b; for it is the sentence that begins there, with its inclusion of the word *self*, that first prompted Rieger to suspect the presence of a second speaker. Indeed this sentence supplies the only grammatical evidence that can be put forward for a change of speakers, and it is my opinion, as it was Kluge's long ago, that there is no other change, at least throughout the fully dramatic part of the poem. But I suspect that the final lines, beginning with the hypermetric verses in line 103, are an epilogue somewhat like that of *The Wanderer*, in which the poet, as master of ceremonies, makes his own comments by way of bringing down the curtain and mediating between the audience and the fully dramatized characters who have spoken hitherto. I take the first speaker to be an experienced seafarer; the second, a younger man who has not yet been to sea and may or may not intend to make an actual voyage; for his philosophic temper and his avowed concern for the joys of the Lord allow us to suppose that he would speak of any great spiritual enterprise under the figure of a voyage.

I have discussed this whole problem at length in the essay

referred to above (p. 80), and must ask those who desire further explanation to consult it. Here I will say only that anyone who prefers to read the poem as a monologue can readily ignore the quotation marks and marginal directions. In my own opinion, much the best of the many interpretations of the poem as a monologue is that of Dorothy Whitelock, "The Interpretation of *The Seafarer*," *Early Cultures of North-West Europe* (H. M. Chadwick Memorial Studies), Cambridge, 1950, pp. 259–272. She believes that the single speaker is a religious man, a *peregrinus pro amore Dei*, who has chosen a life of seafaring and exile abroad as a means of mortifying the flesh and preparing himself for the joys of the life to come. Such characters there were in Anglo-Saxon England, and Professor Whitelock gives ample documentation in support of her theory. She argues very plausibly that such a person would be able to discourse feelingly of life at sea and yet philosophize about ultimate realities in imagery that has nothing to do with seafaring. This may well be so. I have proposed a different theory mainly because I am troubled about the grammatical implications of lines 33b–35, because I am not convinced of the psychological consistency of the discourse when read as a monologue, and still more because I think a poem so remarkably imaginative as this in its individual passages should have a more carefully controlled form than can readily be found in it if everything it contains is attributed to a single speaker. I think the form I have postulated enables one to find a significant progression of themes and contrast of characters; but the evidence for it is by no means incontrovertible.

There is an excellent edition of the poem—which in addition to its formal peculiarities has in some spots a distressingly corrupt text—by Mrs. I. L. Gordon, Methuen's Old English Library, 1960, upon which I have relied heavily in preparing this edition, and to which the reader is referred for bibliography, for a sane and perceptive introduction, and for a very rich and often delightful series of notes.

Notes

15. *wreċċan lāstum,* "on the paths (or with the steps) of an exile." The theme is relevant, as shown by its proper occurrence at line 57; but the imagery here is confusing, for the notion of frequenting, or remaining on, the sea (*sǣ wunode*) seems essentially static and to that extent inharmonious with the activity of *lāstum* even if one is untroubled by the idea of walking the waves. Since there is one verse too many or too few at this point, I am inclined to cast out *wreċċan lāstum* as a stock phrase that has been carelessly added. Note that the next verse alliterates on *w* and forms an excellent second half-line for 15a. Thus, if we leave out the stock expression the passage becomes flawless in meaning and in meter.

24. *þæt* is a pronoun, object of *beġeall,* referring vaguely perhaps to the scene.

25. *ūriġ-feðra* does not alliterate and is too much like 24a to be right. Mrs. Goldsmith's suggestion, *hyrned-nebba,* applied elsewhere to the eagle, is apt and may be correct, but I am not sure the poet would have imitated so closely the rhythm and grammatical form of 24a. Perhaps *īsiġ-* and *ūriġ-feðra* were really alternate readings of 24a, and something totally different has been lost at 25a.

33b–35. "Truly (or indeed), thoughts are even now beating against my heart, urging that I myself make trial of the high (or deep) seas, the tumult of the salt waves." I accept Mrs. Gordon's suggestion that *heortan* is the object of *cnyssaþ*; but those who take *heortan* as a genitive with *ġeþōhtas,* and *cnyssaþ,* in the sense "urge," as comparable to verbs of saying or commanding, governing the clause only as object, may well be right. The real question is whether *self* does or does not need to imply that the speaker has never been to sea before. Scholars have differed on this point, but it seems to me that the odds are greatly in favor of that implication, and that therefore the speaker at this point is not the man who has been speaking hitherto.

38. *el-þeodiġra eard.* This expression has become a *cause célèbre.* If we take this section of the poem as having to do with ordinary voyaging (and at least on the surface it should), the words in question mean simply "the land of foreigners," those who are foreigners in relation to the speaker. But since this speaker later refers in an obviously metaphorical way to "this dead life on land," scorning not simply the landlubber but the worldling, whether he stays at home or puts to sea, it is possible that *el-þeodiġra eard* will bear a second, metaphorical meaning based on the doctrine that men are exiles on earth and the virtuous among them may hope to return to their proper home in heaven. Thus the phrase would mean "the home-land of those who are strangers on earth," and if so, the speaker is intimating already that heaven is his destination—though I heartily agree with Mrs. Gordon that he is not at the point of death. The notion that *el-þeodiġra eard* means heaven was put forward with a number of pertinent quotations from Old English homilies and their patristic sources by G. V. Smithers, "The Meaning of *The Seafarer* and *The Wanderer*," *Medium Ævum*, XXVI (1957), 137–153 (especially 147–151). I cannot agree that this is the only meaning of the expression, but I think it may be one meaning.

48–49. "The groves burst into bloom, adorn the manors, make beautiful the meadows; the world hastens on." The onset of summer is associated with the onward rush of time, which warns the prospective voyager to set forth before it is too late. The second half of the poem encourages one to extend the meaning to include the thought that the end of the world itself is not far off. J. E. Cross has connected the passage very interestingly with Gregory the Great's interpretation of a saying of Jesus about the figtree and the end of the world. See his note, "On the Allegory in the Seafarer," *Medium Ævum*, XXVIII (1959), 104–106.

53. The mournfulness attributed to the cuckoo may be a Celtic fancy. See Mrs. Gordon's Introduction, p. 17. Whatever its origin, the notion is here made part of the speaker's sense of foreboding.

56. I follow Mrs. Gordon in accepting Grein's emendation, *sēft-ēadiġ*.

58 ff. In this extraordinarily intense and imaginative passage the speaker's soul is likened to a bird that soars out over the waters, sights the far country of its desire, and comes back, a lone flier, ravenous with hunger for what it has seen, to urge the man himself to follow. In the article mentioned above I have suggested that the imagery is appropriate to an eagle.

64b–66. Professor Whitelock showed conclusively, in the article mentioned above, that this is the central statement of the poem, and that if one grasps its significance one cannot dismiss what follows as an interpolation.

68. *þeġna ġehwelcum*. The manuscript reading, *þinga gehwylce,* "in every circumstance," is a familiar formula used elsewhere in Old English poetry and not unintelligible here; but I think it is a careless substitution for the much more pertinent formula with which I have replaced it. The sentence as emended means, "Ever one of three things, for every man, before his last day, becomes a cause of uncertainty: sickness or old age or deadly violence will wrest the life from him who is fated to pass away." The *þeġna* supplies an antecedent for *his* in 69.

69. I follow Mrs. Gordon in accepting Grein's emendation, *tīd-dæġe*.

72 ff. In general my text and interpretation follow Mrs. Gordon, who is responsible for the emendation *biþ* in 72. But I begin a new sentence at 74, making *þæt* a pronoun, object of *ġewyrċe,* anticipating the explanatory clause at 77. The emendation *fremum* is Kenneth Sisam's.

97 ff. This passage was reconstructed by Kenneth Sisam in the *Review of English Studies*, XXI (1945), 316–317. He noticed in it a general resemblance to Psalm 48 in the Vulgate, 49 in the Authorized Version. Compare the following verses in the latter:

> 6 They that trust in their wealth, and boast themselves in the multitude of their riches;
>
> 7 None of them can by any means redeem his brother, nor give to God a ransom for him. . . .
>
> 16 Be not thou afraid when one is made rich, when the glory of his house is increased;
>
> 17 For when he dieth he shall take nothing away.

Mrs. Gordon slightly modifies Sisam's translation as follows: "Though brother will strew with gold the grave for his brother born, bury [him] beside the dead with various treasures, that (i.e. the gold) will not go with him; nor can gold be a help to the soul that is full of sin in the presence of the terrible power of God, when he hoards it beforehand while he is still alive on earth." For further discussion see Sisam's article and Mrs. Gordon's note.

103. Mrs. Gordon translates this very persuasively: "Great is the terrible power of God, before which the earth will turn aside." She aptly compares *Apocalypsis* 20:11: *a cuius conspectu fugit terra* (Revelation 20:11: "from whose face the earth . . . fled away). The line serves well as the first line of the epilogue, making a solemn pronouncement on a theme glancingly mentioned by the previous speaker.

109–110. Although I accept in general Mrs. Gordon's interpretation, I assume that *mōde*, to which *þæt* refers, is understood as the object modified by the adjectives in 110: "A man must govern a headstrong spirit and keep it steady, and unfailing in its pledges, pure in its ways." Consequently we must not translate *mōde* as "temper."

111–112. I have modified the word-order of Holthausen's emendation, which seems plausible in spite of Mrs. Gordon's objection if we translate somewhat as follows: "Every man should govern with moderation his affection toward one he loves and his malice toward one he hates." What follows is corrupt, but it seems to be a continuation of the same thought: Even though a man should see his friend done to death by an enemy, he must restrain his grief and also be slow to wreak vengeance on the slayer; for men cannot control their destinies nor be held wholly responsible for their actions.

Deor

This dramatic lyric, spoken by a scop who has had his own misfortune in the world of heroic legend and whose repertory is filled with the sorrows of other famous persons, is as remarkable for its craftsmanship as for its spirit. The unevenly spaced refrain is given gradually increased meaning by the number and variety of illustrations in the first five sections; then, after a delay, it assumes a final, quite unexpected poignancy. The poem has been edited by Kemp Malone, Methuen's Old English Library, 1933; fourth edition, 1966. Since 1933 Professor Malone has made an important discovery about the probable content of the story of Mæþhild and Geat. See his essay, "On *Deor* 14–17," *Modern Philology*, XL (1942), 1–18, reprinted in his *Studies in Heroic Legend and Current Speech*, edited by S. Einarsson and N. E. Eliason, Rosenkilde and Bagger, Copenhagen, 1959, pp. 142–157. His thoughts on the Þeodric of line 18 are extended in another essay in the same collection, pp. 116–123, "The Theodoric of the Rök Inscription," first published in 1934. M. W. Bloomfield, "The Form of *Deor*," *PMLA*, LXXIX (1964), 534–541, suggests that the refrain owes something to Old English charms. If so, the poet has transformed exorcism into wisdom.

Notes

1. *Wēland.* The story of Weland the smith, maker of Beowulf's corselet and of many a famous sword, is told at some length in a poem in the Poetic Edda, the *Vǫlundarkviða*, and even more elaborately, but differently, in the Norwegian saga of Dietrich von Bern, the *Þiðrekssaga*. From these two we can piece together an outline that fits the implications in the first two stanzas of *Deor*. Weland, as a young man, came to work for a certain king named Niþhad, who, greedy for his wonderful productions and wanting to prevent his escape, took him by surprise and cut his hamstrings. Weland, in revenge, lured the two sons of Niþhad to his smithy, killed them, and made bowls out of their skulls, gems out of their eyeballs, and brooches out of their teeth. He presented these objects to Niþhad as masterpieces of his art. Later he ravished Niþhad's daughter, Beaduhild. Finally, having made a coat of feathers with the help of his brother Egill, he escaped, perching on the roof of Niþhad's palace long enough to tell him all he had done. Niþhad sickened and died. A son was born to Beaduhild, and within a few years she was reconciled to Weland, with whom she went to live as his wife. Their son, named Widia, was to become a notable adventurer.

1. *be wearnum,* "by hindrances," in allusion to the hamstring-ing. I have chosen this emendation from among many that have been proposed for the manuscript reading, *be wurman,* because its meaning is plausible and I can offer a conjecture to explain the scribe's mistake. The scribe spelled the smith's name *Welund,* though everywhere else in Old English it is spelled Weland or Welond. This suggests that he may have been copying from an earlier manuscript in which the scribe made his *a*'s with an open top, so that they could only with careful scrutiny be distinguished from *u*'s. Open-top *a*'s of this sort can be seen in the Leningrad MS of Bede and elsewhere. If the scribe mistook *a* for *u* in

Weland, he could have misread the next word, *warnum* (the Anglian spelling of *wearnum*) as *wurnum* and, not understanding this, have produced *wurman*, which he may or may not have regarded as a spelling of *wyrmum*, dative plural of *wyrm*, "snake." The spelling *wurm-* for *wyrm-* is common in Late West Saxon manuscripts, but does not appear elsewhere in the Exeter Book. If *be wyrmum* is by chance the right reading, it may, as Kemp Malone has suggested, be a reference to gold snake-rings or to swords with serpentine decoration, either rings or swords being thought of as products of Weland's smithy and a cause of Niþhad's covetousness.

5–6. A witty allusion to the hamstringing, as if the supple sinews, being cut, were equivalent to bonds. [1] The preposition *on* governs the accusative *hine*. The plural *nīeda* is used concretely to mean physical restraints, fetters; though of course these are figurative fetters.

7. Freely, "That (the misfortune just alluded to) has passed over; so may this (whatever is troubling any of us now)." For the curious impersonal construction with genitive, see the glossary, *ofergān*, *magan*, and *þes*.

14–17. This obscure passage, in which *māna* is a normalized form of Malone's emendation, *mōne*, for MS *monge*, may be translated, "We have learned that the lamentations of Mæþhild, the lady of Geat, grew unbounded, so that her sorrowful love deprived her of all sleep." The formulaic *wē . . . ġefrugnon*, "we have learned," frequently encloses part of the statement it in-

---

[1] I am not persuaded by Karl Jost's recent suggestion that the sinew-bonds be taken literally on the assumption that the poet did not know the story of the hamstringing and was thinking of Judges 16:7, where, according to the Vulgate, Samson tells Delilah (falsely) that he can be bound with *septem nerviceis funibus, necdum siccis et adhuc humentibus*, "seven thongs made of sinews, not yet dry and still moist." *Festschrift zum 75. Geburtstag von Theodor Spira*, ed. H. Viebrock and W. Erzgräber (Heidelberg: Carl Winter, 1961), 86–87.

troduces, though nowhere else does it enclose the beginning of a that-clause. Malone, in the article mentioned above, has very persuasively urged that Mæþhild and Geat are the principals in a story told in slightly differing versions in two ballads, one Norwegian, the other Icelandic. In the Norwegian version, Gaute finds his bride Magnhild (Icelandic Gauti and Magnhild) in tears because she foresees that she will drown in a certain river during her wedding journey. In spite of precautions she falls into this river at a bridge, but Gaute, calling for his harp, plays on it so strongly that Magnhild rises up, still seated on her horse, escaping altogether from the power of the water-demon who had tried to capture her. In the Icelandic version, Gauti succeeds in recovering only her dead body. The names correspond pretty well, since Scandinavian *Gaut* is the same as Old English *Ġēat*, and in Old German the name-element *māþ* (OE *mǣþ*), "honor," became confused with *maht*, "power," which corresponds in meaning to Scandinavian *magn*. The OE *Mǣþ-* thus points to Germany rather than Scandinavia as the source of this poet's knowledge of the story.

18. *Þēodrīċ* is perhaps the legendary representative of Theodoric, son of Clovis, who ruled the Franks from 511 to 534. Many centuries later, in Germany, a fantastic story had grown up about a hero named Wolfdietrich, who, though his adventures began in the East, is commonly identified with this Theodoric or his son. In the late version of the legend Wolfdietrich spends many years as an exile in a foreign city named Meran, evidently taken to be the well-known city in the Tyrol. Possibly a much earlier form of the legend, otherwise unknown to us, made Theodoric an exile, ruling unhappily over the city of a foreign people called the Mærings. Kemp Malone, who has supported this interpretation, believes that the Mærings of the legend were originally Visigoths, who had held territory in Gaul before they were overcome by Clovis. In that case it might even be supposed that our Þeodric ruled the Mærings as a conqueror and it was they who

were unhappy; but the poet gives us little to go on, and the
exile theory is a bit more probable. Other scholars have supposed
that Þeodric is the great Ostrogoth, who in legend, as Dietrich
von Bern, spent long years in exile among the Huns—but not, so
far as we know, in any city connected with a people called
Mærings.

21. *Eormanrīc* is the famous Ermanaric of history, king of the
Goths for a long period until his death in 375. He was the power-
ful ruler of a vast empire stretching from the Baltic to the Black
Sea, but the stories of his tyrannical behavior—especially his
savage treatment of his son, his wife, and several of his nephews,
under the influence of a wicked counselor—appear to belong wholly
to legend, and to have accumulated gradually until they emerge
in Norse saga and Middle High German epic of the twelfth and
thirteenth centuries. In the *Þiðrekssaga* Ermanaric has become
king of Rome and uncle of Theodoric of Verona (Bern). Added
to other crimes against his kin is his responsibility for Theodoric's
thirty-year exile among Attila's Huns. The Old Norse *Lay of
Hamthir (Hamðismál)* in the Edda and the *Vǫlsungasaga* represent
older and different traditions, as does *Deor*. The Old English
Widsith, still older, lays stress on Eormanric's munificence and
mentions almost parenthetically his dangerous temper. In *Beo-
wulf* we have one brief allusion to his threatened vengeance
against the outlaw Hama, who appears to have stolen from him
a necklace of great value and run away from his *hete-
nīðas*. Here in *Deor* his tyranny afflicts everyone in his realm.

26. *ofercumen wǣre*. Observe that *ofercuman* here is used in
the same impersonal way as *ofergān* in the refrain. See the
glossary.

28. The inverted order here introduces a supposition: "If a
man sits full of sorrow."

37. *Dēor*. This character was presumably invented by the poet,

since he is not otherwise known; but he connects himself with persons who figure in a very ancient legend, a version of which in Middle High German, contained in the poem *Kudrun*, comes closer than the Norse versions to explaining the allusion to Heorrenda along with the Hedenings. King Heden laid plans to steal a famous beauty, Hild, from the watchful care of her father, King Hagen. He took with him some helpers, including the giant Wate (still talked of as Wade in Middle English) and a wonderfully talented minstrel named Horant (the Heorrenda of *Deor*). This man so captivated Hild by his singing and harping that she consented to elope with Heden. In the Norse versions, which are older and differently descended, the result is a tragic pursuit and an endless battle between Heden and Hagen, over which Hild, true to her name, presides; but in *Kudrun* we have a more romantic version in which the lovers escape. We may judge that, in the fiction implied here, Heorrenda supplanted Deor in anticipation of his aid in the seduction, or else as a reward for it. In any event Deor was overwhelmed by two forces at once, the sensational artistry of Heorrenda and the spell of Hild.

The main versions of the Hild story, including that which appears in *Kudrun*, are interestingly summarized by R. W. Chambers in *Widsith, A Study in Old English Heroic Legend*, Cambridge, 1912, pp. 100–109.

Old English Versification

With Particular·Attention to the Seven Poems

The study of versification in any ancient poetry may have several objectives. The most important of these for the lover of poetry is to recapture as nearly as possible the actual sound and movement of the verse as it was uttered by the poets themselves and their most accomplished contemporaries; and concurrently, if the lover is also a critic, to know enough about the prosodical rules to appreciate the poet's skill. But Old English poetry was composed in accordance with a now obsolete tradition. No contemporary has left us an account of its prosody, and the surviving manuscripts, remarkable as they are for their time, fall far short of the accuracy we desire. The first task for modern scholars has been to discover enough about the versification as commonly practiced to guide the editor in lineating his text and clearing it of obvious corruption. Observation of basic rules and classification of syllabic patterns have enabled us to distinguish verses and to determine whether or not a given verse conforms to the usual practice. The metrical rules *consciously* observed by the poets are not fully known. Still less certain are the basic rhythm by which the poets were guided as they composed, and the particular rhythms, or the range of acceptable rhythms, of the spoken verses.

In spite of these uncertainties, the present sketch sets forth, in addition to some more or less incontestable facts about the construction of Old English verses, what I believe is a probable theory of the basic rhythm and a survey of its principal variations, especially as they appear in the seven poems here edited. Elsewhere I have shown the grounds for this theory and exhibited in detail its application to the three thousand odd lines of *Beowulf*.[1] I have also provided readings to illustrate the rhythm

1 *The Rhythm of Beowulf*, New Haven: Yale University Press, 1942; second, revised edition in paperback, 1966.

on two phonograph records, one for the seven poems and another
for *Beowulf.* [2]

The Old English poets inherited from their Germanic ances-
tors a single verse form. They applied it to all genres, and modi-
fied but never abandoned it. Two verses, each conforming to one
of several approved types, are bound together by a carefully con-
trolled system of initial rhyme, loosely called alliteration. The
form is often referred to as the alliterative long line, because in
modern editions the pair of verses is printed as a single line,
usually with a space in the middle to separate the first half-line
from the second; but the form was invented before the literary
period, and when poems came to be written down, the scribes
copied them continuously across the page as if they were prose,
marking the metrical form, if at all, merely by points between
verses. [3] Hence, although it is convenient to speak of lines and
half-lines, the poets themselves would have thought rather of
verses and verse-pairs. In what follows the first half-line will
sometimes be called the "on-verse"; the second, the "off-verse." [4]

It is necessary to consider as a metrical entity each member of
the verse-pair as well as the combination of the two. [5] A single

[2] These records are published by Educational Audio-Visual, Inc., Pleasant-
ville, New York. The seven poems are recorded on both sides of a twelve-
inch disc containing selections from *The Dream of the Rood* and *The Battle
of Maldon* and the other five poems complete except for two and a half
corrupt lines near the end of *The Seafarer.* The selections from *Beowulf* are
on one side of a ten-inch disc. The other side contains selections from
Chaucer, read by the late Helge Kökeritz.

[3] Even Latin poetry at this period was usually written continuously across
the page, the verses being marked by punctuation only. See, for example, the
treatment of Bede's alphabetic elegiacs in the Moore MS. of his history, f.
86^v. The Leningrad MS., f. 100^v, is exceptional in starting each verse on a
new line.

[4] German *Anvers* and *Abvers.* German scholars were the pioneers in analyz-
ing Old Germanic verse, and their terminology has had wide influence. Some
writers in English prefer to speak of the "*a*-verse" and the "*b*-verse."

[5] The unpaired verses that occur now and then in the manuscripts usually
point to scribal error. There is one poem, however, the lyric *Wulf and
Eadwacer* in the Exeter Book, in which the verses are arranged in three
unequal groups, each of which is closed in thought and form by an unpaired
verse with double alliteration.

verse invariably consists of one or more complete words, and its
metrical integrity is usually marked by some degree of syntactical
separation from its neighbors and by its conformity to one among
several familiar syllabic patterns. The rules governing on-verse
and off-verse are basically similar and some verses are inter-
changeable, but in the on-verse the poets favor certain alli“era-
tive and syllabic patterns which they carefully avoid in the off-
verse. As a result, the majority of the pairs actually employed are
metrically irreversible.

As in modern blank verse and simple couplet forms, patterns
that extend beyond the line or verse-pair are irregular and there-
fore not metrical but syntactical and rhetorical. A tendency to-
ward stanza form has been pointed out in the commentary on
Cædmon's Hymn, but it is only a tendency. The refrain in *Deor*,
itself a rarity, closes verse groups of markedly unequal length.

In most poems a great deal of the rhythmic interest arises from
the varying relation between the syntactical and metrical patterns.
The syntactical coherence of the single verse is rarely disturbed, [6]
but that of the pair, the long line, is frequently relaxed or
negated. Clauses and sentences may run on from verse to verse,
now in accordance with the metrical pairing, now in opposition
to it. Enjambment of this sort varies in frequency and degree
from passage to passage and poem to poem. Cædmon's Hymn, as
one would expect from its extreme brevity and its lyrical feeling,
is mostly end-stopped; yet even here a syntactical counter-move-
ment is introduced in the middle of the third line. What is more
surprising is the prevalence of end-stopped lines in *The Battle
of Maldon*. Only now and then—as in Offa's speech in lines
230–243—do we find a succession of heavy medial pauses coupled
with a running on at the end of the line.

The verses themselves may be of two main kinds. Much the
commoner of these is central to the entire Germanic tradition
and is called the "normal" form. The other, being fuller and

---

[6] That is, the boundaries of words and phrases within the verse are usually
less conspicuous than those between verses. Among the occasional exceptions
is *Wanderer* 64b.

weightier, is called "hypermetric." [7] It may have been no part of the Germanic heritage but an invention of the Old English poets prior to the eighth century. If so, they must have passed it along to the Old Saxons of the continent, for we find it employed with great frequency in two Old Saxon poems of the ninth century, the *Heliand* and the fragmentary *Genesis*. Since both forms are represented in *The Dream of the Rood*, *The Wanderer*, and *The Seafarer*, both must be described, but much the greater part of our attention will be devoted to the normal form.

The Normal Verses

1. Alliteration

Some of the finer details of the alliterative technique depend for their understanding on a thorough acquaintance with the varying structure of the verses. Nevertheless it is convenient to begin with alliteration. It is almost the first thing we notice in Old English poetry, the poets themselves had to pay constant attention to it, and it serves the modern investigator as a provisional guide to the controlling stresses of the verses. Both normal and hypermetric forms employ it, and much of what follows applies to both; but certain generalizations apply with greater accuracy to the normal form.

The alliteration with which we are here concerned is a strictly regulated device for linking verses in pairs regardless of their syntactical relation. As such it is limited to the initial sounds of stressed syllables, [8] and is more accurately described as a rhyming of initial consonants, what is called vocalic alliteration being a

[7] Sometimes "expanded" or "swelling" (German *Schwellvers*), but the first of these two terms is ambiguous because of its application to certain variations of the normal verses.

[8] Thus, in *Brunanburh* 13—*secga swāte/siþþan sunne upp—siþþan* does not participate in the conventional alliterative scheme (though of course its *s* can be heard), because, as a conjunction, it is subordinate to the noun *sunne* and the adverb *upp*.

special, negative instance rather than an exception. Among initial consonants the rhyming is usually exact: *b* with *b*, *d* with *d*, and so forth; but the palatal and the guttural *c*—the one sounded like *k*, the other like the modern *ch*—were still accepted as rhymes in spite of the sharp phonetic difference that had developed between them. [9] The same is true of the palatal and the guttural *g*, and here the examples are more numerous. [10] The poet of *Maldon* is exceptional in distinguishing the two forms. [11] When a syllable begins with two or more consonants, all may alliterate (as do those beginning with *sw* in *Maldon* 118), but usually only the first is required to do so. Exceptional are the combinations *sc*, *sp*, and *st*, each of which normally alliterates only with itself. [12]

What is called *vocalic* alliteration depends, not on the likeness of initial vowels, but on the absence of initial consonants. Any

[9] Examples, even in *Beowulf*, are not very common, partly because words of the substantive class beginning with *c* are not very numerous in the poetry, and most of those that do appear have the *k*-sound in all dialects. Three examples in the normalized text of *The Seafarer* depend on *ċeald*, "cold," which was pronounced *cald* in Anglian, the probable dialect of the poet; and one in *The Wanderer* involves the doubtfully palatal *c* of the accusative *ceare*. There are only two persuasive instances in this book: *Seafarer* 5, involving *ċēol*, "ship"; and *Maldon* 76, involving the proper name *Cēola*.

[10] E.g., *Brunanburh* 44; *Rood* 7, 16, 18, 39, 77, 146 (with West Saxon *ġealg*, not with Anglian *galg*); *Wanderer* 22, 35, 52, 73; *Seafarer* 40, 62, 83, 92, 101; *Deor* 15.

[11] In *Maldon* the guttural alone alliterates in some twenty lines (13, 32, etc.); the palatal alone in two (84, 274). In lines 32 and 192 there would be double alliteration in the off-verse if the two sounds were equated, whereas both lines alliterate regularly if only the guttural sound is considered. Evidently the poet wished to observe a distinction. Hence in lines 100 and 265, where the palatal *g* heads the first stressed syllable of each member of the pair, the guttural *g* of the second stressed syllable of the on-verse is probably not to be included in the alliterative scheme.

[12] For example, *sc* alliterates in *Brunanburh* 11, 19, *Rood* 54, and *Maldon* 40, 56, 98, 136; *st* in *Rood* 30, 40, 62, 71 and *Maldon* 19, 25, 122, 127, 249, 301; *sp* (the rarest) in *Maldon* 34, 137. In *Maldon* 271, *stunde* is probably not intended to alliterate with *sealde*, for what attracts attention is the end-rhyme, on which I comment below.

two stressed syllables beginning with vowels are considered suffi-
ciently alike to alliterate with each other, no matter whether the
vowels are the same or different. Indeed, the poets generally avoid
the alliteration of identical vowels, and make no distinction be-
tween simple vowels and diphthongs. Typical examples are the
fourth line of Cædmon's Hymn, where *ēce* alliterates with *ōr*, and
the first line of *Brunanburh*, where *Æðelstān* alliterates with
eorla. Evidently, then, vocalic alliteration has nothing in common
with assonance. Some theorists believe that it originated at a time
when a stressed syllable beginning with a vowel was preceded by
a glottal stop—the slight coughing sound produced by closure of
the glottis. This is a phenomenon that has been observed locally
among Germanic and other speakers, and it would have provided
a recognizable substitute for an ordinary consonant. It seems
equally possible, however, that the mere directness of attack on
the vowel, the absence of the expected consonant, was appre-
hended as a likeness; for an initial consonant checks or stops the
breath and produces a distinctive noise as a prelude to the un-
checked sonority of the vowel. The unpreluded sonority of a
stressed vowel can be felt, by contrast, as a distinctive feature.

The poets were generally very careful about the number and
position of the alliterating syllables. Most verses have two
syllables that are more strongly stressed than the others. In the
off-verse the first of these two must alliterate and the second must
not. [13] In the on-verse one or both may alliterate, but the choice
is not entirely unrestricted. The first syllable regularly alliterates
unless it is decidedly weaker than the second; [14] and in certain
emphatic variations, where both syllables are heavily stressed,

[13] Exceptions are very rare in the stricter poems, and the few that turn
up in the manuscripts may be the fault of the scribes. Four more or less
plausible exceptions appear in *Maldon* 45b, 75b, and 288b (where the second
stressed syllable alliterates instead of the first), and 29b (where both stressed
syllables alliterate).

[14] So, in Cædmon's Hymn 4a and 8a, *ēce* takes precedence of *Dryhten* be-
cause they are both of the substantive class and *ēce* comes first. In line 1a, on
the other hand, the infinitive *herian*, though it comes last, takes precedence
of the adverb *nū*. In *Maldon* 80a, 242a, and 298a the rule is broken, for it
is the second of two grammatically equal words that carries the alliteration.

double alliteration is almost obligatory. Hence, if we consider only the four strongest syllables in the line or verse-pair, and represent those that alliterate by *a*, those that do not by *x* and *y*, the following patterns will represent the usual practice. Each of the three is illustrated by a line of Cædmon's Hymn, with accents to mark the most heavily stressed syllables (whether or not they are *equally* stressed) and bold-face type for the alliteration:

(1) a a : a x   **M**étodes **m**éahta   and his **m**ód-ġeþánc

(2) a x : a y   **éċ**e Drýhten,   **ó**r astéalde

(3) x a : a y   Nú sculon **h**érian   **h**éofon-ríċes Wéard

When the principal alliteration is limited to one of the two strongest syllables in the on-verse, as in the second and third patterns above, it is sometimes supplemented by alliteration of a different letter on the syllables designated as *x* and *y*. The second pattern, thus modified, gives what is called "crossed" alliteration; the third, "transverse" alliteration. If we designate the supplementary alliteration by *b*, we have the following patterns:

(4) Crossed alliteration: a b : a b

Nórþ-manna brégu,   níede ġebǽded   (B 33) [15]

lángung-hwíla.   Is mē nū lífes hýht   (R 126)

grýre-léoða súm.   Þā æt gúðe slóg   (M 285)

þe þā wrǽc-lástas   wídost lécgaþ   (S 57)

(5) Transverse alliteration: b a : a b [16]

Swèlċe þā ġebróðor   béġen ætsámne   (B 57)

Hwæðre iċ þær líċgende   lánge hwíle   (R 24)

Èode þā ġesíerwed   séċg to þam éorle   (M 159)

Occasionally, even when the on-verse has double alliteration, there is a third syllable with strong secondary stress that alliterates with the second stressed syllable of the off-verse:

[15] Now and hereafter, as in the glossary, the poems are designated as follows: C = Cædmon's Hymn, B = *The Battle of Brunanburh*, R = *The Dream of the Rood*, M = *The Battle of Maldon*, W = *The Wanderer*, S = *The Seafarer*, and D = *Deor*.

[16] The comparative weakness of the first stress in the following examples is indicated by the reversed slope of the accent. In the second example the trisyllabic *licgende* carries the conventionally necessary stresses of the verse.

(6) a a b : a b

    báðian brím-fùglas, brǽdan féðra   (W 47)

    héowon héaðu-lìnda hámora láfum   (B 6)

There is no name for this pattern; and it is even more likely to be accidental than crossed or transverse alliteration, for in all three of these variations the basic alliterative requirement is already satisfied by the syllables designated as *a*. In most instances of transverse alliteration the *b*-rhyme involves a decidedly weaker syllable. Yet it is likely enough that the extra alliteration, even if not deliberately sought, was welcomed when it occurred.

2. End-rhyme

End-rhyme was not a regular feature of traditional Germanic verse. Its consistent use as a means of linking verses appears first in Latin hymns. Yet it occurs as an embellishment, in *addition* to alliteration, in *Beowulf* and other relatively early poems. It was used in this way by Cynewulf on several occasions—most notably in a personal passage near the end of his *Elene*—and by the author of the *Rhyming Poem* in the Exeter Book, where the effort to achieve both rhyme and alliteration throughout leads to frequent obscurity in the diction. Among the poems in this book, it is limited to four lines in *The Battle of Maldon*, two of which (identical except for the names) merely repeat a weakly stressed though dissyllabic ending:

    Byrhtnōþ maðelode, bord hafenode   (42)

    Byrhtwold maðelode, bord hafenode   (309)

    æfre ymbe stunde hē sealde sume wunde   (271)

    Siġebyrhtes brōðor and swīðe maniġ ōðer   (282)

What is interesting about the last two of these lines is that the alliteration is unorthodox in one and of secondary interest in the other, and that the syllabic patterns, though not entirely irregular, strongly suggest the rhythmic influence of rhymed couplets. [17]

---

[17] Internal rhymes (*bord-ord,* M 110; *weall-steall,* W 88) and rhetorical repetition (*lǣne,* W 108-109) belong in other categories. The occasional rhyming of unstressed endings is usually of no interest. In *Seafarer* 48–50a and 95–96 it is a natural consequence of the rhetorical parallelism.

3. The Syllabic Patterns

If we were able to trace the evolution of normal verses from
primitive Germanic times we might find, as some investigators
have surmised, that an Indo-European heritage of regular
octosyllabic verses, each consisting of four accentual trochees, had
been gradually differentiated as the language changed into the
extraordinary variety of verse-patterns we encounter. That
variety, however, was already established long before the period
with which we are concerned. Not only most of the patterns, but
many of the actual verses, since they appear in more than one of
our extant poems, must have been inherited from the preliterary
period. Indeed, it is the presence of this traditional element that
best accounts for the high degree of order we find in the midst
of the variety. It is not likely that the poets achieved this order by
mastery of a complicated set of rules. Such rules as they had were
probably unsystematic, mere rules of thumb. Lettered or un-
lettered, they worked with a store of inherited verse-formulas,
and fashioned new verses, as we may suppose, more by imitation
than by rule. An intuitive sense of a basic rhythm—sharpened,
perhaps, by use of the harp as an accompaniment—may often
have guided their choice. Nevertheless the order revealed by
analysis is sufficiently remarkable.

A fundamental classification of the various syllabic patterns
was made by Eduard Sievers, first for the Old English *Beowulf*,
then for the whole range of Old Germanic poetry.[18] Other
classifications have been devised from time to time, and some of
them have merit, but the Sievers classification has been so widely
adopted by editors that it is better known than any other. It has

18 The ground-breaking study, still a model of induction and exposition,
is the first part of a continued article, "Zur Rhythmik des germanischen
Alliterationsverses: Erster Abschnitt, Die Metrik des Beowulf," *Beiträge zur
Geschichte der deutschen Sprache und Literatur*, X (1885), 209–314. The in-
clusive and standard treatment is his *Altgermanische Metrik*, Halle, 1893.
Sievers later changed his mind about the rhythmic implications of his analy-
sis, but his classification of the verses according to the main stress-patterns
remains basic.

been, and may well remain, of great service to the textual critic. In itself, it does not tell us by what rhythm the verses are to be read, but no theory of the rhythm has much chance of being correct if it does not take due account of the features to which the Sievers classification calls attention.

As a basis for his analysis, Sievers took the natural word-accent and sentence-stress of Old English and the other Germanic languages as he had come to know them from his grammatical studies. These had to be modified occasionally, but were mainly confirmed by the alliterative patterns and the statistical evidence of the verses themselves, once the most common patterns had been identified. With minor exceptions, Old English shared with the other Germanic languages a fixed word-accent, the first syllable receiving the chief accent except for the prefixes of verbs, a few of the prefixes of substantives (*ġe-*, *be-*, and occasionally *for-*), and the first element in certain compound adverbs, prepositions, and conjunctions (*to-samne*, *on-ġēan*, *on-weġ*, *for-þam*, etc.). Within the phrase or clause, stress fell on the more important words according to a grammatical hierarchy. Nouns, adjectives, infinitives, and participles generally take precedence of finite verbs and adverbs, and these in turn tend to be stronger than personal pronouns, prepositions, conjunctions, and the un-emphatic demonstrative or definite article. Both position and specific meaning can, however, change the ordinary rank of a word. A post-positive preposition ranks as a rather emphatic adverb and frequently alliterates. A finite verb, if it denotes a significant action, may rival a noun.

Among stressed syllables, Sievers found it necessary to distinguish two classes, the long and the short. A stressed syllable is long if it contains a long vowel or a long diphthong, or is closed by a consonant; otherwise it is short. One consonant is enough to close a syllable at the end of a word or member of a compound; medially, two consonants are required, because there is no opportunity to pause on a single consonant in that position. Thus *God* qualifies as a long syllable, but the first syllable of *Godes* is short, while the first syllable of *mannes* is long. Since

the relatively unstressed syllables can be pronounced less dis-
tinctly, and their vowels, if long when stressed, can be shortened,
Sievers did not consider their grammatical length, and indeed
found no evidence that the poets were consistently attentive to it.

Even for the stressed syllables, Sievers did not believe that there
was a fixed ratio, either in ordinary speech or in verse, between
long and short. The conventional *length* of a syllable must be
distinguished from what is often called its *burden*. Every
syllable has a certain burden, a certain number of sounds of a
certain degree of difficulty, and burdens vary widely. When words
are uttered rhythmically, burden may help to determine the
rhythm by helping to regulate the pace of the series or by im-
posing a peculiar obstacle at a certain spot so as to produce a
different configuration of the rhythm. But burden becomes a
paramount factor only when we try to utter a series of syllables
as fast as possible. This we rarely do in reciting poetry, though we
shall find ourselves approaching that limit when we try to pro-
nounce the syllables in some of the more crowded Old English
measures. Now it is true that short syllables have very little bur-
den and that long syllables have more—sometimes a great deal
more. But the distinction between the two, in languages where it
is recognized, has become conventional, and depends on an al-
most opposite sort of test to that which determines burden. We
ask, not how quickly a syllable can be uttered, but whether or not
it can be uttered much more *slowly* than usual without losing its
character or becoming ridiculous. Sievers brought this out when
he recommended the terms *dehnbar* and *undehnbar*, "extensible"
and "non-extensible," for the conventional longs and shorts.[19]

For the analysis of the syllabic patterns of the verses, Sievers
made use of three key terms: *Hebung*, *Nebenhebung*, and *Sen-
kung*, which are usually translated as "lift," "half-lift," and
"drop." A lift consists of a long stressed syllable or its equivalent;
that is, usually, a short stressed syllable and its successor, the two
together constituting a "resolved" lift; but in some circumstances,
a short stressed syllable alone. A half-lift is the same as a lift ex-

19 *Altgermanische Metrik*, pp. xii and 23.

cept that its stress is secondary in comparison to a neighboring lift. A drop consists of a single syllable or a group of syllables (sometimes as many as four or five) which are relatively unstressed by comparison with neighboring lifts or half-lifts. To represent the syllables of a verse in notation, Sievers designated the lift as $\acute{-}$ (a long stressed syllable), $\cup$ (a short stressed syllable), or $\underset{\smile}{x}$ (a resolved lift, consisting of a short stressed syllable and its successor). He designated the half-lift as $\acute{-}, \cup$, or $\underset{\smile}{x}$, and each syllable in a drop as simply x.

Nearly every normal verse in Old English contains at least four syllables, a few contain as many as nine or ten, and the average number in most poems is between five and six. Among the very numerous verses with four syllables, Sievers found five principal stress-patterns, which he designated, in order of frequency, by the first five letters of the alphabet. These are the basis of his five types. By counting resolved lifts and polysyllabic drops as single members, he found that most verses of more than four syllables can be said to have only four members and can be assimilated to the types established by those with four syllables. Some verses, however, have five members so arranged as to seem like verses of type A or type D, rarely type E, with one extra drop. These were classified as A* (expanded A), D* (expanded D), E* (expanded E). The great majority of verses of types A* and D* occur as on-verses with double alliteration. Finally, a few verses otherwise resembling types A, D, or D* have one or two extra unstressed syllables before the first lift. These extra syllables, since they are not needed for the completion of the regular pattern, were treated as "anacrusis" (German *Auftakt*), optional preludes to the verse proper.

An additional feature of the Sievers classification was the assumption that each verse, having two lifts and either four or five members, consisted of two feet, each containing one lift with or without additional members. In my opinion, this feature of the system has been an obstacle to the understanding of the basic rhythm of Old English verse and must be replaced by the rhythmically significant division into measures; but it is retained in the following table.

THE SIEVERS TYPES [20]

Type A: Basic form, *lift, drop, lift, drop.*

A 1: Lifts virtually equal, no weighty syllables in the drops. Alliteration on first lift or (in on-verse) on both lifts. The first drop may have as many as five extra syllables; the second has only one. The minimal form with four syllables is very common:

$\acute{-}$ x | $\acute{-}$ x : ēċe Dryhten (C 4a).

With resolution:

$\underset{\smile}{\acute{}}$x x | $\underset{\smile}{\acute{}}$x x : cyning and æðeling (B 58a).

With anacrusis and five syllables in the first drop (a rare maximum): [21]

x | $\acute{-}$ x x x x x | $\acute{-}$ x : ġebiddaþ him to þissum bēacne (R 83a).

x | $\underset{\smile}{\acute{}}$x x x x x | $\acute{-}$ x : ġebæd iċ mē þā to þam bēame (R 122a).

A 2a: A half-lift, consisting of one long stressed syllable or its resolution, replaces the first drop:

$\acute{-}$ $\grave{-}$ | $\acute{-}$ x : unrīm herġes (B 31b).

$\acute{-}$ $\underset{\smile}{\grave{}}$x | $\acute{-}$ x : ferhþ-loca frēoriġ (W 33a).

For the variation with a short second lift, see A 4 below.

A 2b: A half-lift replaces the second drop:

$\acute{-}$ x | $\acute{-}$ $\grave{-}$: fǣġer feorh-bold (R 73a).

$\acute{-}$ x x | $\acute{-}$ $\underset{\smile}{\grave{}}$x : healde his hord-cofan (W 14a). [22]

---

[20] The subtypes are those distinguished by Sievers, except that subtype A 4 has been added to bring together all verses of type A in which the second lift consists of a single short syllable, and C 1 includes the resolved forms distinguished by Sievers as C 2, so that my C 2 corresponds to his C 3. (I adopted the same changes for the catalogue of rhythmic variations in *The Rhythm of Beowulf*.)

[21] Although these two verses have double alliteration, they tend toward the subtype A 3 because the second lift is stronger than the first. The combination *ġebæd iċ* is almost a single word, and *-bæd* should therefore be considered a short syllable.

[22] This resolved form is often indistinguishable from subtype D*2, under which I have repeated this verse and listed some other examples of which the classification is equally doubtful. The doubt reflects a weakness of the classification and has nothing to do with the authenticity or the rhythm of the verses concerned. In *The Rhythm of Beowulf*, for convenience of reference, I listed all such verses under D*2.

A 2ab: Half-lifts replace both drops. Not exemplified in these poems. Two good examples from *Beowulf* are:

⏑́ ⏑́ | ⏑́ ⏑́ : brēost-hord blōd-rēow (1719a).

⏑́ ⊍x | ⏑́ ⏑́ : nȳd-wracu nīþ-grim (193a).

A 3: The first lift weaker than the second, alliteration on second lift only. An introductory type properly restricted to the on-verse: [23]

⏑̀ x x | ⏑́ x : Nū sculon herian (C 1a). [24]

⏑̀ x x x x x | ⏑́ x : Þūhte mē þæt iċ ġesāwe (R 4a).

This subtype may have a half-lift instead of the final drop, as in A 2b:

x | ⊍x x x | ⏑́ ⏑́ : Ġewiton him þā Norþ-menn (B 53a).

A 4: Here I group variants of the three subtypes above in which the second lift consists of a single short syllable: [25]

Short A 1 : ⊍x x x | ⏝ x : fæġere ġetrymed (M 22b). [26]

Short A 2a: ⏑́ ⏑́ | ⏝ x : Bord-weall clufon (B 5b).

⊍x ⏑́ | ⏝ x : (Hēr) Æðelstān cyning (B 1a).

Short A 3 : x | ⏑́ x x | ⏝ x : ġesiehþ him beforan (W 46a).

Type A* (expanded A): *Lift, half-lift, drop, lift, drop.* The first drop distinguishes this rather rare variant from A 2a:

[23] I use a reversed accent to indicate the weakness of the first lift. Occasionally a lift of this sort shares the alliteration, as in subtype A 1, but most of the minor words (conjunctions, prepositions, etc.) lack synonyms and cannot easily be avoided, so that their occasional participation in the alliterative scheme may be accidental. A polysyllabic first drop is usual in this subtype. Some very short and weak exceptions are mentioned below in connection with the use of initial rests.

[24] The ending *-ian* of weak verbs of the *first* class has consonantal *i* (*j*), like the modern English *y* in *year*, and is therefore monosyllabic, whereas in weak verbs of the *second* class, though the ending is spelled the same way, the *i* forms a separate syllable and usually takes secondary accent in the poetry.

[25] The only frequent and obviously approved form in the poetry is short A 2a, of which other examples occur in this book at R 110b, R 117b, W 45b, and S 1b. Short A 1 and A 3 were perhaps tolerated but usually avoided.

[26] The participle normally had only one *m*, but the manuscript, now lost, apparently gave it two, perhaps on the analogy of the infinitive, and it may be that the author pronounced the verse with a long penult.

$\acute{-}\acute{-}$x | $\acute{-}$x : lid-menn to lande (M 99a) .

　　　Byrhtnōþ mid beornum (M 101a) .

$\acute{-}$ $\underset{\smile}{\smile}$x x | $\acute{-}$x : Lēofsunu ġemǣlde (M 244a) .

　　　earfoða ġemyndiġ (W 6b) .[27]

Type B: Basic form, *drop, lift, drop, lift.* Alliteration on the first lift alone or (in the on-verse) on both lifts.[28] The first drop may have as many as five or six syllables; the second is limited as follows:

B 1: The second drop has only one syllable:

x $\acute{-}$ | x $\acute{-}$: Hē ǣrest scōp (C 5a) .

　　　þā middan-ġeard (C 7a).[29]

x x $\underset{\smile}{\smile}$x | x $\acute{-}$: and his sunu forlēt (B 42b) .

x x x x x $\acute{-}$ | x $\underset{\smile}{\smile}$x : swā hē ǣr on þam bēame dyde (R 114b) .

Occasionally the second member of a compound occurs in the second drop and may be treated as a half-lift:

x x $\acute{-}$ | $\acute{-}$ $\acute{-}$: and ˙mīn mund-byrd is (R 130b) .

B 2: The second drop has two syllables: [30]

x $\acute{-}$ | x x $\acute{-}$: Mē sendon to þē (M 29a) .

x x x $\acute{-}$ | x x $\acute{-}$: and eall þēos mǣre ġesceaft (R 12b) .

x x x x x $\underset{\smile}{\smile}$x | x x $\acute{-}$: þāra-þe him biþ eġesa to mē (R 86b) .

---

[27] A doubtful instance, for the second syllable of *earfoða* would probably have been pronounced weakly enough in this position to be felt as part of a drop. The same is probably true of the second syllable of *ǣrende* in M 28a, *ǣrende to þam eorle*, which would otherwise be clumsily overburdened. The examples with proper names are supported by numerous parallels in other poems but the second element of the name may have been so weakly stressed as to cause these verses to be associated with type A 1. The same may be said of R 86a, M 261b, and M 25b.

[28] A form like A 3 with alliteration on the second lift alone is conceivable but the possible instances are extremely rare and can be classified differently.

[29] Sievers recognized that the second lift may be filled by a syllable that would normally be much weaker than the first, but he thought it should be reckoned as a full lift in order to give proper dignity to the second foot.

[30] Examples with three syllables in the second drop are rare and of doubtful authenticity. *Seafarer* 40b, 41a, and 41b are among these examples, but it will be noted that the preposition *to* is unnecessary and is actually not present in the otherwise parallel verse, 40a. If *to* is authentic, we probably have a minor license, a stretching of the measure for the sake of rhetorical emphasis.

The unusually weighty syllables of the second drop in the follow-
ing verses are probably to be spoken with reduced force or re-
tarded tempo: [31]

    x ⸍ | ⸍ x ⸍ : nē Anlāf þȳ mā (B 46b) .

    x x ⸍ | ⸍ x ⸍ : Þā þǣr Byrhtnōþ ongann (M 17a).

        oþ þæt Heorrenda nū (D 39b) .

Type C: Basic form, *drop, lift, lift, drop*. Alliteration usually on
the first lift alone, occasionally (in the on-verse) on both lifts.
The first drop may have as many as five or six syllables, the
second only one syllable:

  C 1: The second lift consists of one long syllable or its resolu-
tion:

    x ⸍ | ⸍ x : fram cnēo-māgum (B 8a) .

    x x ⏑x | ⸍ x : and þæt spere sprenġde (M 137a) .

    x x x ⏑x | ⏑x x : þam-þe þǣr bryne þolodon (R 149b) .

    x x x x x ⸍ | ⸍ x : þonne hit ǣniġ mǣþ wǣre (M 195b) .

  C 2: The second lift consists of one short stressed syllable: [32]

    x ⸍ | ⏑ x : on camp-stede (B 49a) .

    x x ⸍ | ⏑ x : ofer brād brimu (B 71a) .

    x x x x x x ⸍ | ⏑ x : Ne þurfon mē ymbe Stūrmere (M 249a) .

The second lift may be much weaker than the first, as when it is
supplied by the dissyllabic ending of a weak verb of the second
class:

    x x x ⸍ | ⏑ x : þe wile ealgian (M 52a) .

    x x x x x ⸍ | ⏑ x : þæt hē usiċ ġeweorðode (S 123a) .

These forms are probably conventionally accepted survivals from
prehistoric times when the endings were *ōjan and *ōde respec-
tively.

Type D: Basic form, *lift, lift, half-lift, drop*, or *lift, lift, drop*,

---

[31] Sievers was probably right in regarding such verses as variations of type
B rather than ordinary instances of type E preceded by heavy anacrusis,
especially since even light anacrusis before type E was normally avoided.
The context does not favor classification of the last two verses as hypermetric.

[32] Resolution of the first lift is much rarer in C 2 than in C 1. In the
seven poems there are only four examples (M 199a, S 58b, S 104a, and S 118b).

half-lift. In both patterns the syntax normally brings the last three members closer to one another than to the first member. When the drop is final it is limited to one syllable. When it comes next to last it may have two syllables. Alliteration, when single, is on the first lift alone. In the on-verse it may be on both lifts.

D 1: The half-lift is in third position and long: [33]

   ´ | ´ ´ x : Fréa ælmihtiġ (C 9b).

        hríþ hréosende (W 102a).

   ⌣x | ´ ´ x : scadu forþ éode (R 54b).

   ⌣x | ⌣x ´ x : lucon lagu-stréamas (M 66a).

D 2: The half-lift is in third position and short:

   ´ | ´ ⌣ x : weorc Wuldor-Fæder (C 3a). [34]

        self cunnie (S 35b). [35]

   ⌣x | ´ ⌣ x : nearu niht-wacu (S 7a).

   x | ´ | ´ ⌣ x : behéold hréow-ċearig (R 25a).

   ´ | ⌣x ⌣ x : bord hafenode (M 42b). [35]

D 3: The second lift is short; the half-lift, in third place, long. A very rare variant, occurring a few times in the older poems and scarcely at all in the later ones. There is but one example in the seven poems:

   ´ | ⌣ ´ x : reord-berendum (R 89b). [36]

D 4: The half-lift comes at the end:

---

[33] Resolution of the half-lift is very rare. It occurs in none of the seven poems and only once, doubtfully, in *Beowulf*: *milts ungyfeðe*, 2921b, where the stress on *un-* is optional and may better be subordinated to that of the root syllable. The verse would then be classified as A 1.

[34] At the date of Cædmon's Hymn, *Wuldor* could be pronounced as either one syllable, *Wuldr*, or two syllables, *Wuldor*, the vowel having been supplied to ease pronunciation after the loss of the earlier ending. Here it should probably be treated as a monosyllable.

[35] This subtype, as an off-verse, is the favorite resting-place for weak verbs of the second class, though they also appear occasionally in the on-verse and in other types.

[36] The indicated stress-pattern is almost impossible to produce unless the penult is held longer than necessary so as to produce an effect of syncopation. I think most speakers in the historic period would have said *réord-bérendùm*. The burden of the medial syllable, even if it were unstressed, would have added needed weight to the verse.

  ⏌ | ⏌ x ⏌ : hār hilde-rinc (B 39a) .

    bord ord onfēng (M 110b) .

    hrīm hrūsan band (S 32a) .

  ◡x | ⏌ x ⏌ : cyning ūt ġewāt (B 35b) .

  ⏌ | ⏌ x ◡x : Bærst bordes læriġ (M 284a) . [37]

Type D* (expanded D). Like D in its various forms, with the addition of a drop of one or two syllables (rarely more) after the first lift. Expanded D 3 does not occur, either here or in *Beowulf*. [38] The expanded type occurs almost exclusively in the on-verse, where it regularly has double alliteration.

  D*1:

  ⏌ x | ⏌ ⏌ x : sellan sǣ-mannum (M 38a) .

  ◡x x | ⏌ ⏌ x : eaforan Ēadweardes (B 7a) .

  ⏌ x | ◡x ⏌ x : hēowon here-flīeman (B 23a) .

  x | ⏌ x | ⏌ ◡x x : behangen hrīm-ġicelum (S 17a) .

  ⏌ x x | ⏌ ⏌ x : Wōdon þā wæl-wulfas (M 96a) . [39]

  ⏌ ⏌ x | ⏌ ⏌ x : Anwealda ælmihtiġ (R 153a) . [40]

  D*2:

  ⏌ x | ⏌ ◡ x : beorna bēag-ġiefa (B 2a) .

    ġielleþ ān-floga (S 62b) . [41]

  ⏌ ⏌ | ◡x ◡ x : Byrhtnōþ maðelode (M 42a; cf. M 309a) . [42]

The following verses could perhaps be classified as A 2b with resolution because of the even balance; but uncertainty of classi-

---

[37] Resolution of the half-lift is very rare. It occurs only twice in *Beowulf* and once, in the verse here cited, in the seven poems.

[38] A possible instance in *Beowulf*, *Wuldur-cyninge*, 2795a, can be read with monosyllabic *Wuldr-* or classified as A 1 in spite of the long penult.

[39] Note the very rare triple alliteration. A somewhat comparable instance occurs in *Beowulf* in a verse of type E, *syn-snǣdum swealh*, 743a. Both instances, though perhaps accidental, come at moments of heightened emotion.

[40] A sort of double D, highly exceptional but rhythmically sound and appropriate as an honorific.

[41] The only off-verse of this subtype in the seven poems.

[42] This formula, with other compound names, occurs twenty-five times in *Beowulf*. It is more logical to classify it as D*2 than as A 2ab, because there is a variation with a monosyllabic noun, *Weard maðelode* (*Beowulf* 286a), and also because the inflectional ending is descended from **-ōde*. Note the D 2 off-verse that follows in *Maldon, bord hafenode*.

fication does not entail doubt of authenticity or any difference of rhythm:

$\acute{-}$ x x | $\acute{-}$ ◡ x : healde his hord-cofan (W 14a) .

Ieldu him on fareþ (S 91a) .

$\acute{-}$ x x x | $\acute{-}$ ◡ x : Offa þone sǽ-lidan (M 286a) .

Wōriaþ þā wīn-salu (W 78a) .⁴³

x | ◡x x | $\acute{-}$ ◡ x : Onġietan sceal glēaw hæle (W 73a) .

D*4:

$\acute{-}$ x | $\acute{-}$ x $\acute{-}$: wēriġ, wīġes sǽd (B 20a) .

wǽpen upp ahōf (M 130b) .⁴⁴

hungor innan slāt (S 11b) .⁴⁴

$\acute{-}$ x | ◡x x $\acute{-}$: drēoriġ daroða lāf (B 54a) .

cwīðdon Cyninges fiell (R 56a) .

$\acute{-}$ x | $\acute{-}$ x ◡x : Bearwas blōstmum nimaþ (S 48a) .

x | $\acute{-}$ x | $\acute{-}$ x x $\acute{-}$: onwendeþ wyrda ġesceaft (W 107a) .

x | $\acute{-}$ x | $\acute{-}$ x x ◡x : alīefan landes tō fela (M 90a) .

Type E: Basic form, *lift, half-lift, drop, lift.* The first two members are usually more closely related to each other than to the fourth member. The drop may be either enclitic or proclitic. It may have two syllables, one enclitic, the other proclitic; rarely are both enclitic. The alliteration may be on the first lift alone, or (in the on-verse) on both lifts.⁴⁵

$\acute{-}$ $\acute{-}$ x | $\acute{-}$: andlangne dæġ (B 21a)

mann-cynnes Weard (C 7b)

æsc-holt ascōc (M 230b)

◡x $\acute{-}$ x | $\acute{-}$: heofon-rīċes Weard (C 1b) .

$\acute{-}$ ◡x x | $\acute{-}$: Ælfwine þā cwæþ (M 211a) .

$\acute{-}$ $\acute{-}$ x | ◡x : Norþ-manna bregu (B 33a) .

$\acute{-}$ $\acute{-}$ x x | $\acute{-}$: wæl-reste ġeċēas (M 113b) .

◡x $\acute{-}$ x x | $\acute{-}$: fela ealra ġebād (R 125b) .

⁴³ The penult of the verb here has certainly lost the secondary accent it usually receives in the poetry.

⁴⁴ These are the only off-verses of subtype D*4 in the seven poems. In the older poetry *wǽpen* and *hungor* could be treated as monosyllables, so that such verses as these would have had the pattern of unexpanded D 4.

⁴⁵ Highly irregular is *scield-burg tobrocen* (M 242a) , in which *b* alliterates.

Very rarely the half-lift consists of a single short syllable:

$$\acute{-} \smile \text{x} \mid \acute{-} : \text{earfoðu drēag (D 2b)}.$$
$$\text{earfoða dǣl (D 3ob)}.$$

Type E* (expanded E). Sievers placed in this class some verses of a very uncommon pattern which could be likened to type E with an extra drop after the first lift.[46] There are three such verses in the seven poems, all off-verses with single alliteration on the first lift:

$$\acute{-} \text{x} \acute{-} \text{x} \mid \acute{-} : \text{Wyrd biþ full arǣd (W 5b)}.$$
$$\text{Swimmaþ eft on-weġ (W 53b)}.$$
$$\text{ēċan līfes blǣd (S 79b)}.$$

In spite of the alliteration, which suggests D*4, one might place here the following on-verse—

$$\acute{-} \text{x} \acute{-} \text{x x} \mid \acute{-} : \text{hrūsan heolstre bewrāh (W 23a)}$$

—because the first two words go together; but if so the half-lift should be elevated to the rank of the full lifts, and the pattern is one for which Sievers did not expressly provide. The verse just quoted from *The Seafarer* is syntactically similar and calls for the same treatment in spite of having only single alliteration. See below, p. 123.

Such, then, are the Sievers types of the normal verses. A few verses that appear in company with normal verses yet do not precisely fit any of the types are listed and discussed below, pp. 127 ff.

4. The Basic Rhythm and its Variations

The classification made by Sievers does not tell us all we need to know to achieve a satisfactory recitation of the poetry. It is even misleading in certain details, such as the division into feet of seemingly divergent, even contrary forms, and occasional exaggeration of natural stresses to meet the requirements of these falsely imagined feet. Verse rhythm does require us to modify natural stresses in partial recognition of metrically established ex-

---

[46] There are at least three such verses in *Beowulf*. See *The Rhythm of Beowulf*, pp. 318 and 371.

pectations, but if we misconceive the meter we modify them wrongly. On the whole, however, Sievers put the stresses in the right place, and the distinction he made between lifts and drops, though exaggerated, is essentially true to the nature of the language. The Sievers types help us to generalize what is at first a bewildering variety of syllabic sequences. Taken together with the obviously careful use of alliteration, the types bespeak a fundamental orderliness such as we expect in a well-developed art. The types have helped us to recognize and compare various patterns, to describe them concisely, to know which patterns were preferred, and to detect irregularities. But this orderliness in the midst of variety suggests that there ought to be a basic rhythmic order to contain all the variations. We need, on the one hand, a higher generalization than the types provide, and on the other, a greater particularity. We must be able to deal sensitively with all the syllables, those in the drops as well as those in the lifts.

It is my belief, founded on experimental readings, that the rhythmic basis of every normal verse, whether on-verse or off-verse, is a pair of dipodies, or four-beat measures, of the form $| \text{í } 1 \text{ ì } 1 | \text{í } 1 \text{ ì } 1 |$, where the figure 1 represents the unitary beat governing a time interval equal to the usual quantity of a short stressed syllable, while the accents mark the primary beat at the beginning of the measure and the secondary beat in the middle of it. If we substitute musical notation for numbers and designate the unitary beat by an eighth-note, we shall have two measures of 4/8 time. As with musical rhythms, the basic rhythm can be greatly varied by combining and subdividing beats, by substituting rests (measured silences), and now and then replacing two beats by three of proportionately reduced quantity (1 1 by $\frac{2}{3}$ $\frac{2}{3}$ $\frac{2}{3}$). The normal verses of *Beowulf* can be spoken in accordance with this rhythm, as I have tried to show in *The Rhythm of Beowulf*, and so can all other normal verses, including those in the seven poems. Before entering into detail, however, I must explain my use of a few technical terms and notational devices.

Rhythm as here considered is an ordering, in time, of the

dynamic pulses of speech. [47] The relative intensity of these
pulses and the relative intervals of time between them are the
physical sources of the rhythm, though they are only an approxi-
mation, sometimes a crude one, of the order perceived by the
mind. Every clearly articulated syllable has a crest of intensity,
usually at the onset of the vowel, that serves as a point of meas-
urement for the ear. In a rhythmic sequence of syllables, the in-
terval between the dynamic crest of a syllable and that of its
successor, as compared with neighboring intervals, is the
quantity of the syllable in that particular sequence. [48] Some
crests are stronger than others and these are distinguished as
accents. They mark the regularly recurrent intervals we designate
as measures or parts of measures. The rhythm we are considering
calls for primary accents on every fourth beat to mark the meas-
ures and secondary accents half way between to mark half-
measures. Comparatively weak syllables can receive rhythmic ac-
cents without distortion of meaning if they are spoken at the
time when an accent is expected. For instance, if we utter the
first line of Cædmon's Hymn according to the following rhythm,

Nú scùlon hériàn   héofon-rìces Wéard

| 2   1 1 | 2   1 ∧ | 1   1   1 1 | 2   ∧ |

(where a caret marks a rest equivalent to one beat, or the
multiple of one indicated by the subscript number), we need not
exert a great deal of force in uttering the first syllable of *sculon*
and the second syllable of *herian* (pronounced as two syllables
with consonantal *i*) in order to feel that they have received

[47] William Thomson defines it more generally as "an ordering of blows."
See *The Rhythm of Speech* (Glasgow: Maclehose, Jackson and Co., 1923), p.
28. This is a work to which I am much indebted. It is full of eccentricities and
hard to use, but Thomson had trained himself to hear speech rhythms with
remarkable sensitivity and to record them accurately.

[48] Thus the rhythmic "syllable" is not the same as the grammatical one.
In the verse *ēċe Dryhten*, for example, the boundaries of the rhythmic syl-
lables are approximately indicated by the following slashes: *ēċ/e Dr/yht/en*.
The second "syllable," extending from the crest of *e* to that of *y*, includes
not only the two consonants of the third grammatical syllable, but whatever
period of silence there may be between the two words.

secondary accent. Merely uttering them at the right time helps to convey the impression. They should naturally have less intensity than the first syllable of *rīces*, which may be said to have *stress*. Similarly, *Nū*, though it deserves a modicum of stress, is inferior in that respect to the first syllables of *herian* and *heofon*, and to *Weard*. Yet *Nū* has the primary accent of the first measure by virtue of its relation, in time as well as intensity, to *sculon*.

Verse rhythm usually requires us to modify in this way the contrasts between syllables that deserve relatively heavy stress in their own right and those that do not. A reader of the line under discussion will automatically adjust the dynamic force of the accents if he pays equal attention to the rhythm and the meaning. But for analytical purposes I find it useful to distinguish between accents that are bestowed largely for the sake of the rhythm and those that are demanded by the meaning as well. The latter are properly stronger than the others and are therefore marked with double accents, ʺ for primary, ˮ for secondary. In general, those that receive double accents are those that are distinguished as lifts or half-lifts by Sievers, including those that regularly bear alliteration. I exclude, however, the relatively weak syllables that Sievers designates as lifts primarily for the sake of the meter. Accordingly I mark the first line of Cædmon's Hymn as follows:

Nú scùlon hérìàn   héofon-rìces Wéard.

| 2 1 1 | 2 1 ∧| 1 1   1 1 | 2   ⚲ |

The distinction is only in part a matter of auditory perception. No one need be disturbed if his ear refuses to distinguish all the grades of intensity that the notation might seem to imply. The chief service of the double accents is to bring out the interplay of the perfectly regular (because empty) basic rhythm we imagine and the variously weighted words and phrases that give it partial expression without sacrifice of their individual character.

My treatment of syllabic quantity results from an effort to reconcile the natural demands of the individual syllable with those of the basic rhythm. I take 1 as the normal quantity of a short stressed syllable, 2 as the normal quantity of a long stressed syllable. Both long and short stressed syllables in crowded measures can be compressed to half their usual length, the short to $\frac{1}{2}$, the long to 1—even, in very rare instances, to $\frac{2}{3}$, the quantity of one beat in a triplet, though this theoretical shortening may be offset by compensatory retardation of the tempo. The short syllables cannot, in my opinion, be extended beyond their normal quantity, 1, but the long can sometimes be extended to 3 or 4, the quantity of a full measure, by intoning the long vowel, lingering on one or more of the consonants (including sometimes a consonant that belongs to the next grammatical syllable), or filling out the time with a rest. Unstressed syllables (including some that take secondary accent in virtue of their position) generally *require* no more than the quantity 1 and are sometimes reduced to $\frac{1}{2}$, but proclitics and enclitics must be distinguished. A proclitic syllable, whether or not it is a separate word, tends to be followed quickly by the stressed syllable it introduces, so that its dynamic crest is at least as close to the one that follows as to the one that precedes. Practically, this means that its quantity is limited to 1 unless it is an independent monosyllable preceded by an initial rest, as I explain below. Enclitics, on the other hand, can often be extended, either by lingering on a closing consonant or filling out the time with a rest, or else by deliberate utterance of the opening consonant of the next grammatical syllable. In the line quoted above, the second syllable of *herian* requires no more than the quantity 1, but we can supplement it with a rest of the same quantity, or linger on the *n* enough to justify assigning it the quantity 2. The effect is then what might be called a *legato* reading, which is desirable when the sense runs on closely. Some enclitics, when thus supplemented, can have the quantity 3, but it must be understood that they are always uttered completely enough for recognition within the time of the quantity 1.

It is relatively easy to utter the verses of types A, D, E, and their expanded variants in conformity to the basic rhythm. More than half of the verses in most Old English poems are of type A, so that the rhythm we assign to them will be especially influential. The following table shows my reading of the principal subtypes of A and of A*:

A 1: ế̇cè Drÿhtèn (C 4a)

|2 2 |2 1 ∧ |

hőrd and hāmas (B 10a)

| 2 ∧ 1 |2 1 ∧ |

glấd òfer, grűndàs (B 15a)

|2 1 1 |2 1 ∧ |

flőtenà and Scőttà (B 32a)

|1 1 1 1 |2 1 ∧ |

fǽ̇ġe tò ġefế̇ohtè (B 28a)

|$\frac{4}{3}$ $\frac{2}{3}$ 1 1 | 2 1 ∧ |

Ġebǽd i̇c mē þầ to þam bế̆amè (R 122a) ⁴⁹

1 | $\frac{2}{3}$ $\frac{2}{3}$ $\frac{2}{3}$ 1 $\frac{1}{3}$ $\frac{2}{3}$ | 2 1 ∧ |

A 2a: mắnn-cÿnn sế̇càn (R 104b)

|2 2 |2 1 ∧ |

fế̇rhþ-lòca frế̆orìġ (W 33a)

|2 1 1 |2 1 ∧ |

A 2b: Sế̇ldlī̇c wǽs se sí̆ġe-bĕ̈am (R 13a)

| 1 1 $\frac{4}{3}$ $\frac{2}{3}$ | 1 1 2 |

A 3: Swél̇ce þǽr ĕac se frő̇dà (B 37a) ⁵⁰

| 1 $\frac{1}{3}$ $\frac{2}{3}$ $\frac{4}{3}$ $\frac{2}{3}$ | 2 1 ∧ |

Ġewíton hìm þā Nő̇rþ-mĕ̀nn (B 53a)

1 |1 1 1 1 | 2 2 |

A 4 (short A 2a) : Bố̇rd-wĕ̀all clűfon (B 5b)

| 2 2 |1 1 𝄽 |

A 4 (short A 1) : fǽ̇ġerè ġetrÿmed (M 22b)

|1 1 1 1 | 1 1 𝄽 |

A 4 (short A 3) : ġesíehþ hìm befő̇ran (W 46a)

1| 2 $\frac{4}{3}$ $\frac{2}{3}$ | 1 1 𝄽 |

---

⁴⁹ The grammatically almost parallel verse, *ġebī̆ddaþ hìm to þissum bĕ̈acnè* (R 83a), seems to me to require the indicated accents and to be essentially unreadable without a breach of rhythm or a drastic change of tempo. Such awkward verses are exceedingly rare.

⁵⁰ The *essential* pattern of the first measure requires the utterance of three syllables in the first half and two in the second. If the reader manages this he will approximate the specified rhythm, which readers of music will recognize as a variation of a measure consisting of two triplets.

A*:   líd-mĕnn to lándè   (M 99a)

| 2 $\frac{4}{3}$ $\frac{2}{3}$ | 2   1 $\wedge$ |

Léofsùnu ġemǽldè   (M 244a)

| 2 $\frac{2}{3}$ $\frac{2}{3}$ $\frac{2}{3}$ | 2   1 $\wedge$ |

When we turn from type A to the other four types, we find that they have one characteristic in common: they are particularly suited to the reception of the three-member[51] compounds or combinations of words in which the language, especially the poetic language, abounds. Type A 2 and A* can accomodate a compound such as *ferhþ-loca* with short penult, but more often even this form is found in types C 2, D 2, and D*2. Compounds such as *wræc-lāstas* and simple trisyllables such as *hrēosende*, with the first two syllables long, are found in types C 1, D 1, D*1, and E. Compounds such as *hilde-rinc* and combinations such as *wīġes sǽd*, *mǽre ġesceaft*, *wundra ġehwǽs* are found in types B, D 4, and D*4.[52] In types D and E the three-member words or groups are offset by a single lift; in D* by a lift and a drop; in B and C by an introductory drop.

Type E, in which the isolated lift is at the end, is readily adjusted to the basic rhythm by prolonging this lift or adding a rest:

mănn-cy̆nnes Wéard   (C 7b)

| 2   1   1 | 2   𝄼 |

Nŏrþ-mànna brégu   (B 33a)

| 2   1   1 | 1   1   𝄼 |

wǽl-rèste ġecḗas   (M 113b)

| 2   1 $\frac{1}{2}$ $\frac{1}{2}$ | 2   𝄼 |

The rare E* crowds the first measure but can be spoken without much difficulty:

Wy̆rd biþ fùll arǽd   (W 5b)

| $\frac{4}{3}$ $\frac{2}{3}$ $\frac{4}{3}$ $\frac{2}{3}$ | 2   𝄼 |

---

[51] I use this expression instead of trisyllabic in order to include extra syllables resulting from resolution or dissyllabic drops between lifts.

[52] It must not be supposed that three-member words and combinations of words are the only ones that can appear in any of these types. Verses of type B, in particular, often have a different syntactical structure.

ēċan līfes blǣd   (S 79b) [53]

|1 1   1 1 | 2   𝄋 |

Type D is a little harder because the isolated lift comes first; and in order to adjust it to the rhythm as well as to emphasize its partial separation from the three-member group that follows, the reader must either prolong it or supplement it with a rest: [54]

D 1:   Frēa ǣlmìhtiġ   (C 9b)

　　　| 2 𝄋 | 2   1   1 |

D 2:   nēaru nïht-wàcu   (S 7a)

　　　|1   1 𝄋 | 2   1   1 |

D 3:   rēord-bērendùm   (R 89b)

　　　| 4 |1 1   1   ∧|

D 4:   hār hïlde-rinc   (B 39a)

　　　|2 𝄋 | 4/3 2/3   2 |

D*1:   sēllàn sǣ-mànnum   (M 38a)

　　　|2 2 |2   1   1 |

The rhythms of the other varieties of D* can readily be inferred since they differ from those of the unexpanded type only in the first measure, which is filled out like that of the simpler forms of type A.

The three types of verses that have now been considered, A, D, and E, all begin with a lift (except for the few in which the lift is preceded by a syllable or two of anacrusis), and the feet marked by Sievers correspond to the measures of my interpretation, though the implications are different, for Sievers did not think the feet of his analysis were isochronous. Up to this point, moreover, my interpretation of the rhythm is substantially the same as that of Andreas Heusler, whose influence in Germany

[53] I have marked what is usually a half-lift with double primary accent because I think we are dealing with a variation that the Sievers scheme does not allow for, though it is a natural one. In effect, the compound measure has been replaced by two simple ones, but we keep the expected compound in mind. See *The Rhythm of Beowulf*, revised edition, pp. xx–xxiii.

[54] For a fuller treatment of this problem, see *The Rhythm of Beowulf*, revised edition, pp. xvii–xx.

has rivaled that of Sievers. [55] Types B and C, which remain to be considered, begin with a drop of one or more syllables, and like Heusler I find it necessary to postulate measures that do not correspond to Sievers' feet; but the rhythms I recommend for these verses are not for the most part at all the same as Heusler's.

The Sievers patterns for types B and C can be generalized as follows by using dots to indicate the possibility of extra syllables in the drops and remembering that the long syllable of any lift may be resolved:

B: x . . . . . ´ | x . ´
C: x . . . . . ´ | ˘ x

We notice at once that the feet designated by Sievers cannot well be the same as measures. Rhythmic measures, if they are complete, begin with primary accent, for it is the interval from one such accent to the next that we can hear as a measure. Since the first lift in verses of these types is always at least as strong as the second, usually stronger, and bears the alliteration when it is single, the accent of this lift must certainly mark the beginning of a measure. To replace the Sievers feet by measures we must therefore place one bar before the first lift:

B: x . . . . . | ´ x . ´
C: x . . . . . | ´ ˘ x

The position of the other bar may vary.

In *The Rhythm of Beowulf* I have shown that the frequent resemblance of the last three members of types B and C to the last three of various forms of type D entitles us to treat the second lift designated by Sievers as a half-lift and include all three members in one measure. If we do this we must assume that this measure is preceded by one that is incomplete or lightly filled. If it is incomplete it must begin with a rest. If it is lightly filled it must begin, like the first measure of type A 3, with a weak primary accent. Thus we have such readings as the following:

[55] See his *Deutsche Versgeschichte* (H. Paul's *Grundriss der germanischen Philologie*, VIII), Berlin and Leipzig: Walter de Gruyter, 1925–1929, vol. I, part II, "Der altgermanische Vers," pp. 86–314. The introductory part, pp. 1–85, lays down general principles somewhat like those of William Thomson.

B 1:   Hè ǽrest scŏ̄p   (C 5a)

| 𝄞 2 | 1 1   2 |

        ànd his sŭnu forlḛ̄t   (B 42b) [56]

| 𝄞 1   1 | $\frac{2}{3}$ $\frac{2}{3}$ $\frac{2}{3}$ 2 |

B 2:   þára þe hìm biþ ĕ́gesa to mḛ̄   (R 86b)

| 1 $\frac{1}{2}$ $\frac{1}{2}$ 1   1 | $\frac{1}{2}$ $\frac{1}{2}$ $\frac{1}{2}$ $\frac{1}{2}$ 2 |

C 1:   fràm cnĕ̄o-mă̄gum   (B 8a)

| 𝄞 2 | 2 1 1 |

        ànd þæt spĕ́re sprĕ̄nġde   (M 137a) [57]

| 𝄞 1   1 | 1 1   1   1 |

        þónne hit ă̄niġ mǽþ wǣre   (M 195b)

| 1 $\frac{1}{2}$ $\frac{1}{2}$ 1 1 | 2   1 1 |

C 2:   òfer brăd brı̆mu   (B 71a) [58]

| 𝄞 1 1 | 2   1 1 |

        Ne þúrfon mḛ̄ ymbe Stŭ̄rmère   (M 249a)

| 1 | 1 1   1 $\frac{1}{2}$ $\frac{1}{2}$ | 2   1 1 |

The rhythms just described represent the majority of the verses
in types B and C, and among them those calling for initial rests
are much the most numerous. [59] These rests are the chief means
by which my theory of the rhythm escapes difficulties that beset

---

[56] The same rhythm will serve for the unusual verse, *oþ-þæt Heorrenda nū*
(D 39b), but with retarded tempo to allow for the weight of the trisyllabic
name with its two long syllables.

[57] A reader may choose to give extra time to the first syllable of the verb.
If he does, the irregularity will probably seem expressive and therefore
pleasing.

[58] In these crowded measures there is no *rhythmic* difference between C 1
and C 2, but the difference in *burden* is noticeable, because in C 2 the short
penult has its normal and maximum quantity, whereas in C 1 the long
penult is compressed to half its usual quantity. This may sometimes lead
to a slight irregularity, as suggested in the previous note. In the alternative
readings of types B and C discussed below, the rhythms of C 1 and C 2 are
noticeably different.

[59] Unusually light verses of type A 3 may also be read with initial rests;
e.g. R 109a, *on þissum lǣnè* (| ∧ 1 ì 1 | 2́ ì ∧ |), and R 111a, *for þàm wŏ̄rdè*
(| ∧ 1 2̀ | 2́ ì ∧ |).

other theories, notably Heusler's, for whom the syllables of the first drop in the B and C verses are an unmeasured prelude to the verse proper. Initial rests are conspicuous, since they replace syllables marking the expected primary beat of the first measure of a verse, and their frequency in my reading of the poetry makes them a distinctive feature that requires comment. In most poems the rests seem both natural and expressive, because they come at moments when the phrasing permits or demands a pause, so that they help to punctuate a sequence of verses without interrupting the rhythmic flow. I am strongly inclined to believe that they were first introduced in prehistoric times as a natural development from the practice of accompanying the verses with the harp. Precisely how the harp was used is not known, but it might well have served partly to mark the main beats of the verses, and so led performers, when introducing clauses or adding half-separable phrases, to begin with some rather weak syllables after the first beat had sounded, a practice familiar to us in operatic recitative but not in poetry. Once the habit had become established, the harp would not have been needed. [60]

A number of verses of types B and C, however—mainly to be found among those that begin with a monosyllabic drop—cannot well be treated in the manner I have described. The clearest instances are furnished by the comparatively rare verses in which the monosyllable is a mere prefix. Consider the following lines, in which the off-verses belong to type C:

fōlcès ġefīellèd   befōran þissùm   (B 67)

$|2 \quad \frac{4}{3} \quad \frac{2}{3} | 2 \quad \frac{4}{3} \quad \frac{2}{3}|1 \; 3 \quad | 2 \; 1 \quad \wedge |$

þe hē hìm to dūguðè   gedōn hǣfdè   (M 197)

$1 \; | 2 \quad \frac{4}{3} \quad \frac{2}{3} |1 \; 1 \; 1 \quad 1| 4 \; | 2 \; 1 \; \wedge|$

bìtrè brēost-cèare   ġebīden hǣbbè   (S 4)

$|2 \; 2 \quad | 2 \quad 1 \; \frac{1}{2} \quad \frac{1}{2}| 1 \; 3 \quad | 2 \; 1 \; \wedge |$

---

[60] See *The Rhythm of Beowulf*, pp. 88–95. How frequently the harp was still used during the historical period is uncertain. Bede's story of Cædmon supplies the most positive bit of evidence for its use as an accompaniment. Its continued popularity as an instrument is unquestioned. The little harp found at Sutton Hoo and the references to harps in the poetry have encouraged speculation.

The rhythms here indicated can scarcely be doubted, for the prefixes are too weak to fill the second half of a measure, there is no reason to pause between verses, and the balanced treatment of the lifts in the off-verses is satisfactory in itself. Hardly less clear is the following verse where, although the monosyllable is independent enough to be lengthened, if necessary, after an initial rest, the sense is too continuous to justify such treatment:

þæt gé mid ùrum scéattùm   to scípe gángèn   (M 56)

1 | $\frac{4}{3}$ $\frac{2}{3}$ 1 1 | 2 $\frac{4}{3}$ $\frac{2}{3}$ | 1 1 𝄽| 2   1 $\wedge$ |

Or consider the following sequence, where the on-verse is of type B and a direct running on, with balanced treatment of the two lifts, seems easier and more expressive than the alternative:

cýning ùt gewàt   (B 35b–36a)

|1   3 | $\frac{4}{3}$ $\frac{2}{3}$ $\frac{4}{3}$

on féalonè flód

$\frac{2}{3}$ | 1 1 2 | 2 𝄽 |

It appears, then, that a few verses of types B and C must be treated in the manner just described, and that several others may be so treated, the decision resting on the reader's feeling for the movement of the passage. I find myself reading some of these ambivalent verses differently on successive occasions. [61]

Before concluding this survey of the rhythm of the normal verses I must say something of an unclassified remainder. Even in *Beowulf*, our chief model for Old English versification, there are a few verses that occur in a context of normal verses but do not fit any of the Sievers types, some appearing to be slightly deficient, some excessive. Several of these are manifestly corrupt, but others may well be authentic. *The Dream of the Rood* has two such verses, *The Wanderer* two, *The Seafarer* three (to mention only verses that make good sense), and *The Battle of Maldon* at least five.

[61] This problem is more fully treated in *The Rhythm of Beowulf*, pp. 57–64, where certain verses with two syllables in the first drop are included. I regard the following line, with its combination of types C 2 and B 1, as a quite exceptional fusion of two verses into an undivided whole, the on-verse filling only a little more than a measure and the off-verse filling the better part of three measures:

geweórdôde ófer èall wìfà cýnn   (R 94)

1| 2 1 1 |1 1 2 |2 2 | 2   𝄽 |

Several of these verses might be considered hypermetric, since
the last four syllables resemble type A 1 and these are preceded by
two, three, or five minor syllables at the beginning—in every case
too much for ordinary anacrusis. Those who judge by syllabic
patterns alone, or who do not recognize a rhythmic distinction be-
tween normal and hypermetric, would label them hypermetric
without further ado. But, as I explain below, I use the term
"hypermetric" to describe verses that are to be read in ac-
cordance with a different basic rhythm. The verses here in ques-
tion appear among normal verses and can easily be adjusted to
the same basic rhythm as their neighbors. Hence I am inclined to
treat them as minor deviations from, or a combination of, types
B and C:

x x | ⌣ x ⌣ x :   mìd his mícłan mëahte   (R 102a)

        | ♪ 1   1 | 1 1   1   1 |

and similarly,   þæt þǣr mōdiġlīċe   (M 200a)

                  swā nū missenlīċe   (W 75a)

perhaps also,   and his brōðru mid him   (M 191a)

x x x | ⌣ x ⌣ x :   nē ẏmbe áwiht èlles   (S 46a)

        | ∧ 1 1   1 | 1 1   1   1 |

x x x x x | ⌣ x ⌣ x :   Ne scúlon mè on þǣre þéode   (M 220a)

      1 | 1 1 $\frac{4}{3}$ $\frac{2}{3}$ | 1 1   1   1 |

Another, somewhat similar verse has perhaps a slightly different
stress-pattern:

x x | ⌣ ⌣ x x :   ànd on drẏhtlīċestum   (S 85a)

      | ♪ 1   1 | 2 $\frac{2}{3}$ $\frac{2}{3}$ $\frac{2}{3}$ |

Still another is usually considered hypermetric and is certainly
very full, but I prefer to read it in accordance with the normal
rhythm, as if it were D*1 with a remarkably heavy opening:

⌣ x ⌣ x | ⌣ x ⌣ x :   wíntra dǣl on wéorold-ríċe   (W 65a)

     | $\frac{4}{3}$ $\frac{2}{3}$ $\frac{4}{3}$ $\frac{2}{3}$ | 1 1   1 1 |

Finally, there are four verses that resemble type A 3 in that a
number of minor syllables lead up to an alliterating lift, but
there is no final drop, the ending being abrupt like that of type
E:

⌣ x x x | ⌣ :   wǣron mìne fét   (S 9a)

      | 1 1   1 1 | 2 ♪ |

‿x x x x | ‿‿ :   Hwǽðre iċ þùrh þæt gŏ́ld   (R 18a)

| 1 $\frac{1}{3}$ $\frac{2}{3}$ 1   1 | 2   𝄐 |

þǎ hē hæ̀fde þæt fŏ́lc   (M 22a)

| 1   1   1 $\frac{1}{3}$ $\frac{2}{3}$ | 2   𝄐 |

‿x x x x x | ‿‿ :   þǎ on-èfeṇ hira frḗ̈an   (M 184a)

| $\frac{4}{3}$ $\frac{2}{3}$ $\frac{1}{2}\frac{1}{2}$ $\frac{1}{2}\frac{1}{2}$ | 2   𝄐 |

The first of these verses has the same number of syllables and the same rhythm as *þenden hē wið wulf* (*Beowulf* 3027a), and I think all four are authentic. [62]

The Hypermetric Verses

In *The Dream of the Rood*, *The Wanderer*, and *The Seafarer*, as in several other Old English poems, we encounter clusters of verses that appear to exceed the normal metrical limit by several rather weighty syllables. Sometimes these are syllables that can be treated as all or part of a drop, sometimes they include an alliterating lift. Most of the verses resemble normal varieties of type A to which several syllables have been prefixed. A few end like this or that other type, and have similar prefixes. I find it convenient to classify them as HA, HB, etc. if the prefixed syllables include an alliterating lift, and as hA, hB, etc. if they do not. In the following examples, taken from the three poems in this book, the alliteration is distinguished by boldface type, and in the notations, the bar marks the point after which the pattern of a normal verse, or the part of a normal verse that starts with its first lift, may be observed: [63]

HA 1:   ‿x | ‿x‿x : **e**fstan **e**lne miċle   (R 34a)

‿x x | ‿x x‿x : **b**eorn of his **b**rēostum acŷðan

(W 113a)

HA 2a: ‿x x | ‿‿◡̣x‿x : **S**tormas þǣr **s**tān-clifu bēoton

(S 23a)

---

[62] See *The Rhythm of Beowulf*, revised edition, pp. xxx and 321.

[63] Thus, where the comparison is to type B or type C, the bar does not mark the place where the corresponding normal verse would begin.

HA 4: ́x x x x | ́ ́ ⌣x : Ēadiġ biþ sē-þe ēaþ-mōd
                                      leofaþ   (S 107a)

hA 1: x x x x | ́x x ́x : Eall ic wæs mid sorgum
                                      ġedrēfed   (R 20b)

hA 2a: x x x x x | ́ ́ ́x : Ongunnon him þā mold-ærn
                                      wyrċan   (R 65b)

hA 4: x x x x x | ́ ́ ⌣x : Ongunnon him þā sorg-lēoþ
                                      galan   (R 67b)

HB 1: ⌣x x x | ́x ́ : fæġere þurh forþ-ġesceaft   (R 10a)

hB 1: x x x | ́x ⌣x : sōhton him wuldres Cyning
                                      (R 133b)

HC 1: x ⌣x x x | ⌣x ́x : begoten of þæs Guman sīdan
                                      (R 49a)

HC 2: x ⌣x x x x x | ́⌣x : Onġierede hine þā
                                      ġeong Hæleþ   (R 39a)

HD 1: x ́x x x | ́ ́ ́x : Aleġdon hīe þær lim-wēriġne
                                      (R 63a)

hD 1: x x x x | ́ ́ ́x : Ġeseah iċ þā Frēan mann-cynnes
                                      (R 33b)

hD 2: x x x x | ́ ́ ⌣x : þā hīe woldon eft sīðian   (R 68b)

hE: x x x x x | ́ ́ x x ́ : Ġenāmon hīe þær ælmihtiġne
                                      God   (R 60b)

hE*:   x x x x | ́x ́x ⌣x : Behēoldon þær enġel-dryhta
                                      fela   (R 9b as emended)

Almost invariably the strong openings marked *H* are in the
on-verse and have double alliteration, which occurs on the lift
of the opening and the first lift of the normal close. The weak
openings marked *h* are characteristic of the off-verse, and in that
position have single alliteration on the first lift of the normal
close. On the rare occasions (not exemplified in this book) when
weak openings occur in the on-verse, they tend to have double
alliteration on the two lifts of the normal close. The following
off-verse is exceptional:

HA 1: x ́x x | ́x ́x : ġestāg hē on ġealgan hēanne   (R 40b).
The opening of this verse would pass for weak if the alliteration

were on *g*, as might be expected; but it is actually on *st*, and the opening must therefore be considered strong. In general, hypermetric verses alliterate with great regularity at the points indicated. Supplementary alliteration of a different letter occurs now and then on rather prominent syllables, but quite unpredictably.

The rare instances of hypermetric verses that close like type B or type C are troublesome because ambiguous. They are often not clearly distinguishable from normal verses of the same types or, if they have strong openings, from normal verses of type D*. The four *ubi sunt* verses in *The Wanderer* (lines 92–93) have this sort of ambiguity. They conform to the normal types B and C but are heavy enough to be treated as hB and hC. Since they stand by themselves and are not decisively hypermetric in form I prefer to regard them as normal verses, but to read them—the opening verse especially—at a retarded tempo.

It would be a great mistake to suppose that the poets, in composing hypermetric verses, simply took normal verses and added preludes to them. They are constructed as whole verses of another order; yet the resemblance of the close to a normal verse is, I think, a clue to their basic rhythm. By a rather complicated series of inferences (of which I have given some idea in *The Rhythm of Beowulf*) I have come to believe that this rhythm resembles the normal in structure but is twice as long. We have two measures of quadruple time for each verse, but the unitary beat is 2 instead of 1. If we use musical notation and call the normal time 4/8, the hypermetric time is 4/4. Thus the second measure of a hypermetric verse is equal in duration to both measures of a normal verse. Each half of this slower measure is equivalent to one normal measure and can assert a quasi-independence. [64]

The verses already quoted can be adjusted to the basic rhythm as follows:

HA 1:   éfstàn élne mìcle   (R 34a)

          | 4   2   ♩| 2 2   2 1 ∧ |

---

[64] The absence of consistent emphasis at the mid-point of the first measure is one of the reasons for thinking of two double measures rather than four of the normal sort. Another is the position of the alliteration. For full discussion of this problem, see *The Rhythm of Beowulf*, pp. 121 ff.

béorn   of his bréostum acýðan   (W 113a)

| 4 ᴀ 1   1 | 2   1   1 2 1 ∧ |

HA 4:   Éadiġ bìþ sē-þe éaþ-mód lèofaþ   (S 107a)

| 2   2   2   1 1 | 2   2   1 1 ᴀ |

hA 2a: Ongùnnon him þā mőld-ærn wẙrċan   (R 65b)

| ᴀ 1   1   1   1   1 | 2   2   2 1 ∧ |

HB 1:   fǽġere þurh főrþ-ġescēaft   (R 10a)

| 1   1 1 ᴀ 2 | 3   1   2   ᴀ |

hB 1:   sòhton him wűldres Cẙning   (R 133b)

| ᴀ 2   1   1 | 2   2   1 1   ᴀ |

HC 1:   begőten   of þæs Gűman sìdan   (R 49a) [65]

| 1 | 1   3 ᴀ 1   1 | 1   3   2 1 ∧ |

HC 2:   Ongíerede hìne þā ġéong Hǽleþ   (R 39a) [66]

| 1 | 1 1 2   1 1 2 | 2   ᴀ 1 1 |

HD 1:   Alégdon hìe þǽr lìm-wèriġne   (R 63a)

| 1 | 2   2   2   2 | 4   2 1   1 |

hE: Genàmon hìe þǽr ǽlmihtiġne Gòd   (R 60b)

| ᴀ 1   1   1   1 | 2   1 $\frac{1}{2}$ $\frac{1}{2}$ 2 ᴀ |

Hypermetric verses appear in many different contexts and can produce various effects. The extra long quantities that characterize a good many of the strong openings require a half-chanting delivery and can create an effect of deliberation or of measured solémnity. In contrast, the polysyllabic weak openings can seem almost garrulous. In *The Dream of the Rood* they may suggest impulsive outpourings of the speaker's feelings, alternating with the slow openings that arrest movement and bring out the depth of his emotion. At the end of *The Wanderer* and *The Seafarer* the hypermetric verses are associated by their content with gnomic wisdom and may seem somewhat aloof and oracular. In *The Seafarer* they have, in addition, a rather grim intensity. No verse form, however, can be said to have a meaning of its own.

[65] Better, perhaps, with a "semi-strong" opening: | ᴀ 1 ì 1 1 1 | í 3 ì 1 ∧ |.
[66] I avail myself of the last part of the second measure to start the next verse, thus coverting the latter to a normal verse with anacrusis so that it matches the completely normal sequel, line 40a.

Certain forms seem appropriate to certain ranges of emotion, but it is the chief function of any verse form to enhance the specific meanings that are carried by the words, partly by conferring on them the added solemnity of a basic order, partly by admitting the little rhythmic variations that their individuality requires.

Illustrative Notations of Consecutive Passages

In the foregoing account attention has been focused on individual verses. The beginning and end of such analysis, however, is the consecutively composed poem. We must begin with the verse as it occurs in its context, and must test the value of our results by the extent to which they accord with and deepen our understanding of whole passages. As an aid to this kind of testing I have supplied consecutive rhythmic notations for three passages chosen from the first three poems in the book. Much more extensive notations, making use of the traditional musical symbols, will be found in *The Rhythm of Beowulf*. My own way of reading all these poems is illustrated fully on the phonograph record to which I have referred at the beginning of this account.

The student should be encouraged to acquire for himself the art of reading these poems aloud with due attention not merely to rhythm but to the full expression of their meaning. There is no substitute for this kind of poetic understanding, and it is worth striving for even though, with our limited knowledge, it cannot be fully achieved. A step in the right direction can be taken long before the student has mastered the details of Old English versification. The application of a rhythmic notation, with due attention to quantity, requires careful study and long practice, whereas a respectably rhythmic reading of most verses can be accomplished much more simply. If the student will learn to pick out the governing accents, time them with reasonable accuracy, supply rests where accents are missing, and observe a distinction between long and short syllables, he need not work out the quantitative details. They will take care of themselves.

It is good practice to beat time to the measures, bringing the hand down for the primary beat at the beginning of the measure, up for the secondary beat in the middle of it. The effect will be too mechanical but it is a proper beginning. The subtle modulations of an expressive recitation will follow in due course when the basic order is mastered.

Cædmon's Hymn

Nú scùlon hḗriàn   hḗofon-rȉċes Wḗard,
| 2   1 1 | 2 2 | 1 1   1 1 | 2   𝄐 |

Mḗtodès mḗahtà   ànd his mṓd-ġeþànc,
| 1 1 2 | 2   1 ∧ | 𝄐 1 .   1 | $\frac{4}{3}$ $\frac{2}{3}$ 2 |

wḗorc Wúldor-Fǣder,   swà hē wúndra ġehwǣs,
| 2   𝄐 | 2   1 1 | 𝄐 1   1 | 1 $\frac{1}{2}$ $\frac{1}{2}$ 1 ∧ |

ḗċè Drȳhtèn,   ȍr astḗaldè.
| 2 2 | 2 1   ∧ | 3 1 | 2   1 ∧ |

Hè ǣrest scȍp   ȉeldà bḗarnùm
| 𝄐 2 | 1 1   2 | 2 2 | 2 1   ∧ |

hḗofon to hrȍfè,   hǟliġ Scȉeppeǹd;
| 1   2   1 | 2 1 ∧ | 2 2 | 2   2 |

þà mȉddan-ġeàrd   mǟnn-cȳnnes Wḗard,
| 𝄐 2 | 1 1   2 | 2   1 1 | 2   𝄐 |

ḗċè Drȳhtèn,   ǣftèr tḗodè—
| 2 2 | 2 1   ∧ | 2 2 | 2 1   ∧ |

fȉrùm fȍldàn   Frḗa ǣlmȉhtiġ.
| 2 2 | 2   1   ∧ | 2 𝄐 | 2   1 1 |

The Battle of Brunanburh

Lines 1–20a

Ǽðelstǽn cýning,   ḗorlà drýhtèn,

| 1 1 2 | 1 1 𝄞 | 2 2 | 2 1 ∧ |

bḗornà bḗag-ġìèfa,   ànd his brṓðor ḗàc,

| 2 2 | 2 1 1 | 𝄞 1   1 | 1 1   1 ∧ |

Ḗadmuǹd ǽðelìng,   ḗaldor-làngne tír

| 2 2 | 1 1 1   ∧ | $\frac{4}{3}$ $\frac{2}{.3}$ $\frac{4}{3}$ $\frac{2}{3}$ | 2 ∧

ġeslṓgoǹ æt sǽċċè   swḗordà ḗcgùm

1 | 2 1 1 | 2 1 ∧ | 2 2 | 2 2 |

ỳmbe Brṹnanbùrh.   Bṓrd-weàll clṹfon,

| 𝄞 1   1 | 1 1   1   ∧ | 2   2 | 1 1 𝄞 |

hḗowòn hḗaðu-lìnda   hǽmorà lǽfùm

| 2 2 | 1 1 1 1 | 1 1 2 | 2 1 ∧ |

ḗaforàn Ḗadweàrdes,   swā hìm ġe-ǽðele wǽs

| 1 1 2 | 2   1 1 | ∧   1 $\frac{4}{3}$ $\frac{2}{3}$ | $\frac{2}{3}\frac{2}{3}$ 2 |

fràm cnḗo-màgum   þæt hìe æt cǽmpe òft

| 𝄞 2 | 2   1 1 | ∧ 1   1 1 | $\frac{4}{3}$ $\frac{2}{3}$ 2 |

wìþ lǽðra ġehwòne   lǽnd eǽlgòden,

| 𝄞 2 | 1 $\frac{1}{2}$ $\frac{1}{2}$ 1 1 | 2 𝄞| 2 1 1 |

hṓrd and hǽmàs.   Hḗttènd crṹngon,

| 2 ∧ 1 | 2 1 ∧ | 2 2 | 2 1 ∧|

Scṓttà lḗodè   and scíp-flṓtan,

| 2 2 | 2 1   1 | 2 𝄞| 1 1 𝄞 |

fǽġè fḗollòn.   Fḗld dḗnnòde

| 2 2 | 2 1   ∧ | 2 𝄞| 2 1 1 |

sḗcgà swǽtè   sìþþan sṹnne ùpp

| 2 2 | 2 1 ∧| 𝄞 1   1 | $\frac{4}{3}$ $\frac{2}{3}$ 1   ∧|

òn mṓrgen-tìd,   mǽrè tṹngòl,

| 𝄞 2 | 1 1 2 | 2 2 | 2 1 ∧ |

glắd òfer grűndàs,   Gốdes cằndel bẻorht,

|2   1 1 |2   1 ∧ |1 1 1 1 2   𝄞|

ḗċès Drỹhtnès,   òþ sẽo ắðele ġescẻaft

|2 2 |2 2 |𝄞 1   1 |½ ½½ ½ 2 |

sẳg to sẻtlè.   Þằr læ̇ġ sḗcg mằniġ

|3   1 |2 1 ∧| 𝄞 1   1 |2   1 1 |

gẳruṁ aġḗetèd,   gűma Nốrðẻrna

|2 1   1 |2 1   ∧ |1 1 𝄞| 2 1 1 |

òfer sċïeld scòten,   swèlċe Scỹttisc ẻἁc,

|𝄞 1 1 |2   1 1 |𝄞 1   1 |1 1   1   ∧|

wẻrìġ, wïġes sẳd.

|2 1 ∧| 1 1   2 |

The Dream of the Rood

Lines 1–23

Hwằt, iċ swḗfna cỳst   sḗcgàn wïllè,

|𝄞 $\frac{4}{3}$ $\frac{2}{3}$ |$\frac{4}{3}$ $\frac{2}{3}$ 2 |2 2 |2 1 ∧|

hwằt mè ġemằttè   to mïdrè nïhtè,

|2   1 1 |2 1   1 |2 2 |2 1 ∧|

sìþþan rḗord-bḕrend   rḗstè wűnodòn.

|𝄞 1 1 |2   1 1 |2 2 |1 1 2 |

Þűhte mè þằt iċ ġesẳwè   sḗldlïcre trẻo

|1 $\frac{1}{3}$ $\frac{2}{3}$ $\frac{2}{3}$ $\frac{2}{3}$ $\frac{2}{3}$| 2 1 ∧ |2 1 1 |2 ∧

on lỹft lẳdàn   lẻohtè bewűndèn,

|1 |2 𝄞| 2 1 ∧| 2 1 1 |2 1   ∧|

bẻamà bẻorhtòst.   Èall þằt bẻacen wằs

|2 2 |2 2 |𝄞 1 1 |1 1 $\frac{4}{3}$

begốten mid gốldè;   gïmmàs stốdòn

$\frac{2}{3}$ |1 2   1 |2 1 ∧ |2   2 |2 2 |

fẳġere æt fốldan scẳatum,   swèlċe þằr fïfe wằron

|1 1 1 𝄞 2 |2 2   2 2 |𝄞   1 1 2 |2 2   2 2 |

úppe   on þam éaxl-ġespànne.   Behèoldon þǣr
|2   2🔔1   1 |2 1 1   2 1∧| 🔔 1 1 1 1   2

énġel-dryhta féla,
|$\frac{4}{3}$ $\frac{2}{3}$ 1 1 1 1 🔔|

fǣġere   þurh fórþ-ġesceàft;   ne wæs þǣr hùru
|1 1 1🔔 2 |3   1 2   🔔 |∧ 1 1   1 2 2

fràcuðes ġeàlga,
|1 1 2   2 1

ac híne þǣr behéoldòn   hǽlġè gǽstàs,
1 |1 1 $\frac{4}{3}$ $\frac{2}{3}$| 2 2 |2 2 |2 1 ∧|

ménn òfer móldàn   and èall þeos mǣre ġesceàft.
|2   1 1 |2 2 |∧ 1   1   1 |1 $\frac{1}{2}$ $\frac{1}{2}$ 2 |

Séldlìc wæs se síġe-bèam,   and ìc sýnnum fàg,
|1 1 $\frac{4}{3}$ $\frac{2}{3}$ |1 1 2 |∧ 1 2 |1 1 $\frac{4}{3}$

forwúndòd mid wǎmmùm.   Ġesèah ìc wúldres trèo
$\frac{2}{3}$ |2 1   1 |2   2 |∧ 1 1 1 |1 1 2 |

wǣdùm ġewéorðòd   wýnnùm scìnàn,
|2 $\frac{4}{3}$ $\frac{2}{3}$ |2 1 ∧ | 2   2 |2 $\frac{4}{3}$

ġeġíered mid góldè;   ġímmàs hǽfdòn
$\frac{2}{3}$|1 2   1 |2 1 ∧ | 2   2 |2 $\frac{4}{3}$

bewríġen   wéorþlìce   Wéaldèndes trèo.
$\frac{2}{3}$ |1 1   🔔 |2   1 1 | 2   1 1 |2 🔔 |

Hwǣðre ìc þùrh þæt góld   onġíetan mèahtè
|1 $\frac{1}{2}$ $\frac{2}{3}$ 1   1 |2 ∧ 1 |1 3 |2 1∧|

eármrà ǽr-ġewìnn,   þæt hit ǽrest ongànn
|2   2 |$\frac{4}{3}$ $\frac{2}{3}$ 2 |🔔 1 1 |$\frac{2}{3}$ $\frac{2}{3}$ $\frac{2}{3}$ 2 |

swǣtan on þā swìðran hèalfe.   Èall ìc wæs
|2 2🔔1 1 |2 2   2 1 ∧ |🔔 1 1   1

mid sórgum ġedrèfed;
1 |2 1 1 2 1 ∧ |

fórht ìc wæs for þǣre fǣġeran ġesìhþe.   Ġesèah
|3   1   1   1   1 1 |1 1 $\frac{4}{3}$ $\frac{2}{3}$2 1 ∧|🔔 1 2

ìc þæt fúse bèacen
1 1 |2 2 2 2 |

wḗndan   wǣdum and blḗoum: hwílum hit wǣs

| 2   2   🄰 | 2   1   1   2   1   ∧ | 2   1   1   2

                                      mid wǣtan bestíemed,

                                2 | 2   1   1   2 $\frac{4}{3}$

beswíled   mid swǣtes gǎnge,   hwílum mid

$\frac{2}{3}$ | 1 1   🄰   2 | 2 2   2   1   ∧ | 🄰   2   1   1

                                     sínce ġeġíerwed.

                                | 2   1   1   2   1 ∧ |

GLOSSARY

The order is alphabetical. The diagraph *æ* is treated as *ae*, falling between *ad* and *af*. The voiceless spirant *þ*, interchanging medially with voiced *ð*, follows *t* as a separate letter. Words beginning with the prefix *ġe-* are listed according to their stems; for example, *ġe-beorg* follows *beorg*.

The treatment of compounds is unusual. All words separated into two elements by hyphens in the text of the poems (unless the first element is merely an unstressed prefix, as with *ġe-* when the stem begins with a vowel, or *oþ-* when the stem begins with *þ*) are registered according to their separate elements and also as compounds. Thus *brim-fuglas, Wanderer* 47, is listed according to its elements, *brim* and *fugol*; but also, under the first element, *brim*, the whole compound is listed and defined, and under *fugol* there is a cross-reference to the compound. The student is advised to learn the simple elements rather than the compounds, for the poets use a comparatively limited group of elements to produce a great variety of compounds, most of which can be interpreted successfully by anyone who knows the meaning of the elements. At the same time there are often several possible meanings in an element, and now and then subtleties in the combinations that require careful interpretation. It is therefore safer to define the compound as well as its elements, making sure that the definition fits the immediate context. Most of the compounds are nominal or adjectival, but even such minor combinations as *for-þon, on-weġ, sē-þe,* and *þā-ġiet* are treated in the same way for the sake of consistency.

Hyphenation has not been extended in the text to mere prefixes and suffixes, and therefore such words as *anforht* and *fǣrlīce* are treated like simple words even though it is easy to separate their elements. In the glossary itself hyphenation has been extended to prefixes for the sake of clarity, and cross-references are employed to connect prefixed with unprefixed forms.

Prefixes are ordinarily left undefined, since full definitions would fill a great deal of space. Most of them appear also as separate words and are likewise familiar in modern English. Exception is made on behalf of the very common prefixes *ġe-* and *a-*, because they do not appear independently and their meanings, though sometimes important, are elusive. Those who desire further guidance should consult the Bosworth-Toller *Anglo-Saxon Dictionary* and *Supplement*, and the *Oxford English Dictionary*.

Verbs are cross-referenced with particular care, in order to enable the student to keep track of, and compare, the simple verb and its prefixed variations. The unprefixed form is used as a guide, by cross-reference, to the prefixed forms. Hence it is always entered even if it does not actually occur in the poems.

As a further aid to the student, class-numbers are assigned to the verbs, and the principal parts of all the strong and preterite-present verbs are spelled out, along with those of a few particularly troublesome weak verbs. The principal parts will be found under the unprefixed verb if it actually occurs in the poems; otherwise under one or more of the prefixed forms.

Nouns that do not belong to the main declensions (masculine and neuter *a*-stems, feminine *ō*-stems) are classified either as weak (wk.) or by stems: *ja*-stem, *i*-stem, *u*-stem, etc. This will not always be of practical assistance to the student, but often it will guide him (by way of his reference grammar) to the reason for an unusual ending or the presence of *i*-mutation in the stem-vowel. Adjectives are similarly treated, though the useful distinctions are fewer. The *ja-/jō*-stems are marked simply "ja-stem"; the *wa-/wō*-stems simply "wa-stem". All others follow the regular *a-/ō*-declension, except for *cwic(u)*, which is marked "u-stem".

Familiarity with *i*-mutation and the vowel-gradation exhibited most obviously in the strong verbs enables one to associate a number of words that would otherwise appear to be unrelated. For this reason attention has been called to a good many of the unmutated base-words on which weak verbs of the first class (characterized by the prehistoric ending *-jan with its regular mutating power) are formed, and to a few of the more conspicuous and helpful gradational correspondences.

Abbreviations

The poems are cited according to the order of the texts, by initial and line-number: C (Cædmon's Hymn); B (Brunanburh); R (Rood); M (Maldon); W (Wanderer); S (Seafarer); D (Deor).

Immediately following the boldface entry of a word is a grammatical notation. Nouns are classified by gender (*m., f.,* or *n.*) and also, as mentioned above, page 142, by the prehistoric stem-endings indicating their declension if they are not the regular *a*- or *ō*-stems. The weak declension (*n*-stems) is marked *wk.* before the specification of gender.

Verbs are classified as follows:

> *v.1* to *v.7* = strong verb, class 1 to class 7 (Arabic numbers).
> *wk.v.I* to *wk.v.III* = weak verb, class I to class III (Roman).
> *pret.-pres.v.* = preterite-present verb.
> *anom.v.* = anomalous verb.   *contr.v.* = contract verb.

The other parts of speech are designated by easily recognized abbreviations: *pron., adj., adv., prep., conj., interj.; poss.* for possessive, *rel.* for relative, *num.* for numeral; *comp.* for comparative, *superl.* for superlative. On the designation of stem-endings for certain adjectives, see above, page 142.

Declensional forms of nouns are described by case (*n., v., g., d., a., i.* for nominative, vocative, genitive, dative, accusative, instrumental) and number (*s., p.,* for singular, plural) in that order (*ns., gs.,* for nominative singular, genitive singular, etc., with period after the second letter only). Adjectives have a third letter for the gender: *nsm.* for nominative singular masculine, etc., but this is omitted for the genitive and dative plural, where there is never any distinction of gender in the endings. When there is need to give case alone or number alone, fuller abbreviations are used (*nom.*, *gen.*, *dat.*, *acc.*, *instr.*; *sg.*, *pl.*; and *part. gen.* for partitive genitive). The combinations *dis.* and *dip.* mean dative or instrumental, singular and plural respectively. This formula is used for nouns with dative case-endings when they stand alone (without prepositions) in an apparently instrumental function. Nouns with such endings following prepositions are said to be dative unless there is clear evidence (from an adjective or article) that they are instrumental.

Verb-forms are marked *inf.* (infinitive), *pres. part.* (present participle), *pp.* (past participle), or according to tense (*pres.* or *pret.*), person and number (*1s.* for first person singular, *1p.* for first person plural, etc.). The mood is not specified if it is indicative. Imperatives are marked *imper.* (*s.* or *p.*), and subjunctives, *subj.* Occasionally there is reason to indicate whether a verb is transitive (*trans.*) or intransitive (*intrans.*), or that it is used absolutely (*absol.*).

After the main entry, its classification, and a definition, the particular forms occurring in the texts are cited. If the form is the same as the main entry, it is not repeated. If it differs by simple addition of an ending, a dash for the uninflected entry is followed by the letters to be added; if the change is partly internal, the whole form is given. For example, under *burg, f. cons.-stem*, the notation *as. M 291* means, accusative singular *burg*, Maldon 291; *dp.—um* means, dative plural *burgum*; but for *ap.* (accusative plural) the internally altered form *byrig* is given entire.

Occasionally, when a form already indicated is repeated, only its initial is given. Thus, following citation of the form *abrēoðe*, *a. his anginn* stands for *abrēoðe his anginn*.

Among other, commonly received abbreviations are *OE* for Old English, *Gmc.* for Germanic, *cf.* for *confer* (compare), *q.v.*

for *quod vide* (which see). In certain grammatical descriptions, *w.* stands for with.

Dictionaries and Grammars

For full definition with illustrative quotations from prose and poetry, the student must consult Joseph Bosworth, *An Anglo-Saxon Dictionary*, edited and enlarged by T. Northcote Toller, 1882–1898, and the *Supplement* by Toller, 1908–1921, both volumes published at Oxford by the Clarendon Press, reprinted 1929 and 1954 and still available; often called "Bosworth-Toller" for short. Both volumes must be consulted for a given word. Since a number of Old English texts have been edited since the completion of Toller's *Supplement* and others are still unedited, no dictionary is complete. The most up-to-date for its list of words and the handiest for quick reference is *A Concise Anglo-Saxon Dictionary* by J. R. Clark Hall, 4th ed. with a Supplement by Herbert D. Meritt, Cambridge University Press, 1960. Of great value as a partial concordance to the poetry is C. W. M. Grein's *Sprachschatz der angelsächsischen Dichter*, newly edited by F. Holthausen and J. J. Köhler, Heidelberg: Carl Winter, 1912–1914. A complete concordance, based on the texts of the Krapp-Dobbie *Anglo-Saxon Poetic Records*, is in preparation by J. B. Bessinger, Jr. Useful for etymology is F. Holthausen, *Altenglisches etymologisches Wörterbuch*, Heidelberg: Carl Winter, 1934; 2nd ed. with bibliographical supplement, 1963. For all words that have survived in the language after 1100, the thirteen-volume *Oxford English Dictionary* is often of great value. Middle English forms of these words, if not the latest on record, are sometimes entered for cross-reference, but the main entry is under the *latest* spelling.

The fullest and most authoritative grammars are A. Campbell, *Old English Grammar*, Oxford: The Clarendon Press, 1959, and Karl Brunner, *Altenglische Grammatik, nach der angelsächsischen Grammatik von Eduard Sievers*, 3rd ed., Tübingen: Max Niemeyer, 1965 (usually called "Sievers-Brunner").

A

ā, adv. *always, ever;* M 315; S 42, 47.

a- (or ā-). unstressed verbal prefix of various origin (Æ-, OR-, AN-, etc.) and various meaning (*up, on, from, away,* etc.), but often modifying only slightly the meaning of the unprefixed verb.

a-bēodan, v.2. *announce, deliver (a message);* imper. s. abēod, M 49 (absol. use); pret. 3s. abēad, M 27. [Cf. bēodan.]

a-brēoðan, v.2. *fail, come to naught;* pres. 3s. subj. abrēoðe, M 242 (a. his anginn, *may his conduct have an evil end*—Gordon). [BRĒOÐAN, BRĒAÞ, BRUÐON, .BROÐEN, without the usual grammatical change, ð to *d.*]

ac, conj. *but;* R 11, 43, 115, 119, 132; M 82, 193, 247, 252, 269, 318; S 47.

a-cweċċan, wk.v.I. *shake, brandish,* pret. 3s. acweahte, M 255, 310. [CWEĊĊAN (Gmc. *CWACJAN), CWEAHTE, CWEAHT; cf. CWACIAN, wk.v.II, *quake.*]

a-cweðan, v.5, trans. *speak, utter;* pres. 3s. acwiþ, W 91. [Cf. cweðan.]

a-cȳðan, wk.v.I. *make known, manifest;* inf. W 113. [Cf. ġe-cȳðan.]

ādl, f. *disease, sickness;* ns. S 70.

æfen(n), n. ja-stem (also m.). *evening.* æfen-tīd, f. i-stem. *evening hour;* as,—e, R 68. (Possibly ap., *in the evening hours,* but tīd sometimes has as. —e like the ō-stems.)

æfre, adv. *ever;* B 66; D 11; æfre

ymbe stunde, *ever and anon, repeatedly,* M 271 [see ymbe].

æftan, adv. *from behind;* B 63.

æfter, prep. *after.* (a) w. dat. (temporal), R 65; M 65. (b) w. acc. (marking object of affection), *with longing for,* W 50.

æfter, adv. *after(wards);* C 8; S 77 (i.e., *after death*). æfter-cweðende, pres. part., pl., as noun, *those speaking afterwards (speaking of a man after his death);* gp. —cweðendra, S 72.

æġhwelċ, pron. and adj. *each, every (one).* — as pron. w. part. gen., nsm. M 234 (w. ūre, *of us);* asm. —ne, R 86 (w. gp. ānra, *each one).* —as adj., nsf. R 120. [ā, *ever,* plus ġe-hwelċ, q.v.]

æġðer, pron. *each (of two), either;* nsm. M 133. —conj. æġðer . . . and, *both . . . and,* M 224. [Shortened from ÆĠHWÆÐER, ā plus ġe-hwæðer, *each of two*].

ælmihtiġ, adj. *almighty;* nsm. C 9; R 39, 93, 98, 106, 153, 156; asm. —ne, R 60. [ÆL-, combining form of eall, *all,* plus mihtiġ, *mighty.*]

æniġ, pron. and adj. *anyone, any.* — pron., nsm. R 110, 117; M 70; dsm. —um, R 47. — adj., nsf. M 195; gsm. æniġes, S 116.

ær, adv. *before, formerly, already;* R 118, 137, 145; M 60; W 43, 113; S 102; D 41; — giving pluperf. value to past tense, R 114, 154; M 158, 198, 290. ær-ġewinn, n.

former struggle, agony; as. R 19. [See ǣror, ǣrest.]

ǣr, prep. w. dat. *before,* S 69. **ǣr-þon,** conj. *before,* R 88.

ǣr, conj. w. subj. *before;* M 61 (correl. w. **ǣr,** adv.) , 279, 300; W 64, 69; S 74.

ǣrende, n. ja-stem. *message;* as. M 28.

ǣrest, adv. superl. *earliest, first;* C 5; M 124, 186; R 19 (þæt hit **ǣrest** ongann, *in that it had straightway begun*[?]);—þā . . . **ǣrest,** *when first, as soon as,* M 5.

ǣrn, n. *dwelling, house.* See mold-**ǣrn.**

ǣrnan, wk. v.I. *cause (a horse) to run; gallop;* pret. 3p. **ǣrndon,** M 191. [Gmc. *RANNJAN, causative based on RANN, second gradation of RINNAN, v.3, *run;* in OE the *r* in these forms was frequently metathesized.]

ǣror, adv. comp. *earlier,* R 108.

ǣr-þon, see **ǣr,** prep.

ǣs, n. *food, carrion;* gs. —es, B 63; M 107.

æsc, m. *ash (-wood).* —(a) *spear (of ash);* as. M 43, 310; gp. —a, W 99.

æsc-holt, n. *(ash-wood) spear;* as. M 230. — (b) *ship (of ash):* **æsc-here,** m. i-stem, *army coming in ships; viking army;* ns. M 69. (The cognate Old Norse ASKR was applied to the typical viking warship.)

æt, prep. w. dat. *at, in, by;* B 4, 8, 42, 44; R 8, 63; M 10, 39 (æt ūs, *at our hands, from us*), etc. (16 times); W 111; S 7.

ǣterne, see **ǣtren.**

æt-foran, prep. w. dat. *before, in front of,* M 16. [Cf. be-foran.]

æt-gædere, adv. *together, in unison.* bū-tū æ., *both together,* R 48; samod æ., *in joint action together,*

both together, W 39. [Cf. to-gædere, usually with sense of interaction or interrelation or meeting rather than mere association or simultaneity.]

ǣtren, ǣterne, adj. *poisoned, deadly;* nsm. **ǣterne,** M 146; asm. **ǣtrenne,** M 47. [Properly **ǣtren,** later ǢTTREN, from ĀTER, poison. The odd form **ǣterne** was perhaps influenced by norðerne, sūðerne, etc., or by some old poetic use of a weak form, ǢTRENA, metathesized as ǢTERNA.]

æt-samne, adv. *together;* bēġen æ., *both together,* B 57.

æt-wītan, v.I, w. dat. *reproach;* inf., M 220, 250. [Cf. ġe-wītan.]

æðele, adj. *noble;* nsm. M 280; nsf. wk. B 16; asm. wk. æðelan, M 151.

ġe-æðele, adj. *befitting noble descent;* nsn. B 7.

æðeling, m. *nobleman, prince;* (as title) *member of the royal family, prince;* ns. B 3, 58; *Prince,* ds. —e, R 58; (broadly) gp. —a, S 93.

æðelu, n. ja-stem, pl. *descent, (noble) origin;* ap. M 216.

ǣwisc, adj. *ashamed.* **ǣwisc-mōd,** adj. *ashamed in spirit;* npm. —e, B 56.

a-feallan, v.7. *fall, be laid low (in death);* pp. **afeallen,** nsm. M 202. [Cf. feallan.]

a-flīeman, wk.v.I. *put to flight;* pret. 3s. **aflīemde,** M 243. [Cf. ġe-flīeman.]

a-fȳsan, wk.v.I. (a) *urge forward, impel;* pp. **afȳsed,** nsm. R 125; (b) *drive away;* inf. M 3. [Cf. fȳsan.]

āgan, pret.-pres. v. *have, possess;* inf. M 87; pres. 1s. **āg,** M 175; 3s. **āg,** R 107; S 27 (as aux. w. pp.); 3s. subj. **āge,** W 64; 1p. subj. **āgen,** S 117; pret. 1s. **āhte,** D 38; 3s **āhte,** M 189; D 18, 22. — neg. **nāgan,**

have not; pres. 1s. **nāg**, R 131. [ĀGAN, ĀG, ĀGON, ĀHTE.]

a-ġiefan, v.5. *give, render;* pret. 3s. **aġeaf**, M 44; pp. **aġiefen**, nsn. M 116. [ĊIEFAN, ĊEAF, ĊĒAFON, ĊIEFEN.]

a-ġietan, wk.v.I. *destroy (by shedding blood);* pp. **aġieted**, nsm. B 18. [Base-word ĊEAT, as in pret. s. of ġēotan, q.v.]

a-hafen, see **a-hebban**.

a-hēawan, v.7. *cut down;* pp. **a-hēawen**, nsm. R 29 [Cf. hēawan.]

a-hebban, v.6. *raise, lift up;* pret. 1s. **ahōf**, R 44; 3s. M 130, 244; 3p. **ahōfon**, R 61; fig. (with ref. to lifting up the voice), *utter loudly;* pret. 1p. **ahōfon**, M 213; pp. **ahafen**, nsm. M 106. [Cf. hebban.]

āhte, see **āgan**.

a-lecgan, wk.v.I, *lay;* pret. 3p. **aleġdon**, R 63. [Cf. lecgan.]

a-liefan, wk.v.I. *allow;* inf. M 90. [Base-word lēaf, f. *permission;* cf. ge-liefan.]

amen, Lat. (from Hebrew, *verily);* (as closing formula) *may it be so!* S 124.

a-mierran, wk.v.I. *cripple, wound;* pret. 3s. **amierde**, M 165. [Base-word *MEARR; cf. ĠE-MEARR, n. *hindrance.*]

ān, pron. and adj. *one;* — as pron., asm. —ne, M 117; gp. —ra, w. **æghwelċ, ġehwelċ,** *each one, everyone.* R 86, 108; — as adj., asm. —ne, M 226. **ān-floga**, wk. m. *solitary flier;* ns. S 62. **ān-haga**, wk. m. *one who dwells alone; a solitary; a friendless man;* ns. W 1; as. —n, W 40. [For the element -HAG- see **haga**.]

āna, adv. *alone,* R 123, 128; M 94; W 8. [Often used adjectivally after noun or pron. as if nsm. wk.

of **ān**, but extended to other cases and genders.]

and, conj. *and;* C 2, and frequently in the other poems. [Spelled *and* or *ond* when written out in the MSS., but usually abbreviated as 7.]

anda, wk. m. *enmity, spite;* ds. —n, W 105.

and-lang, adj. *entire* (with reference to a period of time or a spatial dimension); asm. —ne, B 21. [*and-*, *against, corresponding,* plus **lang**, *long;* here the prefix is stressed; the same word with stress on **lang** gave modern "along."]

and-swaru, f. *answer;* as. —**sware**, M 44. [*and-*, *against, counter,* plus **SWARU**, *asseveration;* cf. SWERIAN, v.6, *swear.*]

an-forht, adj. *(very) frightened, terrified:* nsm. R 117. [**an-**, stressed form of **on**, here intensive. MS. has variant spelling *un-*, which obscures contrast with negative **un-**, R 110. Cf. forht, unforht.]

an-ġinn, n. *beginning; action, conduct;* as. M 242. [Cf. **on-ġinnan**.]

an-hyġdiġ, adj. *strong-minded;* nsm. D 2. [Probably intensive **an**-rather than **ān**-, *single.*]

an-mēdla, wk. m. *pomp, glory;* np. —n, S 81. [Base-word **mōd**, q.v.]

an-rǣd, adj. *resolute;* nsm. M 44, 132. [Uncertain whether first syllable is intensive prefix **an**- or **ān**, one, indicating singleness of purpose.]

an-sīen, f. i-stem. *appearance, face;* ns. S 91. [Cf. **wǣfer-sīen, ġe-sīene**, and ġe-sēon.]

an-wealda, wk. m. *ruler, Lord;* ns. R 153. [Cf. wealdan.]

ār, m. *messenger;* ns. M 26.

ār, f. *grace, favor, mercy;* ns. S 107;

as. —e, W 1, 114; *honor, glory,* as.
—e, D 33. **ār-hwæt,** adj. *abounding
in glory, glorious;* npm. —e,
B 73. (See note in Campbell's ed.
of B, p. 121.)

a-ræd, adj. *determined, inexorable*
(?); nsf. W 5. [The word is not
very well attested. In poetry only
here. Perhaps a shortened form of
A-RÆDED; cf. **rædan.**]

a-ræran, wk.v.I. *rear, erect;* pp.
arǣred, nsm, R 44.

a-rīsan, v.1. *arise;* pret. 3s. **arās,** R
101. [RĪSAN, RĀS, RISON, RISEN.]

a-sægde, see **a-secgan.**

a-scacan, v.6. *shake;* pret. 3s. **ascōc,**
M 230. [SCACAN, SCŌC, SCŌCON,
SCACEN.]

ġe-āscian, wk.v.II. *learn (by asking);*
pret. 1p. —**āscodon,** D 21.

a-secgan, wk.v.III. *say, speak out,
tell;* inf. W 11; pret. 3s. **asægde,**
M 198. [Cf. **secgan.**]

a-settan, wk.v.I. *set, set up, place;*
pres. 3s. subj. **asette,** R 142; pret.
3p. **asetton,** R 32. [Cf. **ġe-settan.**]

a-stāg, see **a-stīgan.**

a-stellan, wk.v.I. *establish;* pret. 3s.
astealde, C 4. [STELLAN, STEALDE,
STEALD; cf. **on-stellan.**]

a-stīgan, v.1. *ascend;* pret. 3s. **astāg,**
R 103. [Cf. **ġe-stīgan.**]

a-styrian, wk.v.I. *remove;* pp. **astyred,**
nsm. R 30. [STYRIAN, STYREDE,
STYRED, *stir, move;* from *STURJAN,
related to **storm,** m. *storm.*]

a-swebban, wk.v.I. *put to sleep (kill);*
pp. **aswefed,** npm. —e, B 30.
[SWEBBAN, SWEFEDE, SWEFED; from
*SWÆFJAN; cf. SWÆF, pret. of
SWEFAN, v.5, *sleep.*]

atol, adj. *terrible;* asn. S 6.

āwa, adv. *always,* S 79.

ā-wiht, n. i-stem. *anything, aught;*
as. S 46.

B

ġe-bād, see **ġe-bīdan.**

bæc, n. *back;* as. in **ofer bæc,** *to the
rear, back,* M 276.

bæd, bædon, see **biddan.**

ġe-bǣdan, wk.v.I. *constrain;* pp.
ġebǣded, nsm. B 33.

bǣl, n. *fire;* esp. *funeral fire, pyre;*
ds. —e, S 114.

bǣren, bǣron, see **beran.**

bærnan, wk.v.I, trans. *burn.* See
for-bærnan.

bærst, see **berstan.**

bana, wk. m. *slayer* (whether a per-
son or a thing: "*bane*"); ns. M 299;
gs. —n, R 66 (referring to the
Rood, apparently; Cook emended
to BANENA, gp., referring generally
to those who crucified the Lord).

band, see **bindan.**

baðian, wk.v.II. *bathe;* inf. W 47.

be, stressed form **bī,** prep. w. dat. *by.*
— (a) *by, beside, near;* M 319;
W 80; S 8, 98; **be healfe,** *by the
side (of),* M 152, 318; **bī** (post-
positive), M 182. — (b) *about,
concerning;* S 1; D 35. — (c) *by,
from* (marking agency or source),
D 1; **be þām,** *by that (this),* M 9.

bēacen, n. *sign, portent;* ns. R 6; as.
R 21; ds. **bēacne,** R 83; gp. **bēacna,**
R 118.

beadu, f. wō-stem. *battle;* ds. **beadwe,**
M 185. **beadu-rǣs,** m. *rush of
battle;* ns. M 111. **beadu-weorc,** n.
deed of war; gp. —a, B 48 [The
nominative of **beadu** is not re-
corded as an independent word.]

bēag, m. *ring, crown, necklace* (any
ornament of precious metal bent
or looped together; as a plural, in
formulas, virtually equivalent to
money or *wealth*); ap. — as, M 31,
160. [Cf. **būgan.**] **bēag-ġiefa,** wk. m.

ring-giver (typifying the generous patron) ; ns. B 2; d. or as. —n, M 290.

bealdlíċe, adv. *boldly;* M 311; superl. **bealdlícost,** M 78.

bealu, n. wa-stem. *evil; malice; pain, hardship;* as. S 112 *(malice).*

bealu-síþ, m. *grievous journey or bitter experience;* gp. —a, S 28.

bealu-ware, m. pl. *dwellers in iniquity, evil-doers;* gp. —wara, R 79 (perhaps an error for BEALUWA or BEALWA, gp. of **bealu**).

bēam, m. *tree, wooden beam;* spec., *rood-tree, cross;* ns. R 97; ds. —e, R 114, 122; gp. —a, R 6. [Cf. **siġe-bēam.**]

bearn, n. *child, son;* ns. R 83; M 92, 155, 186, 209, 238, 267, 300, 320; ap. S 93; — ielda bearn, *children of men (the human race, people);* np. S 77; dp. —um, C 5 (var. eorðan b., *children of earth*).

bearu, m. wa-stem. *grove;* np. **bear-was,** S 48.

bēatan, v.7. *beat;* pret. 3p. **bēoton,** S 23. [BĒATAN, BĒOT, BĒOTON, BĒATEN.]

bēċ, see **bōc.**

be-cuman, v.4. *come;* pret. 2p. **be-cōmon,** M 58; 3p., B 70. [The prefix indicates arrival but is not usually to be translated. [Cf. **cuman.**]

be-dǽlan, wk.v.I, w. dat. or instr. *separate (from), deprive (of);* pp. **bedǽled,** nsm. W 20; D 28. [Cf. **dǽlan.**]

be-delfan, v.3. *bury;* pret. 3s. **bedealf,** R 75. [DELFAN, DEALF, DULFON, DOLFEN, *dig.*]

be-drifan, v.1. *cover over, envelop;* pp. **bedrifen,** asm. —ne, R 62. [DRĪFAN, DRĀF, DRIFON, DRIFEN.]

be-droren, adj. w. dat. or instr. *deprived, bereft (of);* nsm. S 16; npm. —e, W 79. [pp. of *BE-DRĒO-SAN; cf. **drēosan.**]

be-foran, prep. w. dat. *before;* B 67 *(earlier than);* W 46 *(in front of).* [Cf. **æt-foran.**]

be-ġeall, see **be-ġiellan.**

be-ġeat, be-ġēaton, see **be-ġietan.**

bēgen, m. dual (bā, f., bū, n.). *both;* nom. B 57; M 182, 183 (by mistake?), 191, 291, 305. [Cf. **bū-tū.**]

be-ġēotan, v.2. *cover (as with liquid);* pp. **begoten,** nsn. R 7; *suffuse, drench;* same form, nsm. R 49. [Cf. **ġēotan.**]

be-ġiellan, v.3. *scream round about* (?); pret. 3s. **begeall,** S 24 (w. acc. þæt, referring perhaps to the cliffs collectively or the scene as a whole). [Recorded here only; cf. **ġiellan.**]

be-ġietan, v.5. *get possession of, conquer;* pret. 3p. **begēaton,** B 73; *keep, hold,* pret. 3s. **begeat,** S 6. [ĠIETAN, ĠEAT, ĠEATON, ĠIETEN; cf. **on-ġietan.**]

be-hangen, see **be-hōn.**

be-healdan, v.7. *behold, gaze at, keep watch over;* pret. 1s. **be-hēold,** R 25, 58; 3p. **behēoldon,** R 9, 11, 64. [Cf. **healdan.**]

be-hindan, prep. w. dat. *behind,* B 60 (postpos.). [Cf. **hindan.**]

be-hōn, contr.v.7, w. dat. -instr. *hang around (with)* ; pp. **be-hangen,** nsm. S 17. [HŌN (from *HANHAN), HĒNG, HĒNGON, HANGEN.]

be-hroren, adj. w. instr. *fallen upon (by), covered (with).* npm. —e, W 77. [pp. of BE-HRĒOSAN, the active verb recorded only as intrans., *fall;* see **hrēosan.**]

be-nam, see **be-niman.**

benċ, f. i-stem. *bench;* ds. —e, M 213.

bend, f. jō-stem. *bond;* see sinu-bend.

be-niman, v.4, w. acc. of person, instr. of thing. *deprive (of);* pret. 3s. benam, D 16. [Cf. niman.]

benn, f. jō-stem. *wound;* np. —a, W 49.

bēodan, v.2. *announce, forebode;* pres. 3s. bēodeþ, S 54. [BEODAN, BĒAD, BUDON, BODEN; cf. a-bēodan.]

bēon-wesan, anom. v. *be;* inf. bēon, M 185; wesán, R 110, 117.

(1) ordinary present forms: 1s. eom, M 179, 317; 2s. eart, M 36; 3s. is, R 80, etc. (8 times); M 31, etc. (4 times); W 106; S 86, 88, 121; 3p. sindon, R 46; W 93; sind, S 64, 80, 86; 3s. subj. sīe, R 112 (see note), 144; M 215; S 122; D 30.

(2) present forms of bēon, used in general statements or with future sense: 3s. biþ, R 86; W 5, etc. (12 times); S 44, 72 (MS. *þæt*), etc. (7 times); 3p. bēoþ, W 49.

(3) preterite forms of wesan: 1s. wæs, R 20, etc. (9 times); M 217; D 36; 3s. wæs, B 7, 40; R 6, etc. (12 times); M 23, etc. (18 times); D 8, 11, 19, 23, 37; 3p. wǣron, R 8; M 110; S 9, 83; 3s. subj. wǣre, M 195, 240; W 96; D 26.

(4) negative forms: pres. 3s. nis, *is not,* W 9; S 39; 3p. nearon, *are not,* S 82 (MS. *nǣron*); pret. 3s. næs, *was not,* M 325.

beorg, m. *hill, mountain;* as. R 32; ds. —e, R 50.

ġe-beorg, n. *defense, protection;* ds. —e, M 31, 131, 245.

beorgan, v.3, w. dat. *protect, save;* pret. 3p. burgon, M 194. [BEORGAN, BEARG, BURGON, BORGEN.]

beorht, adj. *bright;* nsf. B 15; W 94; dsm. wk. —an, R 66; superl.

beorhtost, asm. (uninflected) R 6.

beorn, m. *warrior, man;* ns. B 45; R 42; W 70, 113; S 55; as. M 270; gs. —es, M 131, 160; ds. —e, M 154, 245; np. —as, R 32, 66; M 92, 111, 182; ap. —as, M 17, 62, 277, 305, 311; gp. —a, B 2; M 257; dp. —um, M 101.

bēot, n. *vow* (typically made before battle; hence) *boast; threat;* as. M 15, 27 (on bēot, *threateningly*), 213; W 70. [From *BĪ-HĀT; cf. ġe-hātan, and see Gordon's note on M 27.]

bēotian, wk.v.II. *vow, boast;* pret. 3s. bēotode, M 290.

bēoton, see bēatan.

bēoþ, see bēon-wesan.

beran, v.4. *bear, carry;* inf. M 12, 62; pres. 3s. bereþ, R 118; pret. 3p. bǣron, R 32; M 99; 3p. subj. bǣren, M 67. [BERAN, BÆR, BǢRON, BOREN; cf. oþ-beran and ġe-boren.]

-berend, m. nd-stem. *bearer;* see gār-, reord-berend.

berstan, v.3. *burst;* inf. R 36; pret. 3s. bærst, M 284. [BERSTAN, BÆRST, BURSTON, BORSTEN; orig. BRESTAN, etc. Cf. to-berstan.]

be-slēan, contr.v.6, w. gen. *bereave of (by slaughter);* pp. beslæġen, nsm. B 42. [Cf. slēan.]

be-standan, v.6. *stand around, surround;* pret. 3p. bestōdon, M 68. [Cf. standan.]

be-stīeman, wk.v.I. *make moist, suffuse;* pp. bestīemed, nsm. R 48; nsn. R 22. [Base-word stēam, m. *hot vapor, moisture, blood.*]

be-swīcan, v.1. *betray;* pp. beswicen, apm. —e, M 238. [SWĪCAN, SWĀC, SWICON, SWICEN.]

be-swillan, wk.v.I. *drench;* pp. beswiled, nsn. R 23. (MS. *beswyled* is best interpreted so, with

Dickins and Ross; earlier editors proposed a poorly supported BE-SYLED, *defiled*.)

betera, adj. comp. *better* (declined wk.); nsm. M 276 (as noun); nsn. **betere,** M 31; npm. **beteran,** B 48.

betst, adj. superl. *best;* nsn. S 73 (as noun w. part. gen.).

be-wāwan, v.7. *blow against;* pp. **bewāwen,** npm. **bewāwne,** W 76 (winde b., *beaten by the wind*). [WĀWAN, *WĒOW, *WĒOWON, WĀWEN — only pres. stem and pp. on record.]

be-windan, v.3. *wind (about), encircle, enwrap;* pp. **bewunden,** asn. R 5. [Cf. **windan.**]

be-wrēon, contr.v.1. *put a covering around; cover;* pret. 1s. **bewrāh,** W 23; pp. **bewriġen,** uninfl., R 17, 53. [WRĒON (from *WRĪHAN), WRĀH, WRIGON, WRIGEN; cf. **on-wrēon.**]

bī, see **be.**

bidan, v.1. *remain;* inf. S 30. [BĪDAN, BĀD, BIDON, BIDEN.]

ġe-bīdan, v.1. (a) intrans., *wait;* inf. W 70; (b) trans., *obtain by waiting, live to see; experience, endure;* pres. 3s. **ġebīdeþ,** W 1; pret. 1s. **ġebād,** R 125; M 174; pp. **ġebiden,** uninfl. R 50, 79; S 4, 28.

biddan, v.5. *bid, urge, exhort, ask, pray;* pret. 3s. **bæd,** M 20, 128, 170, 257 (*urged, bade*); pret. 3p. **bædon,** M 87 (*asked*), 262 (*prayed, besought*), 306 (*exhorted*). [Construed w. clause or (M 170) inf., and sometimes acc. of person (M 170, 262). BIDDAN, BÆD, B.ĒDON, BEDEN.]

ġe-biddan, v.5, w. refl. pron. dat. and prep. to, *pray to;* pres. 3p. **ġe-biddaþ,** R 83; pret. 1s. **ġebæd,** R 122.

bieldan, wk.v.I. *embolden, encour-*

age; **bielde,** pret. 3s. M 169, 209 (b. forþ, *incited to advance*), 320; pres. 3s. subj., M 234. [Base-word BEALD, bold.]

bierġan, wk.v.I. *taste;* pret. 3s. **bieriġde,** R 101. [Cf. **on-bierġan.**]

bifian, wk.v.II. *tremble;* inf. R 36; pret. 1s. **bifode,** R 42.

bill, n. *sword;* as. M 162; dp. —um, M 114. **bill-ġeslieht,** m. or n. (*sword-*) *slaughter;* gs. —es, B 45.

ġe-bind, n. *fastening, band; aggregation;* as. in waðuma ġebind, W 24, 57 (*congregated waters? confinement of the waves? waves' embrace?*) [No other occurrences in poetry; cf. **bindan.**]

bindan, v.3. *bind;* pres. 3s. **bindeþ,** W 102; 3p. **bindaþ,** W 18; 3s. subj. **binde,** W 13; pret. 3s. **band,** S 32. [BINDAN, BAND, BUNDON, BUNDEN.]

ġe-bindan, v.3. *bind, hold captive;* pres. 3p. **ġebindaþ,** W 40; pp. **ġe-bunden,** uninfl. (for npm. ĠE-BUNDNE), S 9; nsm. D 24.

bisġu, f. in-stem. *toil, trouble;* as. S 88.

bisiġ, adj. *busy, at work;* npm. —e, M 110.

bismerian, wk.v.II. *mock, revile;* pret. 3p. **bismerodon,** R 48.

biter, adj. *bitter; painful, grievous;* gsm. **biteres,** R 114; asf. **bitre,** S 4, 55 (MS. *bitter*) ; *grim, fierce,* nsm. M 111; apm. **bitere,** M 85. [Orig. *BITR; hence the variation between **bitr-** and **biter-,** which is allowed to stand for possible rhythmic value, though it is probably scribal.]

biþ, see **bēon-wesan.**

blācian, wk.v.II. *grow pale;* pres. 3s. **blācaþ,** S 91.

blǣd, m.(*vital spirit;*) *joy, glory;* ns.

W 33 (foldan b., *earth's glory* — perhaps also *fruitful abundance*; blǣd, f. *blossom, fruit, growth*); S 79, 88; as. D 34; dp. —um, R 149. [blǣd, m. is related to BLĀWAN, v.7, *blow;* blǣd, f., to BLŌWAN, v.7, *bloom.* The first is more frequent in poetry.]

ġe-bland, n. *mixture.* See ēar-ġebland.

blanden, pp. adj. *mixed.* [blandan, v.7.] blanden-feax, adj. *grizzle-haired;* nsm. B 45.

blēo, n. ja-stem. *color;* dip. blēoum, R 22.

bliss, f. *bliss;* ns. R 139, 141; ds. —e, R 149, 153. [From *BLĪþ-s; cf. next word.]

blīðe, adj. ja-stem. *glad, joyful;* isn. R 122; comp. blīðra, nsm. M 146 (*better pleased*).

blōd, n. *blood;* ds. —e, R 48.

blōdiġ, adj. *bloody;* asm. —ne, M 154.

blōstma, wk.m. *blossom;* dip. —um, S 48.

bōc, f. cons.-stem. *book;* np. bēċ, B 68.

boda, wk.m. *messenger;* vs. M 49. [Cf. bēodan.]

boga, wk.m. *bow;* np. —n, M 110. [Cf. būgan.]

bold, n. *dwelling.* See feorh-bold.

bord, n. *shield;* ns. M 110; as. M 15, 42, 62 (or pl.), 131, 245, 270, 283, 309; gs. —es, M 284; gp. —a, M 295; dp. —um, M 101. bord-weall, m. *shield-wall;* as. B 5; M 277.

ġe-boren, adj. (pp., see beran) as noun, *one born in the same family; brother;* dsm. —um, S 98. [Cf. beran.]

bōsm, m. *bosom;* ds. —e, B 27.

bōt, f. *remedy;* as. —e, W 113.

brād, adj. *broad;* asn. M 15, 163; apn. B 71.

brǣc, see brecan.

ġe-brǣc, n. *clash;* ns. M 295. [Cf. brecan.]

brǣdan, wk.v.I. *spread;* inf. W 47. [Base-word brād.]

brǣgd, see breġdan.

brēac, see brūcan.

breahtm, m. *noise, clamor,* gp. —a, W 86.

brecan, v.4. *break;* pret. 3s. brǣc, M 277 (*broke through*—see Gordon's note) ; pp. brocen, ns. M 1 (the noun modified is missing). [BRECAN, BRÆC, BRÆCON, BROCEN; cf. to-brecan.]

breġdan, v.3. *move quickly; draw, pluck out;* pret. 3s. brǣgd, M 154, 162. [BREGDAN, BRÆGD, BRUGDON, BROGDEN.]

bregu, m. u-stem. *sovereign, chief;* ns. B 33.

brēost, n. *breast* (usually pl. where mod. English has sing.) ; dip. —um, R 118; M 144; W 113. brēost-cearu, f. *breast-care, sorrow of heart;* as. —ċeare, S 4. brēost-cofa, wk.m. *the recesses of the breast;* ds. —n, W 18. brēost-hord, n. (*what is treasured in the breast*); *inmost feelings;* as. S 55.

brēoðan. v.2. *waste away.* See a-brēoðan.

brim, n. *sea* (*-surge*); ap. —u, B 71. brim-fugol, m. *seabird;* ap. —fug-las, W 47. brim-lād, f. *sea-passage, voyage;* ds. —e, S 30. brim-līðend, m. nd-stem. *seafarer;* gp. —ra, M 27 (*vikings*). brim-mann, m. cons.-stem. *seaman;* np. —menn, M 295; gp. —manna, M 49 (*vikings*).

bringan, wk.v.1 (pres., strong 3) . *bring;* pres. 3s bringeþ, W 54. [BRINGAN, BRŌHTE, BRŌHT.]

ġe-bringan, wk.v.I. *bring;* pres. 3s. subj. ġebringe, R 139.

brocen, see brecan.

brōðor, m. r-stem. *brother;* ns. B 2; M 282; S 98; np. brōðru, M 191; gp. brōðra, D 8.

ġe-brōðor, m.pl. *brothers* (considered together as children of the same parent); nom. B 57; M 305 (alt. form —brōðru).

brūcan, v.2, w. gen. *enjoy, partake of, use;* inf. B 63; R 144; pres. 3p. brūcaþ, S 88 (b. þurh bisġu, gen. HIRE understood: *gain the use of it by toil*) ; pret. 3s. brēac, W 44. [BRŪCAN, BRĒAC, BRUCON, BROCEN.]

brūn, adj. *brown;* (of metals) *gleaming.* brūn-ecg, adj. *with gleaming blade;* asn. M 163.

brycg, f. jō-stem. *bridge; ford, causeway;* as. —e, M 74, 78. brycg-weard, m. *guard of the causeway;* ap. —as, M 85.

bryne, m. i-stem. *fire;* as. R 149.

brytta, wk.m. *dispenser, giver* (typically w. gen. of a word for treasure, characterizing a generous lord); sinces bryttan, as. W 25 (or gs. if sele-drēoriġ is taken as two separate words).

bryttian, wk.v.II. *divide, distribute;* (hence) *dispose of, enjoy;* inf. B 60.

būgan, v.2. *bow, bend down;* inf. R 36, 42; *turn, retreat;* inf. M 276; pret. 3p. bugon, M 185. [BŪGAN, BĒAG, BUGON, BOGEN: cf. bēag, boga: also for-būgan.]

ġe-bunden, see ġe-bindan.

bune, wk. f. *cup, beaker;* ns. W 94 (as symbol of drinking in the hall).

būr, n. *bower, bedchamber.* būr-þeġn, m. *servant of the bower; chamberlain;* ds. —e, M 121.

burg, f. cons.-stem. *stronghold, stockaded dwelling or manor; walled town, city;* as. M 291 (probably Byrhtnoþ's manor-house; see Gordon's note); D 19; dp. —um, S 28; ap. byriġ, S 48 (less probably np.). burg-ware, m.pl. *keepers of the stronghold, citizens;* gp. —wara, W 86. [Cf. scield-burg.]

burgon, see beorgan.

būtan, conj. (w. subj.) *unless,* M 71; (after negative) *but, except,* S 18.

bū-tū, n. dual. *both;* acc. R 48. [See bēġen and twēġen.]

-byrd, f. i-stem. *what one bears* (cf. ġe-byrd, *birth*) — in compounds, sometimes a social or legal responsibility that one bears. See mund-byrd. [Cf. beran.]

byre, m. i-stem. *opportunity;* as. M 121. [Cf. beran.]

byrġan, wk.v.I. *bury;* inf. S 98. [Cf. beorgan.]

byriġ, see burg.

byrne, wk.f. *corselet, coat of mail;* ns. M 144, 284; as. byrnan, M 163. byrn-wiga, wk. m. *(mailed) warrior;* ns. W 94.

C

cāf, adj. *quick, vigorous, valiant;* asm. —ne, M 76 (c. mid his cynne, *valiant as was his kindred, come of a valiant stock*—Gordon) .

cāflīċe, adv. *valiantly;* M 153.

camp, m. *battle;* ds. —e, B 8. camp-stede, m. i-stem. *battlefield;* ds. B 29, 49.

ġe-camp, m. *battle;* ds. —e, M 153.

candel, f. *candle;* ns. B 15. [From Lat. CANDĒLA, applied to large candles used in churches; hence the application to heaven's candle, the sun.]

cāsere, m. ja-stem (adapt. of Lat. CAESAR) . *emperor;* np. cāseras, S 82.

ćeald, n. *(the) cold;* dis. —e, S 8.

ćeald, adj. *cold;* asn. M 91; dip.
—um, S 10; superl. cealdost, nsn.
w. part. gen. S 33. [Cf. hrīm-, īs-,
winter-ćeald.]

ćeallian, wk.v.II. *call, shout;* inf.
M 91.

ćeariġ, adj. *troubled, sad, sorrowful.*
See earm-, hrēow-, mōd-, sorg-,
winter-ćeariġ.

cearu, f. *care; sorrow, grief, anxiety;*
ns. W 55; as. ćeare, W 9; np.
ceara, S 10. cear-seld, n. *abode of
care;* gp. —a, S 5. [Alt. form caru,
whence mod. "care"; association
with Lat. *cura* had already begun
in OE. On the diphthong of nom.
cearu, which probably did not
have palatal *c* (*ć*), see Campbell,
OE Gram. 208. Cf. brēost-cearu.]

ġe-ćēas, see ġe-ćēosan.

cellod, adj. meaning unknown; asn.
M 283, describing a shield.

cempa, wk.m. *warrior;* ns. M 119.
[Cf. camp.]

cēne, adj. ja-stem. *keen, bold, war-
like;* nsm. M 215; npm. M 283
(or adv. *boldly*); comp. cēnre, nsf.
M 312. [*CŌNJA-.]

ćēol, m. *ship;* ds. —e, S 5.

ćeorfan, v.3. *carve, hew out;* pret.
3p. curfon, R 66. [ĆEORFAN, ĆEARF,
CURFON, CORFEN.]

ćeorl, m. *freeman of the lowest rank,
yeoman, churl* (but less derogatory
than at a later period); ns. M 256;
ds. —e, M 132 (a common VIKING
in contrast to the English earl:
"the earl to the churl").

ġe-ćēosan, v.2. *choose;* pret. 3s.
ġećēas, M 113. [ĆĒOSAN, ĆĒAS,
CURON, COREN.]

ćierm, m. i-stem. *cry, clamor, up-
roar;* ns. M 107.

ćierran, wk.v.I. *turn.* See on-ćierran.

clǣne, adj. ja-stem. *clean, pure;* asn.
S 110.

clamm, m. *grip, fetter;* dip. —um,
S 10.

clēofan, v.2. *cleave, split;* pret. 3p.
clufon, B 5; M 283. [CLĒOFAN,
CLĒAF, CLUFON, CLOFEN.]

clif, n. *cliff;* dp. —um, S 8. [Cf. stān-
clif.]

clipian, wk.v.II. *call out;* pret. 3s.
clipode, M 25, 256.

clufon, see clēofan.

clyppan, wk.v.I. *embrace;* pres. 3s.
subj. clyppe, W 42. [Cf. ymb-clyp-
pan.]

cnāwan, v.7. *know.* See on-cnāwan.

cnearr, m. *ship;* ns. B 35. [Probably
borrowed from, certainly alluding
to, Old Norse KNORR as a specific
term for a viking ship; cf. nægled-
cnearr.]

cnēo, n. wa-stem. *knee;* ds. W 42
(contraction of *CNĒOWE); —fig.,
a step in genealogy: cnēo-mǣġ, m.
*a kinsman in one's genealogical
line; ancestor;* dp. —māgum, B 8.

cniht, m. *young man, youth;* ns. M
9, 153.

cnossian, wk.v.II. *toss, pitch, drive?*
pres. 3s. cnossaþ, S 8. [Recorded
only here. The base-word *CNOSS
is the same as for cnyssan and im-
plies beating or striking; cf. ġe-
CNOSS, *collision;* but perhaps strik-
ing waves rather than rocks.]

cnyssan, wk.v.I. *beat against;* pres.
3p. cnyssaþ, W 101; —fig., *urge in-
sistently, importune,* S 33. [Base-
word *CNOSS; see cnossian.]

cofa, wk.m. *coffer, recess, room.* See
brēost- and hord-cofa.

cōlian, wk.v.II. *cool;* pret. 3s. cōlode,
R 72.

collen-, adj. combining-form, pp. of
a lost verb *CWELLAN, *swell, spring

up, grow big—which has cognates in other languages. **collen-ferhþ**, adj. *stout-hearted, proud, brave;* nsm. W 71.

cōm, cōmon, see **cuman.**

corn, n. *kernel, grain;* gp. —a, S 33.

cræftiġ, adj. *skilled.* See **lēoþ-cræftiġ.**

crēad, see **crūdan.**

cringan, v.3. *fall in battle, perish;* inf. M 292; pret. 3p. **crungon,** B 10; M 302. [CRINGAN, CRANG, CRUNGON, CRUNGEN.]

ġe-cringan, v.3. *fall, perish;* pret. 3s. **ġecrang,** M 250, 324; W 79.

Crist, m. *Christ;* ns. R 56; ds. —e, R 116.

crūdan, v.2. *(crowd,) press on;* pret. 3s. **crēad,** B 35. [Only pres. subj. and pret. 3s. recorded.]

crungon, see **cringan.**

cuman, v.4. *come;* pres. 3s. **cymeþ,** W 103; S 61, 106, 107; 1p. subj. **cumen,** S 118 *(make our way);* pret. 3s. **cōm,** B 37 *(made his way);* R 151, 155; M 65; 3p. **cōmon,** R 57; pp. **cumen,** nsm. R 80; nsf. M 104; —**hwǣr cōm,** pret. 3s. *what has become of, where is,* W 92 (three times), 93. [CUMAN, CŌM, CŌMON, CUMEN; cf. **be-, ofer-cuman.**]

cumbol, n. *banner.* **cumbol-ġehnāst,** n. *collision of banners* (in battle); gs. —es, B 49.

cunnan, pret.-pres. v. *(can,) know, know how;* pres. 3s. subj. **cunne:** w.inf., *know how to,* W 113; w. **gear(w)e,** *know for certain,* W 69 (used absolutely, w. same implication as next), 71 (w. ind. quest.). [CUNNAN, CANN, CUNNON, CŪÐE.]

cunnian, wk.v.II. *test, find out* (by *trial); make trial of, experience;* inf. M 215 (**mæġ cunnian,** *one can find out;* see **magan**); pres. 3s.

cunnaþ, W 29; 1s. subj. **cunnie,** S 35; pret. 3s. **cunnode,** D 1 (w. gen.).

ġe-cunnian, wk.v.II. *explore, make trial of, come to know;* pp. **ġe-cunnod,** uninfl., S 5.

curfon, see **ċeorfan.**

cūþ, adj. *known, familiar;* nsn. D 19; gp. —ra, W 55. [Cf. **cunnan.**]

cwæþ, see **cweðan.**

cweċċan, wk.v.I. *shake.* See **a-cweċċan.**

cweðan, v.5. *say, speak;* inf. R 116; pres. 3s. **cwiþ,** R 111 (future sense); pret. 3s. **cwæþ,** M 211, 255; W 6, 111. [CWEÐAN, CWÆþ, CWǢDON, CWEDEN; cf. **a-, on-cweðan,** and **æfter-cweðende.**]

ġe-cweðan, v.5. *speak;* pret. 3s. **ġe-cwæþ,** M 168.

cwic(u), adj. u-stem. *alive;* pl. as noun, *the living;* gp. **cwicra,** W 9.

cwide, m. i-stem. *speech, discourse.*

cwide-ġiedd, n. ja-stem. *saying, utterance;* gp. —a, W 55 (**cūðra c.,** *familiar utterances*—almost, *familiar accents?*). [Cf. **lār-cwide.**]

cwiþ, see **cweðan.**

cwiðan, wk.v.I. *bewail, lament;* inf. W 9; pret. 3p. **cwīðdon,** R 56.

cymeþ, see **cuman.**

cyne-, adjectival combining-form. *royal.* **cyne-rīċe,** n. ja-stem. *kingdom;* gs. —s, D 26. [From *CUNI-, related to **cyning** and **cynn.**]

cyning, m. *king;* ns. B 1, 35, 58; D 23; gs. —es, R 56 *(King);* as. R 44, 133 *(King);* np. —as, B 29; S 82.

cynn, n. ja-stem. *kind, race, family, kindred;* as. R 94 (**wīfa c.,** *womankind*); gs. —es, M 217, 266; ds. —e, M 76. [Cf. **mann-cynn.**]

cyssan, wk.v.I. *kiss;* pres. 3s. subj. **cysse,** W 42. [COSS, m. *kiss, embrace.*]

cyst, f. i-stem. (a) *the best, choicest;* as. R 1. [Cf. ċēosan.] — (b) *(picked) band;* see **ēorod-cyst.** [But perhaps the word in this second context is unrelated to ċēosan and should be normalized as ċiest, an i-stem from *CÆSTI-, meaning simply *band, troop, crowd.* Cf. Old Norse KOSTR, *pile, heap.*]

ġe-cȳðan, wk.v.I. *make known, declare;* inf. M 216. [Base-word cūþ, q.v.; cf. a-cȳðan.]

cȳþþ, f. iþō-stem. *known region or people, home;* as. —e, B 38, 58. [Base-word cūþ; cf. *"kith* and kin."]

D

dæd, f. i-stem. *deed;* dp. —um, S 41; dip. —um, S 76.

dæġ, m. *day;* as. B 21; M 198 (or endingless locative: on **dæġ,** *upon a [certain] day, one day);* np. dagas, S 80; gp. daga, R 136.

dæġ-weorc, n. *day's work;* gs. —es, M 148. [Cf. dōm-, tīd-dæġ; ġēar-, ġe-swinċ-dagas.]

dæl, m. i-stem. w. gen. *share, portion (of);* ns. D 30; *a good share, a deal (of), many,* as. W 65; D 34.

dælan, wk.v.I. *deal out or share;* pres. 1p. subj. **dælen,** M 33 (hilde d., *should join battle*). [Base-word DÅL, n. *division, portion;* cf. be-dælan.]

ġe-dælan, wk.v.I. *divide, share;* **dēaðe ġedælde,** pret. 3s. *shared with Death,* W 83.

dagas, see **dæġ.**

daroþ, m. *spear;* as. M 149, 255; gp. —a, B 54.

dēad, adj. *dead;* nsn.wk. —e, S 65 (fig.); dp. —um, as noun, *the dead,* S 98.

dēag, see **dugan.**

dēaþ, m. *death;* ns. S 106; D 8; as. R 101; gs. —es, R 113; ds. —e, W 83 (personified).

delfan, v.3. *dig.* See be-delfan.

dēman, wk.v.I., w. dat., *pass judgment on, judge;* inf. R 107. [Base-word dōm, q.v.]

dennian, wk.v.II. *become wet, flow?* pret. 3s. dennode, B 12. [The only occurrence; meaning doubtful. Holthausen, *Altenglisches etym. Wörterbuch,* cites Sanskrit DHANVATI, *flows,* as a possible relative.]

dēofol, m. and n. *(the) devil;* ds. dēofle, S 76.

dēop, adj. *deep;* asn. B 55; dsm.wk. —an, R 75.

dēope, adv. *deeply,* W 89.

dēor, n. *animal;* as. B 64.

dēor, adj. *brave, valiant;* nsm. S 41; dip. —um, S 76.

deorc, adj. *dark* (with various emotional overtones); asn.wk. —e, W 89 (*mysterious and cheerless?*); dp. —um, R 46 (*iron-colored and sinister?*). [For possible influence of the Irish cognate, meaning *red, bloody,* at R 46, see note in Dickins and Ross.]

derian, wk.v.I, w. dat. *injure, harm;* inf. M 70.

dīere, adj. ja-stem. *dear;* nsm. D 37 (w. dat., *dear to*).

dōgor, n. (or m.) *day;* gp. dōgra, W 63.

dol, adj. *foolish;* nsm. S 106.

dolg, n. *wound;* np. R 46.

dōm, m. (a) *doom, judgment;* gs.

—es, R 107; (b) *stipulation, choice;* as. M 38; (c) *favorable judgment, praise, glory, renown;* as. M 129; ds. —e, S 85. **dōm-dæg,** m. *day of judgment;* ds. —e, R 105. **dōm-ġeorn,** adj. *eager for praise;* npm. —e, W 17 (as noun: *men of repute, aspirants to honor*). [Cf. **dēman.**]

dōn, anom. v. *do;* pret. **dyde,** (a) as substitute for a verb previously used: *did,* 3s. R 114; (b) *did, acted* (in a specified manner), 3s. M 280; (c) w. acc. object and **to,** *made to serve as, took for,* 1s. S 20.

ġe-dōn, anom. v., trans. (a) *do, perform;* pp. **ġedōn,** M 197; (b) w. **to,** *bring into a condition,* or *put to a purpose;* inf. S 43 (**to hwon hine dryhten ġedōn wille,** [*as to*] *what the Lord will bring him to* —so Mrs. Gordon, following Miss Whitelock).

dorste, see **durran.**

-drǣdan, v.7. *dread;* only w. prefixes; see **on-drǣdan.**

drēag, see **drēogan.**

drēam, m. *joy, delight, festivity; music, musical entertainment;* ns. R 140; S 80; gs. —es, R 144; dis. —e, W 79; np. —as, S 65, 86; dp. —um, R 133. [Mod. "dream" is a sense not recorded in OE. Cf. **sele-drēam.**]

ġe-drēfan, wk.v.I. *trouble, afflict;* pp. **ġedīefed,** nsm. R 20, 59. [Baseword **DRŌF,** adj. *turbid, troubled.*]

dreng, m. *(viking) warrior;* gp. —a, M 149. [The vikings' own term for their warriors; see Gordon's note.]

drēogan, v.2. *undergŏ, endure;* pres. 3p. **drēogaþ,** S 56; pret. 3s. **drēag,** D 2. [DRĒOGAN, DRĒAG, DRUGON, DROGEN.]

drēoriġ, adj. *(bloody;) sad, dejected;* nsf. B 54 (*dejected—and bloody?*); asm. —ne, W 17 (modifying **hyġe** understood). **drēoriġ-hlēor,** adj. *sad-faced;* nsm. W 83. [Cf. **sele-drēoriġ.**]

drēosan, v.2. *fall, droop, fail;* pres. 3s. **drēoseþ,** W 63. [DRĒOSAN, DRĒAS, DRURON, DROREN; cf. **be-droren.**]

ġe-drēosan, v.2. *fail, come to an end;* pret. 3s. **ġedrēas,** W 36; pp. **ġedroren,** *fallen;* nsf. S 86.

drīfan, v.1. *drive.* See **be-, þurh-drīfan.**

drinc, m. *drink;* see **medu-drinc.**

ġe-droren, see **ġe-drēosan.**

dryht, f. i-stem. *army, host.* See **enġel-dryht.**

dryhten, m. (a) *lord (leader of a dryht);* ns. B 1; S 41; ds. **dryhtne,** D 37; —(b) *the Lord* (used attributively or as a proper name); ns. C 4, 8; R 101, 105, 144; M 148; S 43, 124; D 32; as. R 64; S 106; gs. **dryhtnes,** B 16; R 9 (MS. — emended to **-dryhta),** 35, 75, 113, 136, 140; S 65, 121. [Cf. **mann-, wine-dryhten,** sense (a).]

dryhtlīcest, adj. superl. *most lordly;* dsm. —um, S 85.

dugan, pret.-pres. v. *avail;* pres. 3s. **dēag,** M 48 (future sense). [DUGAN, DĒAG, DUGON, DOHTE.]

duguþ, f. (a) *that which avails, benefit, advantage;* ds. —e, M 197 (**him to d.,** *for their benefit*). —(b) *seasoned retainers;* (less specifically) *military band, company of noble warriors, host;* ns. W 79; S 86; ds. —e, W 97; *(heavenly) host,* dp. — um, S 80. [Cf. **dugan.**]

durran, pret.-pres. v. *dare;* pres. subj.

1s. **durre,** W 10; pret. 1s. **dorste,**
R 35, 42, 45, 47. [DURRAN, DEARR,
DURRON, DORSTE.]

dyde, see **dōn.**

E

ēa, f. cons.-stem. *river.* **ēa-stæþ,** n.
river-bank; ds. **—e,** M 63.

ēa, interj. *O!* **ēa-lā,** interj. *O, lo;
alas!* W 94 (twice), 95.

ēac, adv. *also,* B 2; R 92; S 119.
swelċe ... ēac, *and likewise, also;*
B 19, 30, 37.

ēac, prep. w dat. *in addition to,* M
11.

ēacen, adj. *increased, great; pregnant;* nsf. D 11. [Pp. of obsolescent ĒACAN, v.7, *increase.*]

ēadiġ, adj. *blessed;* nsm. S 107; *prosperous, fortunate;* see **sēft-ēadiġ.**

ēadiġness, f. jō-stem. *beatitude, happiness;* as. **—e,** S 120.

eafora, wk.m. *son, heir, descendant;*
np. **—n,** B 7; ap. **—n,** B 52.

eald, adj. *old;* nsm. B 46; M 310;
wk. **—a,** M 218 (e. **fæder,** *grandfather*); npn. **eald,** W 87; apn. **—
e** (the generalized form, or asn.
wk.), M 47; npm. **—e,** B 69. **ealdġewyrht,** f. i-stem (or n.). *deed of
old, former action;* dp. **—um,** R
100.

ealdian, wk.v.II. *grow old;* pres. 3s.
ealdaþ, S 89.

ealdor, m. *lord;* ns. M 202, 222, 314;
gs. **ealdres,** M 53; ds. **ealdre,** M 11;
—w. limiting gen., *the Lord:* **wuldres ealdor,** ns. R 90; S 123. **ealdor-mann,** m. *nobleman of the
highest rank, "ealdorman";* ns. M
219.

ealdor, n. *life; age, eternity;* ds.
ealdre, S 79 (**āwa to ealdre,** *ever*

for life, for ever and ever). **ealdor-lang,** adj. *age-long, eternal;* asm.
—ne, B 3.

ealgian, wk.v.II. *defend;* inf. M 52
(MS. *gealgean;* see Gordon's note);
pret. 3p. subj. **ealgoden,** B 9.

eall, adj. *all;* nsm. W 74; nsn. R 6
(or adv.) ; W 106, 110; nsf. R 12,
55, 82; W 36, 79, 115; S 86; asn.
R 58, 94; W 60; asf. **—e,** M 304;
S 124; ism. **—e,** D 16; npm. **—e,** R
9 (MS. **—em.** to **fela),** 128; M 63,
203, 207; S 81; np.(n.?) **—e,** S 50
(**ealle þā,** indef. antecedent); apm.
—e, R 37, 74, 93; M 231, 238, 320;
apf. **—e,** M 196; gp. **ealra,** R 125;
M 174; W 63; dp. **eallum,** R 154;
M 233. — as pron., asn. M 256 (**ofer
eall,** see **ofer);** dp. **eallum,** *to all
men,* M 216. [Cf. **ælmihtiġ.**]

eall, adv. *entirely;* R 6 (or adj., nsn.),
20, 48, 62; M 314.

ēar, m. *sea.* **ēar-ġebland,** n. *concourse
of waters, sea-surge;* as. B 26.

eard, m. *land, homeland, country;*
as. B 73; M 53, 58, 222; S 38.
eard-ġeard, m. *(enclosed) plot of
ground, dwelling-place, region;* as.
W 85. **eard-stapa,** wk.m. *landtreader, wanderer;* ns. W 6.

earfoðe, n. ja-stem (also **earfeðe).**
hardship, tribulation, trouble; ap.
—u, D 2 (MS. **—a);** gp. **—a,** W 6;
D 30. **earfoþ-hwil,** f. *time of hardship;* as. **—e,** S 3.

earfoþlīċ, adj. *full of trouble, distressful;* nsn. W 106.

earg, adj. *slack, cowardly;* nsn. M
238. [Cf. **un-earg, ierġþu.**]

earm, m. *arm;* as. M 165.

earm, adj. *poor, destitute, wretched,
miserable;* asm. **—ne,** W 40; npm.
—e, R 68; gp. **—ra,** R 19 (as
noun). **earm-ċeariġ,** adj. *wretched*

and sorrowful, miserably sad; nsm.
W 20; S 14.

earn, m. *eagle;* ns. M 107; S 24; as.
B 63.

ġe-earnian, wk.v.II. *earn, deserve;*
pres. 3s. ġe-earnaþ, R 109.

ġe-earnung, f. *act deserving gratitude
(or other recompense); favor;* ap.
—a, M 196.

eart, see bēon-wesan.

ēastan, adv. *from the east;* B 69.

ēaþ-, combining-form of ēaðe, adj.
and adv. *easy, easily; gentle, gen-
tly.* ēaþ-mōd, adj. *humble, meek,
submissive;* nsm. R 60; S 107.

eaxl, f. *shoulder;* dp. —um, R 32.

eaxl-ġespann, n. *shoulder-beam or
shoulder-joint, intersection;* ds. —
e, R 9.

ebba, wk.m. *ebb-tide;* ds. —n, M 65.

ēċe, adj. ja-stem. *eternal;* nsm. C 4,
8; S 124; gsm. —s, B 16; gsn.wk.
ēċan, S 79; asf.wk. ēċan, S 120.
[From *ŌCJA-.]

ēċe, adv. *eternally, for ever;* S 67.

ecg, f. jō-stem. *edge, (sword-) blade;*
ns. M 60; dip. —um, B 4, 68. ecg-
hete, m. i-stem. *sword-hate, deadly
violence;* ns. S 70. [Cf. brūn-ecg.]

efstan, wk.v.I. *hasten;* inf. R 34;
pret. 3p. efston, M 206. [Base-
word OFOST, f. *haste;* cf. ofostlíċe.]

eft, adv. *again, back, afterwards;* B
56; R 68, 101, 103; M 201; W 45,
53 (MS. *oft*); S 61; eft onġēan,
back again, in reply, M 49, 156.

eġesa, wk. m. *awe, terror; awful
power;* ns. R 86; S 103; ds. —n,
S 101.

eġesliċ, adj. *fearful, dreadful;* nsf.
R 74.

el-, combining-form (from prehist.
*ALJA-, *ALI-), *other, alien, for-
eign.* [Cf. elles.] el-þēodiġ, adj. *of
a foreign country;* gp. —ra, S 38

(as noun: *of foreigners, strangers
—possibly, strangers on earth,* PER-
EGRINI).

ellen, n. (rarely m.), *courage, valor,
zeal, fortitude;* as. on ellen, *val-
iantly,* M 211; ds. mid elne, *val-
iantly,* W 114; is. elne miċle, *with
great zeal,* R 34, 60, 123.

elles, adv. *of another sort; else;* S
46. [gs. of unrecorded adj. *ELL
(from *ALJA-), *other, alien;* cf.
el-.]

ende, m. ja-stem. *end, outermost
part;* ds. R 29 (*edge*). ende-lēas,
adj. *endless;* nsm. D 30.

enġel, m. *angel;* np. englas, R 106;
gp. engla, M 178; dp. englum, R
153; S 78. [Lat. ANGELUS, vulg. AN-
GILUS; pronunciation of *g* in ob-
lique cases uncertain.] enġel-dryht,
f. *host of angels;* gp. —a, R 9 (emen-
dation; an unrecorded compound;
MS. *engel dryhtnes*).

ent, m. *giant;* gp. —a, W 87 (enta
ġeweorc, *work(s) of giants*—a re-
current poetic expression for an-
cient ruins, presumably occasioned
by wonder at the remains of Ro-
man building in Britain).

ēode, ēoden, ēodon, see gān.

eodor, m. *enclosure, dwelling;* np.
—as, W 77.

eoh, m. *war-horse, charger;* as. M
189.

eom, see bēon-wesan.

eorl, m. (a) *nobleman, man (of rank),
leader;* ns. M 51 (partly sense b);
W 84, 114; D 2; ds. —e, W 12;
D 33; ap. —as, W 99; gp. —a,
B 1; W 60; S 72; D 41. (b) *earl*
(a title corresponding to Old
Norse JARL and used in late Old
English times as equivalent to the
native title ealdormann; in M it is
applied exclusively to Byrhtnoþ);

ns. M 6, 51 (partly sense a), 89, 132, 146, 203, 233; gs. —es, M 165; ds. —e, M 28, 159;—referring to Norse JARLS, np. —as, B 31.

eornoste, adv. *resolutely*, M 281.

ēorod, n. *troop* (orig. *of horsemen:* **eoh**, *horse*, plus RĀD, *group of riders*.) **ēorod-cyst**, f. i-stem. *picked company*, or **-ċiest**, f. i-stem. *band of horsemen;* dip. —um, B 21. [See **cyst**.]

eorðe, wk.f. *earth, the earth;* **eorðan**, gs. C 5 (var.); R 37; W 106, 110; S 61, 81, 89, 105; ds. R 42, 74, 137, 145; M 107, 126, 157, 233, 286, 303; S 32 (or as.), 93; as. S 39. **eorþ-scræf**, n. *earth-pit, grave;* ds. —e, W 84. **eorþ-weġ**, m. *earthly way;* ds. —e, R 120. **eorþ-wela**, wk. m. *earthly wealth;* in pl., *earthly riches, worldly goods;* np. —n, S 67.

ēow, see **ġē**.

ēðel, m. *home, native land;* ns. R 156; as. M 52; S 60 (fig., **hwæles** e.) dis. **ēðle**, W 20. [*ōðIL-.]

F

fæder, m. r-stem. *father;* ds. W 115 (*Father*); **ealda fæder**, *grandfather*, ns. M 218. [Cf. **hēah-**, **wuldor-fæder**.]

fǣġe, adj. ja-stem. *fated to die (fey);* nsm. M 119; npm. B 12, 28; M 105; gsm. —s, M 297 (as noun); dsm. **fǣġum**, S 71 (as noun); dsm.wk. **fǣġan**, M 125.

fæġen, adj. *glad, cheerful;* nsm. W 68.

fæġer or **fæġer**, adj. *beautiful, fair;* nsn. **fæġer**, R 73; dsf.wk. **fæġeran**, R 21; **fæġere**, npm. R 8, npf. R 10.

fæġere, adv. *fairly, well;* M 22.

fæġrian, wk.v.II. *make beautiful, adorn;* pres. 3p. **fæġriaþ**, S 48. (Less probably, *become beautiful;* see Mrs. Gordon's note.)

fæġrost, adv. superl. *most pleasantly*, S 13.

fæhþ(u), f. iþō-stem. *hostility, feud;* gs. or as. **fæhþe**, M 225. [Base-word FĀH, adj. *hostile.*]

fǣr, m. *sudden attack.* **fǣr-scaða**, wk. m. *sudden raider* (viking); ds. —n, M 142.

fǣrlīċe, adv. *suddenly, with terrible swiftness;* W 61.

fæst, adj. *firm, fixed.* See **sigor-**, **stede-**, **þrymm-fæst.**

fæste, adv. *firmly, fast;* (a) *so as not to be moved or shaken,* w. **standan**, R 38, 43; M 171, 301; (b) *so as not to be overcome: securely,* M 103; (c) *with firm grasp or restraint,* M 21; W 13, 18.

fæsten, n. ja-stem. *fastness, place of safety;* as. M 194.

fæstlīċe, adv. *stoutly, resolutely;* M 82, 254.

fæstnian, wk.v.II. *make fast, confirm;* inf. M 35.

ġe-fæstnian, wk.v.II. *fasten;* pret. 3p. **ġefæstnodon**, R 33.

fæstnung, f. *firmness, stability, permanence;* ns. W 115.

-fæt, m. uncertain meaning, perhaps related to **fōt;** not the same as FÆT, n. *container, vat;* appears only as second element of **sīþ-fæt**, q.v.

fāg, adj. *colored, stained* (hence *guilty*) ; *decorated;* nsm. R 13 (*stained*); W 98 (*decorated*). [In both instances there may be overtones of FĀH, adj. *hostile, proscribed:* the MSS. spell both words alike, either *fag* or *fah.*]

faran, v.6. *go, pass;* inf. M 88, 156; w. **on,** adv., and dat. of person, *advance* (relatively to someone), *gain upon, overtake:* pres. 3s. **him on fareþ,** *overtakes him,* S 91. [FARAN, FŌR, FŌRON, FAREN.]

faru, f. *expedition, passage.* See **hæġl-faru.**

fēa, adv. (apn. of **fēawe,** adj. npm. *few*), *(few things), little, but little;* R 115. **fēa-sceaftiġ,** adj. *wretched, desolate;* asn. S 26. (The usual adj. is FĒA-SCEAFT, *having few things, destitute;* perhaps it is here modified for figurative application to spiritual poverty.)

feaht, see **feohtan.**

feallan, v.7. *fall;* inf. R 43; M 54, 105; pres. 3s. **fealleþ,** W 63; pret. 3s. **fēoll,** M 119, 126, 166, 286, 303; S 32; 3p. **fēollon,** B 12; M 111. [FEALLAN, FĒOLL, FĒOLLON, FEALLEN; cf. **a-feallan.**]

fealu, adj. wa-stem. *fallow; yellow;* (a) characterizing the appearance of the sea or its waves: the color-notion is uncertain, perhaps merely *dusky;* asm. **fealone,** B 36; apm. **fealwe,** W 46. (b) **fealu-hilte,** adj. ja-stem. *having a yellow (golden) hilt;* nsm. M 166.

feax, n. *hair (of the head);* as adjectival suffix, *haired.* See **blanden-, gamol-feax.**

ġe-feċċan (earlier **-fetian**), wk.v.II (orig. III). *carry off, take, fetch;* inf. M 160 (MS. *gefecgan*) ; pres. 3s. subj. **ġefeċċe,** R 138 (MS. *gefetige*) .

fela, n., indecl. pron. *much, many* (w. part. gen.); nom. R 9 (em. for MS. *ealle*); M 73; acc. R 50, 125, 131; M 90; W 54; S 5; (indicating extent of time) D 38.

ġe-fēlan, wk.v.I. *feel;* inf. S 95. [From *FŌLJAN.]

feld, m. u-stem. *field;* ns. B 12; ds. **-a,** M 241. [Cf. **wæl-feld.**]

fēng, see **fōn.**

feoh, n. *property; money; wealth;* ns. W 108; as. M 39. **feoh-ġifre,** adj. *greedy for wealth;* nsm. W 68.

ġe-feoht, n. *fight;* ds. **-e,** B 28; M 12.

feohtan, v.3. *fight;* inf. M 16, 261; pret. 3s. **feaht,** M 254, 277, 281, 298. [FEOHTAN, FEAHT, FUHTON, FOHTEN; cf. **un-befohten.**]

ġe-feohtan, v.3, trans. *acquire by fighting, win;* inf. M 129.

feohte, wk.f. *battle;* ns. M 103.

fēol, f. *file.* **fēol-heard,** adj. *hard as a file;* apn. **-e** (generalized form), M 108. ("The file was used to test the temper of the blade."— Gordon.)

fēoll, fēollon, see **feallan.**

fēond, m. nd-stem. *enemy;* np. **-as,** R 30, 33; ap. **-as,** R 38; gp. **-a,** S 75 (either secular enemies or devils); dp. **-um,** M 103, 264; ap. **fiend,** M 82. [**fiend** is standard West Saxon for nap. but **fēondas** occurs in poetical texts, esp. those from Anglian sources.]

feorh, n. (rarely m.) *life, soul, spirit;* ns. S 94; as. B 36; M 125, 142, 184; S 71; gs. **feores,** M 260, 317; ds. **feore,** M 194, 259. **feorh-bold,** n. *dwelling of the soul, body;* ns. R 73. **feorh-hūs,** n. *house of the soul, body;* as. M 297. [Cf. **firas.**]

feorr, adv. *far, afar, far away;* M 3, 57; W 26; S 37, 52 ; w. dat., *far from,* W 21; *at a distance in time, long ago,* W 90.

feorran, adv. *from afar,* R 57.

ġe-fēra, wk.m. *companion, comrade; member of a lord's comitatus, re-*

tainer; ns. M 280; ap. —n, M 170, 229; in figurative use, ds. —n, W 30. [Base-word **fōr,** f. *journey;* cf. **faran** and **fēran.**]

fēran, wk.v.I. *go, journey;* inf. M 41, 221; S 37. [Base-word **fōr,** f., corresponding to pret. 1s. of **faran;** see preceding word.]

ferhþ, m. or n. *spirit, soul, heart;* ns. W 54; as. S 26 (here neuter), 37; ds. —e, W 90. **ferhþ-loca,** wk. m. *enclosure of the spirit, breast; thoughts; feelings* (conceived as locked in the breast); ns. W 33; as. —n, W 13. [Cf. **collen-ferhþ.**]

ferian, wk.v.I. *carry, transport;* pret. 3s. **ferede,** W 81; rare meaning, *go;* inf. M 179 (mistake for **fēran?**) [Base-word **FÆR,** n. *a going, passage.*]

fēt, see **fōt.**

feter, f. *fetter;* dip. —um, W 21.

fēða, wk.m. *troop (on foot);* as. —n, M 88. [Related to **fōt.**]

feðer, f. *feather;* ap. **feðra,** W 47.

-feðra, wk.m. *feathered one* (formed from adjectival **-feðer**). See **isiġ-, ūriġ-feðra.** [These compounds have the same form as wk. adjectives but their position in the verse suggests that they are nouns.]

fiell, m. i-stem. *fall, death;* as. R 56; M 71, 264.

fiellan, wk.v.I. *fell, cut down;* inf. R 73. [Cf. **feallan.**]

ġe-fiellan, wk.v.I. (a) *fell, kill;* inf. R 38; pp. **ġefielled,** nsn. B 67; (b) *deprive of (by killing),* w. gen., pp. **ġefielled,** nsm. B 41 (perhaps a mistake for **befielled,** since *be-* normally gives this sense with verbs of killing).

fiend, see **fēond.**

fierd, f. i-stem. *army (on the march);* spec., the local levy organized for the defense of the realm; ds. —e, M 221. **fierd-rinc,** m. *warrior* (of the English levy); ns. M 140.

fīf, num. adj. *five;* npm. **fife,** B 28; R 8.

findan, v.3. *find;* inf. W 26; pret. 3p. **fundon,** M 85. [FINDAN, FAND or FUNDE, FUNDON, FUNDEN; cf. **on-findan.**]

firas, m.pl. *men, human beings;* dp. **firum,** C 9. [Related to **feorh,** q.v.]

flǣsc, n. i-stem. *flesh.* **flǣsc-hama,** wk.m. *fleshly covering, body;* ns. S 94.

flān, m. *arrow, dart;* as. M 269 (generic); gs. —es, M 71.

flēag, see **flēogan.**

flēam, m. *flight* (of a fugitive); as. M 81, 254; ds. —e, B 37; M 186.

flēogan, v.2. (a) *fly;* inf. M 7, 109, 150; pret. 3s. **flēag,** S 17; (b) *flee;* inf. M 275 (instead of **flēon,**—perhaps for extra syllable). [FLĒOGAN, FLĒAG, FLUGON, FLOGEN.]

flēon, contr.v.2. *flee;* inf. M 247; pret. 3p. **flugon,** M 194. [FLĒON (from *FLĒOHAN) FLĒAH, FLUGON, FLOGEN.]

flēotan, v.2. *float; fleet;* pres. part. **flēotende,** as noun, *floating or fleeting one;* gp. **flēotendra,** W 54. (Both senses may be operative if the actual seabirds are confused with the visionary companions.) [FLĒOTAN, FLĒAT, FLUTON, FLOTEN.]

flett, n. ja-stem. *floor* (typically of a hall; hence metaphorical for the life of a noble retainer and also for life on the floor of this earth); as. W 61.

fliema, wk.m. *fugitive.* See **here-fliema.**

ġe-flieman, wk.v.I, *put to flight;* pp.

ġefliemed, nsm. B 32. [Cf. fleam and a-flīeman.]

flōd, m. or n. *flood;* (a) *current, stream, sea;* as. (m.) B 36; (b) *flood-tide;* ns. M 65, 72 (m.).

flōd-weġ, m. *sea-way;* ap. —as, S 52 *(paths of ocean).* [Cf. mere-flōd.]

-floga, wk.m. *flier.* See ān-floga.

flot, n. *water?* (occurs only in prep. phrases, to flote, on flot, *afloat;* might mean the act or state of floating, or water deep enough to float a ship); as. in on flot, B 35, M 41. [Cf. flēotan.]

flota, wk.m. *floater: sailor, viking;* as. —n, M 227; np. —n, M 72; gp. flotena, B 32. [Cf. scip-flota.]

flōwan, v.7. *flow;* pres. part. flōwende, nsm. M 65. [FLŌWAN, FLĒOW, FLĒOWON, FLŌWEN.]

flugon *(fled),* see flēon.

flyht, m. i-stem. *flight;* as. M 71.

folc, n. (a) *people;* ns. R 140; M 45; as. M 54; D 22; gs. —es, B 67; M 202; (b) *army, host;* ns. M 241; as. M 22; ds. —e, M 227, 259 (on folce, on an *[enemy] host?),* 323. folc-stede, m. i-stem. *place of assembly, battlefield;* ds. B 41.

folde, wk.f. *earth, ground, land;* foldan, gs. R 8, 43; W 33; ds. R 132; M 166, 227; S 13, 75; as. C 9; M 54.

folgoþ, m. *(position of) service; office;* as. D 38.

folme, wk.f. *hand;* ds. folman, M 150; dp. folmum, M 21, 108. [FOLM, f., is the commoner form, but M 150, confirmed as ds. by handa, 149, points to wk. folme.]

fōn, contr.v.7. *take, seize;* pret. 3s. fēng, M 10 (to wǣpnum t., *took up arms).* [FŌN. (from *FANHAN), FĒNG, FĒNGON, FANGEN; cf. on-fōn.]

for, prep. w. dat., instr., or acc. *for;* —(a) w. dat. or instr., *in the presence of, before,* R 112; S 101, 103 (for þon, *before which,* or *because of which); because of,* R 21, 111 (unforht for, *unafraid of);* M 64, 89; *for the sake of,* R 113; *in expiation of,* R 99, 146; *for (fear or dislike of),* M 96; *for (fear of losing),* M 259. —(b) w. acc., *for the sake of,* R 93 (see note). for-þon, adv. and conj. (a) adv. *therefore, wherefore,* R 84; M 241; W 17, 64; *indeed,* W 37, 58; S 27, 33 (as for that? but yet?), 39 *(for indeed?),* 58, 72.— (b) conj. *for, because,* S 64, 108. [In S 103, þon is probably a relative pronoun: see above, for (a). The interpretation of for-þon, in S and elsewhere, has been much disputed. The suggestions above are offered without conviction.] for-hwon, interr. adv. and conj. *for what reason, why, wherefore;* as conj., W 59.

fōr, f. *journey.* See sǣ-fōr.

for-bǣrnan, wk.v.I. *burn up, consume* (in fire); pp. forbǣrned, asm. —ne, S 114.

for-būgan, v.2, w. acc. *turn away from, flee from;* pret. 3s. forbēag, M 325. [Cf. būgan.]

for-cūþ, adj. *infamous;* see un-forcūþ, and cf. fracuþ, with stress on first syllable.

ford, m. u-stem. *ford;* as. M 88; ds. —a, M 81.

fore, prep. *for, in place of;* w. acc., S 21; w.dat., S 22. (Possibly we should read hleahtre, dat., for hleahtor, acc. in S 21.)

for-ġiefan, v.5. *give (away), grant;* pret. 3s. forġeaf, R 147; M 139,

148; pp. forġiefen, ap. (m. or n.)
—e, S 93 (given up, consigned).
[Cf. a-ġiefan.]

for-ġieldan, v.3, w. acc. buy off;
pres. 2p. subj. forġielden, M 32.
[GIELDAN, ĠEALD, GULDON, GOLDEN,
yield, give, pay.]

for-grindan, v.3. grind to pieces,
destroy; pp. for-grunden, asm.
uninfl. B 43. [Cf. ġe-grindan.]

for-heard, adj. very hard; asm. —ne,
M 156 (gār understood; stressed
on first syllable).

for-hēawan, v.7. hew down, cut
down; pp. forhēawen, nsm. M 115,
223, 288, 314. [Cf. hēawan.]

for-hogode, see for-hycgan.

forht, adj. afraid, fearful; nsm. R 21;
W 68. [Cf. an-, un-forht.]

forhtian, wk.v.II. be afraid; pres. 3p.
forhtiaþ, R 115 (future sense);
pret. 3p. subj. forhtoden, M 21.

for-hwon, see for.

for-hycgan, wk.v.III (and II). des-
pise, scorn; pret. 3s. forhogode,
M 254. [Cf. hycgan.]

for-lætan, v.7. (a) leave, abandon;
inf. M 2, 208; pret. 3s. forlēt,
B 42; M 187; 3p. forlēton, R 61; (b)
w. inf., let, cause to; pret. 3s.
forlēt, M 149, 156, 321. [Cf. lætan.]

forma, wk.adj. earliest, first; asm.
—n, M 77.

for-maniġ, adj. very many; nsm. M
239 (stressed on second syllable).

for-niman, v.4. carry off, destroy;
pret. 3s. fornam, W 80; 3p. for-
nāmon, W 99. [Cf. niman.]

forst, m. frost; dis. —e, S 9.

for-swelgan, v.3. swallow (up); inf.
S 95. [SWELGAN, SWEALG, SWULGON,
SWOLGEN.]

forþ, adv. forth, away, onward; B
20; R 54, 132; M 3, 12, 170, 205,
209, 225, 229, 260, 269, 297; —

tō forþ, too successfully, too
deeply, M 150. forþ-ġeorn, adj.
eager to advance; nsm. M 281.

forþ-ġesceaft, f. pre-ordained con-
dition; as. R 10 (see note). forþ-
weġ, m. the way forth (into the
hereafter); as. R 125 (MS. ds.
—e,); W 81 (MS. ds. —e).

ġe-forþian, wk.v.II. carry out, ac-
complish; pp. ġeforðod, uninfl.
M 289.

for-þolian, wk.v.II. endure the ab-
sence of, do without, forgo; inf.
W 38. [Cf. þolian.]

for-þon, see for.

for-wegan, v.5. carry off, destroy,
kill; pp. for-weġen, nsm. M 228.
[Cf. wegan.]

for-wundian, wk.v.II. wound (sorely);
pp. forwundod, nsm. R 14, 62. [Cf.
ġe-wundian.]

fōt, m. cons.-stem. foot; gs. —es, M
247; dp. —um, M 119, 171; np.
fēt, S 9. fōt-mæl, n. foot's length;
as. as adv. M 275.

fracuþ, adj. wicked, shameful, pro-
scribed; gsm. —es, R 10 (as noun,
a criminal's).

fram, prep. w. dat. or instr. from;
B 8; R 69; M 185, 187, 193, 252,
316 (the last clearly w. instr.).

fram, adv. away; M 317.

fram-weard, adj. on the way out,
passing away; dsm. —um, S 71.

franca, wk.m. spear; as. —n, M 140;
ds. —n, M 77. [Originally a spear
favored by the Franks, but in
poetry equated with gār; see Gor-
don's note on M 77.]

frēa, wk.m. (a) lord; as. —n, M 259;
ds. —n, M 12, 16, 184, 289; (b)
the Lord; ns. C 9; as. —n, R 33.

frēfran, wk.v.I. comfort; inf. W 28;
S 26 (MS.feran). [Base-word
frōfor, q.v.]

ġe-fremman, wk.v.I. *perform, bring about, accomplish;* inf. W 16, 114; pret. 3p. ġefremedon, S 84.

fremu, f. *beneficial action; good deed;* dip. —m, S 75 (MS. frem-man).

frēo, f. ja-stem. *lady;* gs. frīge, D 15.

frēo, adj. ja-stem. *free, noble.* frēo-mǣġ, m. *(noble) kinsman;* dip. —māgum, W 21.

frēod, f. *peace;* ds. —e, M 39.

frēond, m. nd-stem. *friend, loved one, kinsman;* ns. R 144; W 108; np. —as, R 76; gp. —a, B 41, R 132; ap. frīend, M 229. [Standard West Saxon has nap. frīend, but the analogical -as occurs in some poems, esp. of Anglian origin.] frēond-lēas, adj. *friendless;* asm. —ne, W 28.

frēoriġ, adj. *cold, frozen;* nsm. W 33. [Cf. FRĒOSAN, v.2, *freeze.*]

friend, see frēond.

frīge, see frēo, f.

frignan, v.3. *ask;* pres. 3s. friġneþ, R 112 (future sense). [FRIĠNAN, FRǢĠN, FRUGNON, FRUGNEN; parts 1, 3, and 4 were often spelled without G, indicating the pronunciation FRĪN- and FRŪN-.]

ġe-frignan, v.3. *learn* (by asking); pret. 1p. ġefrugnon, D 14; 3p. R 76.

friþ, m. *peace;* as. M 39; gs. —es, M 41 (instr. *force, at peace*—see healdan); ds. —e, M 179.

frōd, adj. *old, wise, experienced;* nsm. M 140, 317 (frōd feores, *advanced in years*); W 90; nsm.wk. as noun, se frōda, *the old campaigner,* B 37.

frōfor, f. *comfort, help, support;* as. frōfre, W 115.

ġe-frugnon, see ġe-frignan.

frymdiġ, adj. *asking, desirous;* nsm.

M 179 (iċ eom f. to þē, *I beseech thee*).

fugol, m. *bird;* ns. W 81. [Cf. brim-fugol.]

full, adj. w. gen. *full (of);* nsf. S 100; asm. fulne, S 113 (w. gen. fȳres according to MS., but some other gen. beginning with *w* seems to be needed).

full, adv. *wholly, fully, very;* M 153, 253, 311; W 5; S 24.

fundian, wk.v.II, w. prep. or adv. (indicating the goal), *direct one's course (to);* pres. 3s. fundaþ, S 47 (sē-þe on lagu fundaþ, *he that will go to sea*); and w. inf. (indicating purpose), R 103 (hider eft fundaþ . . ., mann-cynn sēċan, *he will come hither again to seek mankind*).

fundon, see findan.

furðor, adv. comp. *further;* f. gān, *advance,* M 247.

fūs, adj. (a) *eager (to set out, to press on);* nsm. M 281; asm. —ne, S 50; (b) *hastening;* npm. —e, R 57 (as noun); (c) *brilliant, shining;* asn.wk. —e, R 21 (the meaning "mobile, quickly shifting," suggested by Cook, lacks confirmation from other passages —see note in Dickins and Ross). [Related to fundian; the base of fȳsan.]

fylstan, wk.v.I. w. dat., *help;* inf. M 265.

fȳr, n. *fire;* gs. —es, S 113 (MS. — this reading rejected for faulty alliteration and doubtful sense).

fyrmest, adj. superl. *foremost, first;* nsm. M 323.

fȳsan, wk.v.I, trans. *send forth rapidly; speed, shoot;* pret. 3s. fȳsde, M 269. [The intrans. sense, *hasten,* is not here represented; base-word fūs, q.v.; cf. a-fȳsan.]

G

gǣstlíċ, adj. *ghostly, spectral;* nsn. W 73. [The meaning *ghastly, terrifying* is tempting here and may be correct, but see OED, "ghastly"—the word cannot with certainty be connected with OE gǣstlíċ.]

gafol, n. *tribute;* as. M 61; ds. —e, M 32, 46.

gāl, adj. *gay, wanton.* See **win-gāl.**

galan, v.6. *sing;* inf. R 67. [GALAN, GŌL, GŌLON, GALEN.]

gamen, n. *entertainment;* ds. —e, S 20.

gamol, adj. *old, aged.* **gamol-feax,** adj. *hoary-haired, gray-headed;* nsm. S 92 (as noun).

gān, anom.v. *go;* inf. M 247; imper. pl. gāþ, M 93 (=*come*); pret. 3s. ēode, R 54; M 132, 159, 225, 297, 323; 3p. ēodon, M 260; 3p. subj. ēoden, M 229. [Cf. **ofer-gān.**]

gang, m. *going, passage; flow* (of blood), ds. —e, R 23. [Cf. **upp-gang,** and next word.]

gangan, v.7. *go, move along, proceed;* inf. M 62; **gangan forþ,** *advance;* inf. M 3, 170; **to scipe gangan,** *embark;* inf. M 40 (w. refl. dat. **ūs,** *take to our ships*); pres. 2p. subj. **gangen,** *should embark,* M 56. [GANGAN, ĠEONG, ĠEONGON, GANGEN.]

ġe-gangan, v.7. (*go and*) *get, obtain;* inf. M 59.

ganot, m. *gannet;* gs. —es, S 20.

gār, m. *spear;* ns. M 296; as. M 13, 134, 154, 237, 321; ds. —e, M 138; ap. —as, M 46, 67, 109; dip. —um, B 18. **gār-berend,** m. nd-stem. *spear-bearer, spearman;* np. M 262. **gār-mittung,** f. *encounter of spears;* gs. —e, B 50. **gār-rǣs,** m.

rush of spears, battle; as. M 32.

gāst, m. *soul, spirit;* as. R 49; ds. —e, M 176; np. —as, R 11; gp. —a, R 152.

gāþ, see **gān.**

ġe-, prefix. sometimes signifying *together.* With verbs a sign of completed action, often untranslatable but sometimes distinctive. All words beginning with this prefix are listed according to the first letter of their stems.

ġē, pron. 2nd pers. pl. *ye;* nom. M 32, 34, 56, 57, 59; dat. **ēow,** M 31, 46, 48; 93; acc. **ēow,** M 41.

ġēac, m. *cuckoo;* ns. S 53.

ġealga, wk.m. *gallows, cross;* ns. R 10; as. —n, R 40. **ġealg-trēo,** n. wa-stem. *gallows-tree, cross;* ds. —we, R 146. [Mod. pronunciation from Anglian GALGA.]

ġear, n. *year;* gp. in **ġēara ġēo,** adv. *in years gone by, long ago,* R 28; W 22. **ġēar-dagas,** m.pl. *days of yore, former times;* dp. —dagum, W 44. [The sense here develops in accordance with **ġēara** or **ġēara,** gp. as independent adv. *of yore, formerly.*]

ġeard, m. *yard; enclosed field or plot of ground* (sometimes of great extent). See **eard-, middan-ġeard.**

ġearu, adj. wa-stem. *ready;* nsm. M 274; npm. **ġearwe,** M 72, 100.

ġearulíċe, adv. *readily;* (with verb of perceiving) *clearly;* D 10.

ġearwe, or **ġeare,** adv. *readily;* (with verb of knowing) *clearly, for certain, well;* W 69, 71. [The two spellings represent a long and a short stressed syllable respectively and their alternate use here accords with metrical requirements.]

ġeatu, f. wō-stem. *equipment, gear.*
See here-ġeatu.

ġeō, adv. *of old, formerly;* R 87; S
83; ġēara ġeō, *in years gone by,
long ago,* R 28; W 22. ġeō-wine, m.
i-stem. *friend* (or *lord*) *of former
days;* ap. S 92. [Often spelled *iu*
in the MSS.]

ġēoc, f. *help;* ds. —e, S 101.

ġeoguþ, f. *youth* (as a period of
life) ; ds. —e, W 35; S 40.

ġeōmor, adj. *sad, mournful;* disf. wk.
ġeōmran, S 53.

ġeond, prep. w. acc. *through,
throughout, over;* W 3, 58, 75; S
90; D 31 (wendeþ ġeond, *goes
about through*).

ġeond-hweorfan, v.3. *pass through,
rove through;* pres. 3s. —hweorfeþ,
W 51. [Cf. hweorfan.]

ġeond-scēawian, wk.v.II. *survey;* pres.
3s. —scēawaþ, W 52. [Cf. scēawian.]

ġeond-þenċan, wk.v.I. *consider thor-
oughly, contemplate;* pres. 1s.
—þenċe, W 60; 3s. —þenċeþ, W 89.
[Cf. þenċan.]

ġeong, adj. *young;* nsm. R 39; M
210; nsm.wk. se ġeonga, as epithet,
M 155; asm. —ne, B 44; npm. —e,
B 29.

ġeorn, adj., w. gen. *eager (for);* nsm.
M 107; W 69; npm. —e, M 73. [Cf.
dōm-, forþ-ġeorn.]

ġeorne, adv. *eagerly,* M 123, 206; W
52; (with a verb of seeing, im-
plying careful observation) *well,
clearly;* M 84.

ġeornfull, adj. *eager;* nsm. M 274.

ġeornlīċe, adv. *eagerly,* M 265.

ġēotan, v.2. *pour out, shed* (blood);
pres. part. ġēotende, *dripping*
(with blood), np. R 70 (emenda-
tion adopted by Cook for MS.
reotende; see grēotan for the
alternative here preferred).

[ĠĒOTAN, ĠĒAT, GUTON, GOTEN; cf.
be-ġēotan and a-ġietan.]

ġicel, m. *piece of ice, icicle.* See hrīm-
ġicel.

ġiedd, n. ja-stem. *saying; song, poem.*
See cwide-, sōþ-ġiedd.

ġiefa, wk.m. *giver.* See bēag-, gold-,
māðum-, sinċ-ġiefa.

ġiefan, v.5. *give.* See a-, for-, of-ġiefan.
[ĠIEFAN, ĠEAF, ĠĒAFON, ĠIEFEN.]

ġiefu, f. *gift;* gp. ġiefena, S 40 (with
gōd, *generous of gifts?* or *well-
endowed with natural abilities,
generously gifted?* —Mrs. Gordon
recommends the first, but the
other seems more appropriate) .

ġief-stōl, m. *gift-seat* (the high
seat or throne, from which gifts
were dispensed) ; *the ceremony of
gift-giving;* gs. —es, W 44.

ġieldan, v.3. *yield, give, pay.* See for-
ġieldan.

ġiellan, v.3. (*yell,*) *cry out loudly;*
pres. 3s. ġielleþ, S 62. [ĠIELLAN,
ĠEALL, GULLON, *GOLLEN; cf. be-
ġiellan.]

ġielp, m. or n. *boasting; a boast;* gs.
—es, W 69. ġielp-word, n. *vaunting
word;* dip. M 274.

ġielpan, v.3. *boast;* inf. B 44 (w.
gen.). ġielpan, ġealp, GULPON,
GOLPEN.]

ġieman, wk.v.I, w. gen. *heed, care
for;* pret. 3p. ġiemdon, M 192.

ġierwan, wk.v.I. *prepare, dress,
adorn;* pret. 3p. ġieredon, R 77.
[Base-word ġearu; cf. ġe-, on-ġier-
wan.]

ġe-ġierwan, wk.v.I. *adorn;* pp. ġe-
ġiered, asn. R 16; ġeġierwed, the
same, R 23. [The form without w
is historically correct, the other
analogical, and the alternation
metrically sound.]

ġiest, m. i-stem. *stranger;* np. —as, M 86.

ġiet, adv. *yet.* See þā-ġiet.

ġīeta, adv. *yet;* B 66; R 28.

ġietan, v.5. *get.* See be-, on-ġietan. [ĠIETAN, ĠEAT, ĠĒATON, ĠIETEN.]

ġietan, wk.v.I. *destroy.* See a-ġietan.

ġif, conj. *if,* M 34, 36, 196.

ġīfre, adj. ja-stem. *greedy, ravenous;* nsm. S 62. [Cf. feoh-, wæl-ġifre.]

ġimm, m. *jewel;* np. —as, R 7, 16. [From Lat. GEMMA.]

-ġinnan, v.3. *begin.* Never without prefix. See on-ġinnan.

ġisel, m. *hostage;* ns. M 265.

glēaw, adj. *sagacious, sharp-sighted, wise, prudent;* nsm. W 73.

glēo, n. *joy, merriment; music.* glēo-stafas, m.pl. *signs of joy, joyful salutations, songs?* dp. —stafum, W 52. [See stæf.]

glīdan, v.l. *glide;* pret. 3s. glād, B 15. [GLĪDAN, GLĀD, GLIDON, GLIDEN.]

gnornian, wk.v.II. *mourn, feel sorrow, lament;* inf. M 315; pres. 3s. gnornaþ, S 92.

God, m. *God;* ns. R 39, 93, 98, 106, 156; M 94; as. R 51, 60; M 262; gs. —es, B 15; R 83, 152; S 101. [GOD, n. *(heathen) god.*]

gōd, n. *(that which is) good;* gs. —es, M 176.

gōd, adj. *good;* nsm. M 315; S 40 *(well-endowed, excellent? generous?)* ; asn. M 13, 237; asm.wk. —an, M 187 *(as noun);* dsm. —um, M 4; apm. —e, M 170; asf. in gōde hwīle, *a good while,* R 70. [Cf. betera, betst, sēlest.]

gold, n. *gold;* ns. W 32 (see wunden); S 101; as. R 18; ds. —e, R 7, 16; M 35; dis. —e, R 77; S 97. gold-ġiefa, wk.m. *gold-giver;* np. —n, S 83. gold-wine, m. *friendly patron, bountiful friend* (since the lord

typically gives gold to his loyal retainers); ns. W 35; as. W 22.

grǣdiġ, adj. *greedy;* nsm. S 62; asm. —ne, B 64.

græf, n. *grave;* as. S 97.

grǣġ, adj. *gray;* asn.wk. grǣġe, B 64.

gram, adj. *fierce;* npm. —e, M 262; dp. —um, M 100 (as noun, *foes*).

ġe-gremian or -gremman, wk.v.I. *enrage;* pp. ġegremed, nsm. M 138; np. —e, M 296. [Base-word gram.]

grēot, n. *sand, dust;* ds. —e, M 315.

grēotan, v.2. *weep;* pres. part. grēotende, np. R 70 (MS. *reotende,* from RĒOTAN, v.2, *weep,* lacks alliteration; see ġēotan for alternative emendation). [Only the present stem of this verb is on record.]

grētan, wk.v.I. *approach; speak to, hail, greet;* pres. 3s. grēteþ, W 52. [The base-word *GRŌT has not survived.]

grimm, adj. *grim, fierce, savage;* nsm. M 61; D 23.

grimme, adv. *grimly, cruelly;* M 109.

ġe-grindan, v.3. *grind, sharpen;* pp. ġegrunden, ap. ġegrundne, M 109. [GRINDAN, GRAND, GRUNDON, GRUNDEN; cf. for-grindan.]

griþ, n. *truce, peace;* as. M 35. [A Scandinavian term for a truce based on definite conditions; less general than friþ; see Gordon's note.]

grund, m. *ground; land, surface of the earth; bottom, foundation;* as. M 287 *(the ground);* ap. —as, B 15 *(surfaces of earth; the land);* S 104 (stīðe grundas, *the rocky foundations).* grund-lēas, adj. *bottomless; boundless;* npf. —e, D 15.

ġe-grundne, see ġe-grindan.

gryre, m. i-stem. *terror.* gryre-lēoþ, n. *terrible song;* gp. —a, M 285.

guma, wk.m. *man;* ns. B 18; W 45;

gs. —n, R 49, 146 (generic sing. or late form of pl. **gumena**?); np. — n, M 94; gp. **gumena**, B 50.

gūþ, f. *battle*; as. —e, M 325; gs. —e, M 192; ds. —e, B 44; M 13, 94, 187, 285, 296 (or instr.), 321. **gūþ-hafoc**, m. *war-hawk*; as. B 64. **gūþ-plega**, wk.m. *battle-play*; ns. M 61. **gūþ-rinc**, m. *warrior*; ns. M 138.

H

habban, wk.v.III. *have.* (a) as independent v.; inf. M 236; pres. 3s. **hafaþ**, W 31; S 47; pret. 3s. **hæfde**, M 13, 121, 199 (*held*); D 3. —neg. **næbbe** (ne **hæbbe**), pres. 3s. subj. S 42. (b) as aux. w pp.; pres. 1s. **hæbbe**, R 50, 79; S 4; 2s. **hafast**, M 231; 3s. **hafaþ**, M 237 (MS. **hæfþ**); pret. 3s. **hæfde**, R 49; M 22, 197, 289; D 10; 3p. **hæfdon**, R 16, 52. [West Saxon normally has HÆFST, HÆFÞ, but it has seemed best to adopt the commoner poetic forms.]

hægl, m. *hail*; ns. S 17, 32; dis. —e, W 48. **hægl-faru**, f. *shower of hail, hailstorm* (perhaps with analogy to an army on the march; see **faru**) ; as. —fære, W 105.

hǣlan, wk.v.I. *heal, save*; inf. R 85. [Base-word **hāl**, q.v.]

hæle, or **hæleþ**, m. þ-stem. *man, warrior, hero*; ns. **hæle**, W 73; **hæleþ**, R 39; vs. **hæleþ**, R 78, 95; np. **hæleþ**, M 214, 249; gp. **hæleða**, B 25; M 74; dp. **hæleðum**, W 105. [Originally ns. **hæle**, np. **hæleþ**.]

Hǣlend, m. nd-stem. *Healer, Savior* (translation of "Jesus"); gs. —es, R 25. [Cf. **hǣlan** and **hāl**.]

hǣðen, adj. *heathen;* npm. **hǣðne**, M 55, 181.

hafaþ, see **habban**.

hafenian, wk.v.II. *raise aloft;* pret. 3s. **hafenode**, M 42, 309.

hafoc, m. *hawk;* as. M 8. [Cf. **gūþ-hafoc.**]

haga, wk.m. *hedge, enclosure,* as in **wīg-haga**, q.v.; in **ān-haga** the wk. ending -a, signifies an agent and **hag-** may signify a hedged dwelling (hence "lone-dweller"), but the sense of narrow confinement is appropriate.

hāl, adj. *whole, safe and sound, unhurt;* npm. —e, M 292.

hāliġ, adj. *holy;* nsm. C 6; npm. **hālġe**, R 11; —declined wk. as m. noun, **hālga**, *holy one;* ds. —n, S 122 (*God*); dp. **hālgum**, R 143, 154 (*saints*).

hām, m. *home, dwelling;* as. R 148; S 117; ds. —e, M 292; ap. —as, B 10; —as. as adv. w. verb of motion, *home(ward)*, M 251.

hama, wk.m. *covering.* See **flǣsc-hama**.

hamor, m. *hammer;* gp. —a, B 6.

hand, f. u-stem. *hand;* ns. M 141; as. M 112; S 96; ds. —a, R 59; M 149; ap. —a, W 43; dp. —um, M 4 (see note), 7, 14; W 4.

hār, adj. *gray; hoary, old;* nsm. B 39; M 169; nsm.wk. —a, W 82.

hasu, adj. wa-stem. *dark, dusky.* **hasu-pāda**, wk.m. *dusky-coated one;* as. —n, B 62. (The same in form as a wk. adj. corresponding to strong HASU-PĀD, *dusky-coated.*)

hāt, adj. *hot;* npf. **hāt'** for **hāte**, S 11; comp. **hātra**, npm. —n, S 64 (fig.). **hāt-heort**, adj. *hot-tempered;* nsm. W 66.

hātan, v.7. (a) *command;* pres. 1s. **hāte**, R 95; pret. 3s. **hēt**, M 2, 62,

74, 101; 3p. hēton, R 31; M 30; —(b) *call, name;* pp. hāten, nsm. M 75, 218. [HĀTAN, HĒT, HĒTON, HĀTEN.]

ġe-hātan, v.7. *promise, vow;* pres. 1s. ġehāte, M 246; pret. 3s. ġehēt, M 289.

hē, hēo, hit, pron. 3d pers. *he, she, it,* pl. *they.* hē, nsm. C 3, 5; B 40; R 34, etc. (15 times); M 7, etc. (56 times); W 2, etc. (10 times); S 8 (*it*), 42, etc. (9 times). his, gsm. C 2; B 2, 38, 40, 42; R 49, 63, 92, 102, 106, 156; M 11, etc. (20 times); W 13, etc. (8 times); S 40, etc. (11 times). him, dsm. R 65, 67, 108, 118; M 7, etc. (15 times; refl. in 300); W 1, 10 (w. *þe, to whom*), etc. (7 times); S 13 (w. *þe, to whom*), etc. (11 times); D 1, 3. hine, asm. R 11, 39, 61, 64; M 164, 181; W 32, 35; S 43, 77, 99; D 5. hēo, nsf. W 96; D 10, 11. hire, gsf. D 8, 9. hīe, asf. M 180; S 103 (refl., *itself*); D 16. hit, nsn. R 19, 22, 26, 97; M 66, 137, 190, 195, 240; asn. S 102. hīe, np. B 8, 48, 51; R 32, 46, 48, 60, 63, 64, 66, 67, 68, 115, 116, 132; M 19, etc. (19 times); W 61; S 84. hīe, ap. M 82, 127, 209, 283, 320. hira, gp. B 47; R 31, 47, 155; M 20, etc. (11 times); W 18. him, dp. B 7, 60; R 86, 88; M 66, 197, 198, 265; S 23; refl., B 53; R 31, 63 (see note), 83, 133; S 67, 84 (mid him, *amongst themselves*).

hēafod, n. *head;* as. W 43; ds. hēaf-dum, R 63. [Campbell, *OE Gram.* 574, 4, regards this form as a locatival dat. sg., perhaps instr. in origin; the three recorded instances are all datives with æt; otherwise we find ds. hēafde.]

hēah, adj. *high;* nsm. W 98; asm.

hēanne, R 40; W 82; apm. wk. hēan, S 34 (*high* or *deep*). hēah-fæder, m. r-stem. *God the Father;* ds. -e, R 134.

healf, f. *side;* ds. -e, M 152, 318; as. -e, R 20.

healdan, v.7. *hold, grasp, possess; keep, guard, maintain, control;* inf. M 14, 19, 74, 102, 236; S 109, 111; pres. 3p. healdaþ, S 87; 3s. subj. healde, W 14 (*hold in, keep to himself*); pret. 3p. subj. hēolden, M 20; —w. instrumental genitive, ēow friðes healdan (inf.), *keep you at peace, remain at peace with you?* M 41. [HEALDAN, HĒOLD, HĒOLDON, HEALDEN; cf. be-healdan.]

ġe-healdan. v.7. *keep hold of;* inf. M 167; *keep (unbroken),* pres. 3s. ġehealdeþ, W 112.

heall, f. *hall;* ds. -e, M 214. [Cf. medu-heall.]

heals, m. *neck;.* as. M 141.

hēan, adj. *lowly, abject, downcast;* nsm. W 23.

hēan, hēanne, inflected forms, see hēah.

hēanliċ, adj. *humiliating;* nsn. M 55.

heard, adj. *hard; severe, bitter; hard-fighting, fierce, unyielding;* nsm. M 130 (wīġes heard, *fierce in battle*); asn. M 214; gsm. -es, B 25; gsn. -es, M 266; asm. -ne, M 167, 236; asf. -e, M 33. —comp. heardra, *harder, more resolute,* nsm. M 312; superl. heardost, *bitterest, most severe;* nsn. R 87. [Cf. fēol-, for-, wiġ-heard.]

heardliċe, adv. *fiercely;* M 261.

hearm, m. *grief, sorrow;* gp. -a, M 223.

hearpe, wk.f. *harp;* ds. hearpan, S 44.

hearra, wk.m. *lord;* ns. M 204. [Cf. German HERR. The OE word may have been borrowed from Old Saxon.]

heaðu-, *battle, war* (a word occurring only as the first member of compounds). heaðu-lind, f. *battle-shield (of linden)*; ap. —a, B 6.

hēawan, v.7. *hew*; pret. 3s. hēow, M 324; 3p. hēowon, B 6, 23; M 181. [HĒAWAN, HĒOW, HĒOWON, HĒA-WEN; cf. a-, for-hēawan.]

hebban, v.6. *lift, raise*; inf. R 31. [HEBBAN, HŌF, HŌFON, HAFEN; cf. a-hebban.]

hefiġ, adj. *heavy, oppressive*; dsn. wk. —an, R 61; *sad, depressed*; comp. hefiġran, npf. W 49.

hell, f. *hell.* hell-scaða, wk.m. *fiend of hell*; np. —n, M 180.

helm, m. *covering, helmet*, etc. See niht-helm. [Cf. HELAN, v.4, *conceal, hide*.]

help, f. *help*; as. —e, W 16; ds. —e, R 102.

ġe-hende, prep. w. dat. *near*, M 294 (postpos.). [Base-word hand.]

hēo, see hē.

heofon, m. *heaven*; as. C 6; gs. —es, R 64; ap. —as, R 103; gp. —a, R 45; dp. —um, R 85, 134, 140, 154; M 172; W 107, 115; S 107, 122.

heofon-riċe, n. ja-stem. *kingdom of heaven*; gs. —s, C 1; R 91.

heofonliċ, adj. *heavenly*; asm. —ne, R 148.

hēolden, see healdan.

heolstor, m. *concealment, darkness*; dis. heolstre, W 23. [Cf. HELAN, v.4, *conceal, hide*.]

heonan, adv. *hence, from here*; R 132; M 246; S 37.

-heort, adjectival combining-form of heorte, *heart*. See hāt-heort.

heorte, wk.f. *heart*; ns. M 312; heortan, gs. W 49; ds. M 145; as.

S 11, 34 (obj. of cnyssaþ; or gs. with ġeþōhtas).

heorþ, m. *hearth.* heorþ-ġenēat, m. *sharer of the hearth, member of the chief's household troops, his closest followers*; np. —as, M 204. heorþ-weorod, n. *the body of household retainers*; as. M 24.

hēow, hēowon, see hēawan.

hēr, adv. *here*, M 36, 51, 241, 243, 314; *in this world*, R 108, 137, 145; W 108 (twice), 109 (twice); S 102; *in this year*, B 1 (the typical introduction to an entry in the Chronicle; probably not part of the poem).

here, m. ja-stem. *army*; ds. M 292 (West Saxon variant of herġe, the usual dative); gs. herġes, B 31. here-flīema, wk.m. *fugitive* (from pursuing host); ap. —n, B 23. here-ġeatu, f. *war-equipment*; in law a "heriot," "a feudal service originally consisting of weapons, horses and other military equipments, restored to a lord on the death of his tenant" (see Gordon's note, taking up a suggestion made by C. Brett); as. —ġeatwe, M 48. here-lāf, f. *remnant of an army after a battle; group of survivors*; dp. —um. B 47. [Cf. æsc-here.]

herian, wk.v.I. *praise, extol*; inf. C 1; pres. 3p. subj. herien, S 77. [HERIAN (from *H.ERJAN), HEREDE, HERED.]

hēt, hēton, ġe-hēt, see hātan, ġe-hātan.

hete, m. i-stem. *hate, hostility*. See ecg-hete.

hettend, m. nd-stem. *enemy*; np. B 10. [Cf. HATIAN, *hate*, and HETTAN, *persecute*.]

hider, adv. *hither*; B 69; R 103; M 57.

hīe, see hē.

hieldan, wk.v.I. *bend;* inf. R 45 (w. refl. pron.) [Base-word HEALD, adj. *bent, inclined.*]

hīenan, wk.v.I. *bring low, lay low, afflict;* inf. M 180; pret. 3s. hiende, M 324 (used absolutely: *laid low.*) [Base-word hēan, adj., q.v.]

ġe-hīeran, wk.v.I. *hear, perceive, understand;* inf. R 78; pres. 2s. ġehierst, M 45; pret. 1s. ġe-hīerde, R 26; M 117; S 18.

hild, f. jō-stem. *battle, war;* as. —e, M 33; ds. —e, M 8, 48, 55, 123, 223, 288, 324. hilde-rinc, m. *warrior;* ns. B 39; M 169; np. —as, R 61; gp. —a. R 72.

-hilte, adjectival combining-form, *hilted,* corresponding to ĠE-HILTE, n. ja-stem, *sword-hilt.* See fealu-hilte.

him, see hē.

hindan, adv. *from behind;* B 23. [Cf. be-hindan.]

hīne, hira, see hē.

hīred, m. *household, body of retainers.* hīred-mann, m. *household retainer;* np. —menn, M 261.

his, hit, see hē.

hlāford, m. *lord;* ns. M 135, 189, 224, 240; as. D 39; ds. —e, M 318; *the Lord,* as. R 45. hlāford-lēas, adj. *lordless;* nsm. M 251.

hleahtor, m. *laughter;* as. S 21 (perhaps for ds. hleahtre; see fore).

ġe-hlēapan, v.7. *leap upon, mount;* pret. 3s. ġehlēop, M 189. [HLĒAPAN, HLĒOP, HLĒOPON, HLĒAPEN.]

hlemm, m. ja-stem. *noise (of a blow);* but in inwitt-hlemm, (q.v.) the meaning appears to be *wound.*

hlēo, n. wa-stem. *shelter; protector lord;* ns. M 74; D 41. hlēo-mǣġ,

m. *protecting kinsman; gp.* —māga, S 25.

ġe-hlēop, see ġe-hlēapan.

hlēor, n. *cheek, face;* as adjectival combining-form, -hlēor, *faced.* See drēoriġ-hlēor.

hlēoðor, n. *cry, (bird-) call;* as. S 20. [Cf. next word.]

hleōðrian, wk.v.II. *call out, speak;* pret. 3s. hlēoðrode, R 26.

hliehhan, v.6. *laugh;* inf. B 47; pret. 3s. hlōg, M 147. [HLIEHHAN, HLŌG, HLŌGON,——; cf. hleahtor.]

hlīfian, wk.v.II. *tower, rise up;* pres. 1s. hlīfie, R 85.

hlimman, v.3. *roar, resound;* inf. S 18. [HLIMMAN, *HLAMM, HLUMMON,——.]

hliþ, n. *cliff;* see stān-hliþ.

hlōg, see hliehhan.

ġe-hlystan, wk.v.I. *listen;* pret. 3p. ġehlyston, M 92.

ġe-hnǣġan, wk.v.I. *bring low, abase, humble;* pp. ġehnǣġed, nsm. S 88. [Base-word HNĀG, adj. *low;* cf. hnīgan.]

hnāg, see hnīgan.

ġe-hnāst, n. *collision* (in battle). See cumbol-ġehnāst.

hnīgan, v.1. *bow down;* pret. 1s. hnāg, R 59. [HNĪGAN, HNĀG, HNIGON, HNIĠEN; cf. ġe-hnǣġan.]

hogode, hogodon, see hycgan.

ġe-hola, wk.m. *protector;* gp. ġe-holena, W 31.

hold, adj. *kind, friendly, gracious;* nsm. S 41; asm. —ne, D 39; superl. holdost, *most loyal, devoted;* asn. M 24. [Describes a lord's regard for his followers and also theirs for him; hence the two shades of meaning.]

holm, m. *wave, (high) sea;* pl. *seas, ocean;* as. W 82; gp. —a, S 64.

holt, n. *forest, wood; wooden shaft;*

gs. —es, R 29; M 8. **holt-wudu,** m. u-stem, *trees of the forest;* as. R 91 (MS. *holm wudu*) . [Cf. **æsc-holt.**]

hōn, contr.v.7. **hang.** See **be-hōn.**

hord, n. *treasure, hoard;* as. or ap. B 10. **hord-cofa,** wk.m. *treasure-chest* (i.e. the breast as container of thoughts) ; as. —n, W 14. [Cf. **brēost-hord.**]

hors, n. *horse;* as. M 2.

hræd, adj. *quick, swift, sudden, hasty.* **hræd-wyrde,** adj. ja-stem. *hasty of speech;* nsm. W 66.

hræfn, nı. *raven;* as. B 61; np. —as, M 106.

hræðe, adv. *quickly, soon;* M 30, 164, 288.

hrǣw, n. *corpse;* ns. R 72; as. R 53; ap. B 60.

hrēam, m. *outcry, clamor;* ns. M 106.

hrēman, wk.v.I. *exult;* inf. B 39 (w. gen.) [Cf. Old Saxon HRŌM, *glory;* German RUHM.]

hrēmiġ, adj. *exultant;* npm. **hrēmġe,** B 59 (w. gen.) .

hrēoh, adj. *rough, troubled;* nsm. wk. **hrēo,** (=*HRĒOHA), W 16; asf. **hrēo,** (=*HREŌHE) , W 105.

hrēosan, v.2. *fall;* inf. W 48; pres. part. **hrēosende,** nsf. W 102. [HRĒOSAN, HRĒAS, HRURON, HROREN; cf. **be-hroren.**]

hrēow, f. wō-stem. *sorrow, (rue)* . **hrēow-ċeariġ,** adj. *sorrowful, troubled;* nsm. R 25.

hrēran, wk.v.I. *stir (up) , move;* inf. W 4. [Base-word HRŌR, adj. *vigorous, active;* cf. **on-hrēran.**]

hreðer, m. or n. *breast, bosom* (esp. as the seat of feelings); *heart;* as. S 63; gp. **hreðra,** W 72. **hreðer-loca,** wk.m. *enclosure of the breast or heart: the breast;* as. —n, S 58.

hrīm, m. *rime, (hoar-)frost;* ns. S 32;

as. W 48; dis. —e, W 77. **hrīm-ċeald,** adj. *frost-cold;* asf. —e, W 4. **hrīm-ġicel,** m. *icicle;* dip. —um, S 17.

hring, m. *ring;* ap. —as, M 161 (*gold rings, ornaments*). **hring-loca,** wk. m. *linked ring* (of corselet); ap. —n, M 145. **hring-þegu,** f. *receiving of (gold) rings* (by a liegeman from his lord); ds. —þeġe, S 44.

hrīþ. f. *snowstorm;* ns. W 102. [The only occurrence of the word in OE; the meaning inferred from the context and from Old Norse HRĪÐ, f. *tempest.*]

hrīðiġ, adj. *snow-covered? storm-beaten?* npm. **hrīðġe,** W 77. [Only occurrence; see preceding word.]

hrōf, m. *roof;* ds. —e, C 6.

hrūse, wk.f. *earth, ground;* gs. **hrū-san,** W 23; as. W 102 (MS. has nom. *hruse*) ; S 32.

hryre, m. i-stem. *fall, ruin;* ds. **hryre,** W 7. [One would expect **hryres,** parallel to the two preceding genitives dependent on **ġemyndiġ,** 6; but perhaps a dat. of accompaniment modifying **wæl-sleahta,** "attended by the fall of kinsmen." For the word, cf. **hroren,** pp. of **hrēosan.**]

hū, interr. adv. and conj. *how;* (a) introducing subord. cl., M 19; W 30, 35, 61, 73; S 2, 14, 29, 118; D 12; (b) introducing an exclamation, W 95.

hungor, m. *hunger;* ns. S 11.

hūru, adv. *certainly,* R 10.

hūs, n. *house.* See **feorh-hūs.**

hwā, hwæt, pron. (1) interr. *who what;* (a) in indirect questions, nsm. **hwā,** M 95, 124, 215; asn. **hwæt,** R 116; isn. **hwon,** S 43 (to **hwon,** *to what:* scil. *what end, what service, what fate*); (b) as a relative, asn. **hwæt**, R 2 (MS. **hæt**); M 45; S 56. (2) indef. pron. *someone, something*; nsm. **hwā**, M 71. (3) indef. pron. *each* (normally ġe-**hwā**); asm. **hwone**, M 2.

ġe-**hwā**, ġe-**hwæt**, pron. w. part. gen. *each*; gsn. ġe**hwæs**, C 3; dsm. ġe**hwǣm**, W 63; S 72; asm. ġe**hwone**, B 9.

hwæl, m. *whale*; gs. —**es**, S 60. **hwælweġ**, m. *whale's way, ocean*; as. S 63 (MS. *wæl weg*).

hwǣr, adv. and conj. *where*; (a) interr. adv. R 112; W 92, 93 (five times); (b) rel. conj. *(there) where*, W 26; S 117.

hwæt, adj. *quick, vigorous, active*; nsm. S 40; in certain compounds, *quick at producing, abounding in*. See **ār-hwæt**.

hwæt, interj. *lo!* R 1, 90; M 231.

hwæt, pron. see **hwā**.

ġe-**hwæðer**, adj. *either*; asf. —**e**, M 112.

hwæð(e)re, adv. conj. *nevertheless, but*; R 18, 24, 38, 42, 57, 59, 70, 75, 101.

ġe-**hwelċ**, pron. w. part. gen. *each*; nsm. M 128, 257; S 90, 111; dsm. —**um**, R 108 (**ānra** ġ., *each one*); S 68 (MS. isn. —*e*); ism. —**e**, R 136; W 8; S 36. [Fusion of ġe-**hwā** and **liċ**; cf. **ǣġhwelċ**.]

hweorfan, v.3. *turn, go, take* (or *change*) *one's course*; inf. W 72; pres. 3s. **hweorfeþ**, S 58, 60 (w. comparison to a bird: *flies, takes its flight*). [HWEORFAN, HWEARF, HWURFON, HWORFEN; cf. ġeond-**hweorfan**.]

hwettan, wk.v.I. *whet, incite*; pres. 3s. **hweteþ**, S 63. [Base-word **hwæt**, adj., q.v.]

hwider, interr. conj. *whither*, W 72.

hwīl, f. (*an indefinite period of*) *time, while*. (a) as. —**e** as adv. *for a time*, R 64, 84; D 36; **ealle h.** *all the time, continually*, M 304; **gōde h.** *for a good while*, R 70; **lange h.** *for a long time*, R 24. (b) dp. —**um** as adv. *at times, sometimes*; W 43; S 19; correl. *at one time . . . at another time; now . . . now*, R 22, 23; M 270. (c) **þā hwīle þe**, conj. *while*; M 14, 83, 235, 272. [Cf. **earfoþ-, langunghwil**.]

hwilpe, wk.f. *whaup* (English and Scottish dialect), *curlew*; gs. —**n**, S 21. (See Mrs. Gordon's note.)

hwilum, adv. see **hwīl**.

hwīt, adj. *white*; asm. uninflected (because parenthetical?), B 63. [On the grammar, see Campbell's ed., p. 119. He says **earn æftan hwīt** is parenthetical and therefore ns.]

hwon, instr. of **hwæt**, see **hwā** and **for-hwon** under **for**.

hwōn, pron. w. gen. *little, few*; as. S 28.

hwone, see **hwā**.

hwonne, interr. adv. *when*; as rel. conj. w. subj. *(the time) when*, R 136; M 66 (w. **tō lang**, *too long until the time when*).

hycgan, wk.v.III (and II). *think, consider, be intent* (*on*), *intend, purpose*; inf. M 4; S 117; pres. 3s. subj. **hycge**, W 14; pret. 3s. **hogode**, M 133 (w. gen., *was intent on, purposed*); 3s. subj., M 128; 3p. **hogodon**, M 123. [HYCGAN, HOGDE or HOGODE, HOGD or HOGOD; cf. **for-hycgan**, **stīþ-hycgende**.]

hȳdan, wk.v.I. *hide, hoard*; pres. 3s. **hȳdeþ**, S 102.

ġe-**hȳdan**, wk.v.I. *hide, bury*; pret. 3s. ġe**hȳdde**, W 84.

ġe-**hyġd**, f. and n. i-stem. *thought*,

intention; conception; ns. W 72; S 116.

hyġdiġ, adj. *mindful;* in composition, *minded, disposed.* See **an-, wan-hyġdiġ.**

hyġe, m. i-stem. *mind, thought; soul, spirit; purpose, courage;* ns. M 312; W 16; S 44, 58; ds. M 4; S 96.

hyht, m. i-stem. *joyous expectation, pleasure, bliss;* ns. R 126, 148; S 45, 122.

hyrned, pp. adj. *horned.* **hyrned-nebba,** wk.m. *horny-beaked one,* as. **—n,** B 62. [The same in form as a wk. adj., corresponding to strong HYRNED-NEBB, *horny-beaked; cf.* **īsiġ-, ūriġ-feðra.**]

hyse, m. i-stem, inflected according to ja-stems (with gemination), **hyss-,** *young man, young warrior;* ns. M 152; gs. hysses, M 141; np. hyssas, M 112, 123; ap. hyssas, M 169; gp. hyssa, M 2, 128.

I

iċ, pron. 1st pers. sg. *I;* ns. R 1, etc. (43 times); M 117, etc. (14 times); W 8, etc. (8 times); S 1, 2, etc. (9 times); D 35, 36, 38. **mīn,** gs., only in the rejected emendation, mīn myne wisse, W 27 (but see **mīn,** poss. adj.). **mē,** ds. R 2, 4, 46, 83, 86, 126, 129, 135, 144; M 55, 220, 223, 249, 318 (refl.); S 1, 20 (refl.), 61, 64; D 35, 37, 41. **mē,** as. R 30, 31, 32 (twice), 33, 34, 42, 45, 46, 61, 75, 77, 81, 90, 122, 136, 139, 142; M 29, 252. **meċ,** as. W 28; S 6. [See **wē, wit.**]

īdel, adj. *empty, vain;* nsn. W 110; npn. īdlu, W 87.

ielde, m. i-stem, pl. *men* (conceived

as the successive generations, or men of old); gp. ielda, C 5; W 85; S 77. [Base-word **eald,** *old.*]

ieldu, f. īn-stem. *age, old age;* ns. S 70, 91.

ielfetu, f. *(wild) swan;* gs. **ielfete,** S 19.

iergþu, f. iþō-stem. *slackness;* as. iergþe, M 6. [Base-word **earg,** q.v.]

ierre, adj. ja-stem. *angry, wrathful;* nsm. M 44, 253.

īeðan, wk.v.I. *lay waste, depopulate, destroy;* pret. 3s.īeðde, W 85. [Cf. the rare adj. **ĪEÐE,** *empty, waste,* cognate w. German **ÖDE.**]

īġ, f. jō-stem. (alt. sp. **īeġ,** from *ĒA-JŌ-; see **ēa,**) *watery place, island.* **īġ-land,** n. *island;* is. **—e,** B 66. [Mod. "island" from native ME ILAND, influenced by OF ile from Lat. INSULA, respelled ISLE by Renaissance scholars.]

in-dryhten, adj. *noble, excellent;* nsm. W 12. [This adj. is probably formed from **in-dryhtu,** next below, the prefix indicating a quality inherent in a noble **dryht,** though it is sometimes regarded as an intensive.]

in-dryhtu, f. īn-stem. *nobility;* ns. S 89. [Cf. preceding word.]

inn, adv. *in,* M 58, 157.

innan, adv. *(from) within,* S 11.

inwitt, n. *malice, fraud.* **inwitt-hlemm,** m. *malicious wound;* np. **—as,** R 47. [It is uncertain whether **inwitt** is borrowed from Lat. INVIDIA or of Germanic origin; for the odd meaning of the second element see **hlemm.**]

inwitta, wk.m. *malicious or deceitful one;* ns. B 46. [Cf. preceding word.]

iren, n. ja-stem, *iron, iron blade;* ns. M 253 (**ord** and **iren** as variation

of **wǣpen:** *point* [*of spear*] *and
iron blade;* or, as hendiadys, *iron
point* or *pointed iron?*) .

is, see **bēon-wesan.**

īs, n. *ice.* **īs-ċeald,** adj. *ice-cold;* asm.
—**ne,** S 14, 19.

īsiġ, adj. *icy.* **īsiġ-feðra,** wk.m. *icy-
feathered one;* ns. S 24. [Usually
regarded as a wk. adj., but like
ūriġ-feðra, q.v., it is placed as if
in apposition and can be taken as
a characterizing noun like **hyrned-
nebba,** q.v. The corresponding
strong adj. would be **īsiġ-feðer.**]

L

lā, interj. *lo!* — see **eā-lā.**

ġe-lāc, n. *tossing, play; tumult;* as.
S 35.

lād, f. *way, course.* See **brim-, lagu-lād.**
[Cf. **līðend, lid, lida.**]

lǣdan, wk.v.I. *lead;* inf. R 5 (*extend:*
possibly an error for **lēodan,** v.2,
spring up); M 88. [Base-word **lād,**
as above.]

lǣġ, see **licgan.**

lǣne, adj. ja-stem. *transitory, brief,
fleeting;* ns. W 108 (n. and m.),
109 (m. and f.) ; nsn. S 66; dsn.wk.
lǣnan, R 109 (MS. —**um**), 138.
[Lit. *on loan:* **lǣn,** f. *a loan.*]

lǣran, wk.v.I. *instruct;* pret. 3s.
lǣrde, M 311. [Base-word **lār,** f.,
q.v.]

lǣriġ, m. *rim* (*of shield*)? ns. M 284.
[Perhaps a borrowing from Lat.
lōrīca, corselet, by way of Old
Welsh, with shift of meaning; see
Gordon's note.]

ġe-lǣstan, wk.v.I, w. dat. *support,
help;* inf. M 11; w. acc., *fulfill;*
pret. 3s. **ġelǣste,** M 15. [Base-word
lāst, m., q.v.]

lǣtan, v.7, w. inf. *let, cause to;* pret.
3s. **lēt,** M 7, 140; 3p. **lēton,** B 60;
M 108. [**lǣtan, lēt, lēton,
lǣten;** cf. **for-lǣtan.**]

lāf, f. *remnant;* hamora **lāf,** *what is
left by the hammers of the smith:
a sword;* dip. —**um,** B 6; daroða
lāf, *what is left by the spears: the
remnant that survives after a
battle;* ns. B 54. [Cf. **here-lāf.**]

lāge, lāgon, see **licgan.**

lagu, m. u-stem. *sea, water;* as. S 47
(on l., *to sea*). **lagu-lād** f. *water-
way, sea;* as. —**e,** W 3. **lagu-strēam,**
m. *sea-stream;* np. —**as,** M 66
(tidal streams, coming up the
river) .

ġe-lagu, n.pl. (uniquely recorded,
apparently an inflected form of
****ġe-lǣċ,** n. *lay, layer, material
spread out*), *stretches, expanse;*
ap. in holma **ġelagu,** *expanse of
the seas,* S 64. [Etymologically
distinct from **lagu,** m.; cf. **licgan.**]

land, n. *land;* as. B 9, 27, 56, 59;
gs. —**es,** M 90, 275; ds. —**e,** M 99;
S 66. **land-riht,** n. *land-right* (the
rights and privileges of an estate);
as. D 40. [Cf. **iġ-land.**]

lang, adj. *long;* (in duration) nsn.
M 66; asf. —**e,** R 24; (in stature)
nsm. wk. se **langa** (as distinguish-
ing epithet), *the tall,* M 273. [Cf.
ealdor-lang; also **leng.**]

ġe-lang, adj. w. prep. *on* (Anglian
in), *comprehended in, inseparable
from;* nsn. S 121.

lange, adv. *for a long time.* W 3, 38.

langoþ, m. *longing;* as. D 3.

langung, f. *longing, restless desire,
anxiety;* as. —**e,** S 47. **langung-hwīl,**
f. *time of longing;* gp. —**a,** R 126
(according to Dickins and Ross,
times of weariness of spirit,
accidia; but the dreamer seems

hardly to be blaming himself here).

lār, f. *lore, instruction, knowledge.*

lār-cwide, m. i-stem, *speech of instruction, counsel;* dip. —cwidum, W 38. [Cf. **lǽran**.]

lāst, m. *footstep, track, path;* as. B 22; ds. —e, W 97 (on l., w. dat. *on the track of, behind, after*); dip. —um, S 15 (wreċċan l., *in the paths of an exile*). **lāst-word**, n. *reputation left behind* (after death); gp. —a, S 73 (Mrs. Gordon's definition). [Cf. **wræc-lāst**.]

lāþ, adj. *hostile, hateful, hated;* asm. —ne, S 112 (as noun); dsf. —re, M 90; npm. —e, M 86; gp. —ra, B 9 (as noun, *enemies*); dp. —um, B 22; comp. **lāðre**, asn. M 50; superl. **lāðost**, nsm. R 88.

lēan, n. *recompense.* Cf. **wiðer-lēan**.

lēas, adj. *lacking, deprived of;* npn. —e, W 86 (analogical -e, generalized from the npm.; the npn. of long monosyllables usually has no ending, having lost its original -u; but the extra syllable is metrically necessary; possibly the original version had an archaic -u, but the analogical -e of the MS. is probably authentic); —as suffix, *-less;* see **ende-, frēond-, grund-, hlāford-, wine-lēas**.

lecgan, wk.v.I. *lay;* pres. 3p. lecgaþ, S 57; 3s. subj. lecge, W 42; pret. 3s. leġde, D 5; 3p. leġdon, B 22 (elliptically w. on lāst, *pursued*). [LECGAN, LEĠDE, LEĠ(E)D; baseword LÆĠ; cf. **licgan**; also **a-lecgan**.]

leng, comp. adv. *longer;* M 171. [Cf. **lang**.]

lēode, m. i-stem, pl. *people;* np. B 11; ap. M 37; dp. lēodum, R 88; M 23, 50. [Cf. LĒOD, m. *man, leader;* LĒOD, f. *people, nation.* The plural

lēode is usually assigned to the former.]

lēof, adj. *dear, beloved;* gsm. —es, W 38; dsm. —um, M 319; asm. —ne, M 7, 208 (as noun); S 112 (as noun); dsf. —re, W 97; vsm.wk. —a, R 78, 95; gp. —ra, W 31; superl. **lēofost**, nsm. M 23 (see note).

leofaþ, see **libban**.

lēoht, n. *light;* dis. —e, R 5.

lēoþ, n. *song.* **lēoþ-cræftiġ**, adj. *skilled in song;* nsm. D 40. [Cf. **gryre-, sorg-lēoþ**.]

lēt, lēton, see **lǽtan**.

ġe-lettan, wk.v.I. *hinder;* pret. 3s. ġelette, M 164.

libban, wk.v.III. *live;* pres. 3s. leofaþ, S 102, 107; 3p. libbaþ, R 134; 3s. subj. libbe, S 78; pret. 3p. lifdon, S 85; —pres. part. libbende, m.pl. as noun, *the living;* gp. libbendra, S 73.

liċ, n. *body;* gs. —es, R 63.

-lica, wk. m. *image, likeness;* see **wyrm-lica**.

licgan, v.5. *lie, lie dead;* pres. part. licgende, nsm. R 24; pres. 3s. liġeþ, M 222, 232, 314; 3p. licgaþ, W 78; pret. 3s. læġ, B 17; M 157, 204, 227, 276, 294; 3p. lāgon, B 28; M 112, 183; pret. 3s. subj. lāge, M 279; w. refl. dat., *lie down;* inf. M 319; pret. 3s. subj. lāge, M 300 (see note). [LICGAN, LÆĠ, LĀGON, LEĠEN.]

lid, n. *ship;* gs. —es, B 27, 34. **lid-mann**, m. *shipman, sailor (viking);* np. —menn, M 99; gp. —manna, M 164. [Cf. LĪÐAN, v.l, *sail;* and next word.]

lida, wk.m. *sailor.* See **sǽ-lida**.

liefan, wk.v.I, *allow, permit.* See **a-liefan**.

ġe-liefan, wk.v.I. *believe;* (a) w. subordinate clause as object, pres.

1s. ġelīefe, S 66; 3s. ġelīefeþ, S 27
(w. refl. him, *admits to himself*);
(b) w. on and dat. (or acc.), *be-
lieve in, trust in;* pres. 3s.
ġelīefeþ, S 108. [Base-word LĒAF, f.
leave, permission; cf. a-līefan;
also ĊELĒAFA, wk.m. *belief*.]

līehtan, wk.v.I. *alight;* pret. 3s. liehte,
M 23. [Cf. LĪOHT, later LĒOHT, adj.
light in weight.]

līesan, wk.v.I. *līberate, redeem,
ransom;* inf. R 41; M 37. [Cf.
lēas, adj.; also on-līesan.]

lif, n. *life;* ns. S 65, 121; as. R 147;
M 208; W 60, 89; gs. —es, R 88,
126; S 27, 79; ds. —e, R 109, 138.

lifdon, see libban.

liġeþ, see licgan.

lim₂ n. *limb.* lim-wēriġ, adj. *weary of
limb;* asm. —ne, R 63.

limpan, v.3. impersonal, w. dat.
befall; pres. 3s. limpeþ, S 13.
[LIMPAN, LAMP, LUMPON, LUMPEN.]

lind, f. *linden-wood; shield (of
linden-wood);* as. —e, M 244; ap.
—a, M 99. [Cf. heaðu-lind.]

liðend, m. nd-stem. *sailor.* See
brim-liðend.

loca, wk.m. *lock, link;* see hring-loca;
enclosure, locker; see ferhþ-,
hreðer-loca. [Cf. lūcan.]

lof, n. and m. *praise;* ns. S 73, 78.

losian, wk.v.II. *be lost, fail;* pres. 3s.
losaþ, S 94.

lūcan, v.2. *lock, unite, join;* pret.
3p. lucon, M 66. [LŪCAN, LĒAC,
LUCON, LOCEN.]

lufu, f. *love* (often inflected, as here,
according to the wk. decl. as if
from the rare nom. LUFE); ds.
lufan, S 121; as. lufan, S 112 (not
in MS.). [Cf. sorg-lufu.]

lust, m. *desire;* ns. S 36.

lyft, f. i-stem (also m. and n.) *air;*
as. R 5 (on lyft, *aloft, on high*).

lȳt, indecl. subst., adj. and adv.
little, few; as subst., w. part. gen.,
as. W 31; as adv., S 27.

lȳtel, adj. *little;* isn. lȳtle, B 34.

lytiġian, wk.v.II. *use guile;* inf. M
86.

lȳtlian, wk.v.II. *grow less, dwindle,
diminish;* pres. 3s. lȳtlaþ, M 313.

M

mā, n., w. part. gen. *more;* M 195;
as adv. *more,* B 46. [Cf. mǣst.]

mæcg, m. ja-stem. *man;* gp. —a, B
40 (alt. reading for mēċa).

mæġ, mæġe, see magan.

mæġ, f. þ-stem (gds. and nap. mæġþ),
maiden, woman; ns. W 109.
[Some scholars regard this word
as mǣġ, f. *kinswoman, woman;*
but all instances are in nom. sg.,
so that association with mæġþ, rep-
resented in other cases, is prob-
able. Cf. the variation of hæle
and hæleþ.]

mǣġ, m. *kinsman;* ns. M 5, 114, 224,
287; gp. māga, B 40; W 51. [Cf.
cnēo-, frēo-, hlēo-, wine-mǣġ.]

mæġen, n. *strength;* ns. M 313.

mǣl 1, n. (a) *measure;* see fōt-mǣl;
(b) *time, occasion;* gp. —a, S 36.

mǣl 2, n. *speech;* gp. —a, M 212.
[Unique occurrence with this
meaning, but cf. mǣlan and
mæðel. Gordon's emendation of
MS. þa to gen. pl. þāra permits us
to regard mǣl as neuter in-
stead of feminine, a gender which
is improbable on other grounds.]

mǣlan, wk.v.I. *speak;* pret. 3s.
mǣlde, M 26, 43, 210. [Cf.
maðelian.]

ġe-mǣlan, wk.v.I. *speak;* pret. 3s.
ġemǣlde, M 230, 244.

mǣre, adj. ja-stem. *glorious, famous;*
nsf. wk. R 12, 82; W 100 (*Wyrd*

the mighty?); nsn. (or m.), B 14
(**tungol** is usually neuter in the
poetry but once masc.); dsm.wk.
mǣran, R 69.

mǣrðu, f. iþō-stem. *glorious deed;*
gp. —**a**, S 84.

mǣst, adj. superl. *most, greatest;* asf.
—**e**, M 175; — as noun, n., w.
part. gen. *the greatest (of);* ns. M
223; *the greatest number (of);* as.
S 84. [Cf. **micel**, **mā**, **māra**.]

ġe-mǣtan, wk.v.I, impers. w. dat. of
person. *dream;* pret. 3s. **ġemǣtte**,
R 2.

mǣte, adj. ja-stem. *small, limited;*
isn. R 69, 124. [Cf. METAN, v.5,
measure.]

mǣþ, f. *proper measure, fitness;* ns.
M 195.

mæðel, n. *assembly; speech.* **mæðel-
stede**, m. i-stem. *meeting-place;*
ds. M 199.

mæw, m. i-stem. *mew; seagull;* as.
S 22.

māg-, see **mǣġ**.

magan, pret.-pres. v. *be able, can,
may.* — (a) w. inf., pres. 1s. **mæġ**,
R 85; W 58; S 1; 2s. **meaht**, R 78;
3s. **mæġ**, R 110; M 215 (subjectless
mæġ cunnian, *one can find out, it
can be tested*), 258, 315; W 15,
64; S 94; D 31; impers. w.
ofergān understood, *it may pass
over*, D 7, 13, 17, 20, 27, 42; 3s.
subj. **mæġe**, M 235; pret. 1s.
meahte, R 18, 37; 3s. **meahte**, M 9,
14, 70, 124 (subj.?), 167, 171; S
26; D 11; 1s. subj. (?) **meahte**,
W 26. (b) w. prep. phrase im-
plying an inf. of being or of
motion, pres. 3s. **mæġ** *(can be)*,
S 100; pret. 3s. **meahte** *(could
go)*, M 64. [MAGAN, MÆĠ, MAGON,
MEAHTE.]

magu, m. *(son;) young man, warrior;*
ns. W 92. **magu-þeġn**, m. *(young)
retainer;* np. —**as**, W 62.

man, m. (weakly stressed form of
mann), indef. pron. *one* (used in
ns. only), R 73, 75; M 9; S 109.
[Normally spelled with single *n*
in the MSS., but the same spelling
sometimes serves for the stressed
form.]

ġe-man, see **ġe-munan**.

mān, f. *moan, lamentation;* np. —**a**,
D 14. [The base-word of MǢNAN,
wk.v.I, *lament*, and ancestor of
mod. "moan," but unrecorded in
OE; conjectured by Malone in the
form of a nom.pl. MŌNE, for the
improbable *monge* of the MS.]

ġe-māna, wk.m. *fellowship, meeting;*
gs. (or dis.?) —**n**, depending on
hrēman, B 40. [ĠEMǢNE, adj. *com-
mon;* German GEMEIN.]

manian, wk.v.II. *exhort, remind,
urge;* inf. M 228; pres. 3s **manaþ**,
S 36 (w. clause), 53 (used abso-
lutely).

ġe-manian, wk.v.II. *exhort, admon-
ish, remind;* pres. 3p. **ġemaniaþ**,
S 50 (w. **to** and dat.); pp. **ġe-
manod**, apm. —**e** (agreeing w. þeġ-
nas, obj. of **hafast**), M 231.

maniġ, adj. and pron. *many (a);* —
as adj., nsm. B 17; M 282; D 24;
dsm. —**um**, D 33; asm. —**ne**, M
188, 243; dp. —**um**, R 99; — as
pron., npm. —**e**, M 200; gp. —**ra**,
R 41; dp. —**um**, D 19. [Cf. **for-
maniġ**.]

mann, m. cons.-stem. *man;* ns. R
112; M 147, 239; W 109; S 12, 39;
D 40; as. M 77, 243; D 6; gs. —**es**,
S 116; ds. **menn**, M 125, 319; np.
menn, R 12, 82, 128; M 105, 206;
ap. **menn**, R 93; gp. **manna**, M

195; S 90, 111; dp. **mannum, R
96, 102. mann-cynn,** n. ja-stem.
mankind; as. R 41, 104; gs. **—es,**
C 7; R 33, 99. **mann-dryhten,** m.
(liege) lord; as. W 41. (For this
meaning see Klaeber's glossary to
Beowulf.) [Cf. **brim-, ealdor-, hīred-,
lid-, sǣ-mann;** and **Norþ-mann,** pr.
n.; also **man,** pron.]

māra, comp. adj. *more, greater;* nsn.
māre, B 65; M 313. [Cf. **micel, mā,**
and **mǣst.**]

maðelian, wk.v.II. *make a speech,
speak;* pret. 3s. **maðelode,** M 42,
309.

māðum, m. *gift, treasure, precious
object;* dip. **māðmum,** S 99. **māð-
um-ġiefa,** m. *giver of treasure;* ns.
W 92.

mē, see **iċ.**

meaht, f. i-stem. *might, power;* dis.
meahte, R 102; ds. S 108 (less
probably as., which should have
no ending; possibly ap. *powers,*
since *ġelīefan on* takes acc. more
often than dat.); ap. **—a,** C 2
(Northumbrian *-i;* the West Saxon
-e may be as.) . [The parallel form
MIHT gives mod. "might"; cf. **ma-
gan.**]

meaht, meahte, see **magan.**

mearh, m. *horse, steed;* ns. W 92;
as. M 188; ds. **mēare,** M 239.

meċ, see **iċ.**

mēċe, m. ja-stem. *sword;* as. M 167,
236; gp. **mēċa,** B 40 (alt. reading
MÆCGA, see **mæcg**); dip. **mēċum,** B
24. [A poetical word appearing
only in this Anglian form; West
Saxon *MĒĊE.]

medu, m. u-stem. *mead;* ds. M 212.
medu-drinc, m. *(mead-drink,) mead;*
ds. **—e,** S 22. **medu-heall,** f. *mead-
hall;* ds. **—e,** W 27.

ġe-menġan, wk.v.I. *mingle;* pp. **ġe-**
menġed, W 48 (uninflected; one
might expect apm. **ĠEMENĠDE**).
[Base-word **ġe-mang,** n. *mixture,
throng.*]

meniġu, f. īn-stem. *multitude;* ds.
meniġe, R 112, 151.

menn, see **mann.**

mere, m. i-stem. *sea* (elsewhere also
lake); as. B 54. **mere-flōd,** m. *ocean-
stream;* ds. **—e,** S 59. **mere-wēriġ,**
adj. *sea-weary;* gs. **—werġes,** S 12
(as noun).

ġe-met, n. *measure;* ds. S 111 (mid
ġemete, with moderation).

metod, m. *the measurer,* originally
fate, but in these and most other
poems, God (as ordainer of fate
or creator); ns. S 108, 116; vs. M
175; gs. **—es,** C 2; W 2; S 103; ds.
—e, M 147. [Cf. METAN, v. 5, *mete,
measure.*]

mēðe, adj. ja-stem. *weary;* nsm. R
65; npm. R 69. [From *MŌÐJA-.]

micel, adj. *much, great;* nsm. R 130;
S 103; nsf. R 139; gsn. **micles,** M
217; ds.wk. **miclan,** R 65, 102;
ism. **micle,** R 34, 60, 123 (w. **elne**).
[Cf. **mā, māra, mǣst.**]

micle, isn. of **micel,** n., adv. w.
comp., *much;* M 50.

mid, prep. *with, amid, by,* etc. (1)
w. dat. (instr.) ; (a) of persons act-
ing, moving, or being together:
*(in company) with, together with,
accompanied by;* B 26, 47; R 121,
134, 143, 151; M 51, 79, 101a, 191;
and with latent personification, S
59 (mid **mere-flōde**). (b) of asso-
ciated abstractions: *(in conjunc-
tion) with,* R 149 (twice). (c) *hav-
ing in hold, taking;* M 40, 56. (d)
amid, among; M 23, 76; S 78, 80,
84 (mid **him,** *amongst themselves*) .
(e) of instrumentality: *with, by
means of;* R 7, 14, 16, 20, 22, 23

(twice), 46, 48, 53, 59, 62, 102; M
14, 21, 32, 77, 101b, 114, 118, 124,
126, 136, 138, 226, 228; W 4, 29
(or manner); S 96. (f) of manner:
with, in; B 37; M 68, 179; W 114;
S 111. (2) w. acc., *along with,* S 99
(postpos.).

mid, adv. *in attendance, at the
same time* (an extension of the
preposition), R 106.

midd, adj. *middle, mid;* dsf. midre,
R 2.

middan-ġeard, m. *(this) world, the
earth;* ns. W 62; as. C 7; R 104;
W 75; S 90. [Gothic MIDJUN-
GARD-S, OHG MITTIN-GART; the
the first element related to midd,
adj.; cf. Old Norse MIÐ-GARÐR.]

mierran, wk.v.I. *hinder.* See a-
mierran.

mihtiġ, adj. *mighty;* nsm. R 151;
comp. mihtiġra, nsm. S 116. [Cf.
ælmihtiġ.]

milde, adj. ja-stem. *merciful;* vsm.
M 175.

milds, f. jō-stem. *mildness, mercy,
favor;* as. —e, W 2.

min, poss. adj. *my, mine;* nsm. M
218, 222, 224 (twice), 250; W 59;
S 58, 59; vsm. R 78, 95; nsf. R
130; M 177; gsm. —es, M 53; dsm.
—um, R 30; M 176, 318; asm. —ne,
M 248; W 10, 19, 22; asf. —e, W
9; npm. —e, S 9; apm. —e, W 27
(*my [people]*); apn. —e, M 216.
[Cf. iċ.]

mislīċ, adj. *various, diverse;* dip.
—um, S 99.

missenlīċe, adv. *variously,* W 75 (*in
various places or forms*) ; or
missenlīċ, adj. *various,* npm. —e.
[If the word is taken as an adv.,
its relation to the following
phrase is closer and the flow of

the sentence easier. The alternate
form MISLĪĊE would be metrically
more regular.]

mittung, f. *encounter.* See gār-
mittung.

mōd, n. *mind, heart, spirit, mood;*
ns. M 313; as. W 51; S 12, 108;
gs. —es, S 36, 50; ds. —e, R 130;
W 41, 111; S 109; is. —e, R 122.
mōd-ċeariġ, adj. *sad, troubled in
spirit;* nsm. W 2. **mōd-ġeþanc,** m.
or n. *(mind's) purpose, counsel;*
as. C 2. **mōd-sefa,** wk. m. *heart,
soul, mind, inmost thoughts;* ns.
R 124; W 59; S 59; as. —n, W 10,
19. **mōd-wlanc,** adj. *proud in spirit;*
nsm. S 39. [Cf. æwisc-, ēaþ-, ofer-,
stīþ-, wēriġ-mōd.]

mōdiġ, adj. *bold, courageous, spirit-
ed;* nsm. R 41; M 147; npm.
mōdġe, M 80; W 62.

mōdiġlīċe, adv. *boldly, with a show
of courage;* M 200.

mōdor, f. r-stem. *mother;* as. R 92.

molde, wk.f. *earth;* ns. S 103; as.
moldan, R 12, 82. **mold-ærn,** n.
earth-house, sepulchre; as. R 65.

morgen, m. *morning.* **morgen-tīd,** f.
i-stem, *morningtide;* as. B 14.

mōst, mōste, mōston, see mōtan.

ġe-mōt, n. *meeting, encounter;* ns.
M 301; as. M 199; gs. —es, B 50.

mōtan, pret.-pres. v. *be permitted,
may, must;* pres. 1s. mōt, R 142;
2s. mōst, M 30; 1s. subj. mōte,
R 127; 3s. subj. mōte, M 95, 177;
1p. subj. mōten, S 119 (tō mōten,
may go thither) ; 3p. subj. mōten,
M 180; pret. 3s. mōste, M 272; 3p.
mōston, M 83; 3p. subj. mōsten,
M 87, 263. [MŌTAN, MŌT, MŌTON,
MŌSTE.]

ġe-munan, pret.-pres. v. *remember,
be mindful of;* — w. acc., pres. 1s.
ġeman, R 28; 3s. ġeman, W 34,

90; pret. 3s. ġemunde, M 225 (acc. or gen.) ; 3p. subj. ġemunden, M 196; — w. gen., imper.pl. ġemunaþ, M 212 (emendation; E's transcript has *gemunu þa mæla,* which might indicate acc. originally) . [MUNAN, MAN, MUNON, MUNDE.]

mund, f. *hand, protection.* **mund-byrd,** f. i-stem, *protection* (as a social or legal obligation, such as a king owes to his subjects) ; ns. R 130 *(hope of protection)* .

murnan, v.3. *mourn;* w. for, *trouble about, care for;* inf. M 259; pret. 3p. **murnon,** M 96. [MURNAN, MEARN, MURNON, MURNEN.]

mylen, m. *mill; place where weapons were ground? grindstone?* **mylen-scearp,** adj. *sharp from the grinding?* dip. —um, B 24. [On the various possibilities offered by this uniquely recorded extension of the ordinary meaning of **mylen** (from Lat. MOLĪNA, a mill for grinding grain), see note in Campbell's ed. of B, p. 105.]

ġe-mynd, f. i-stem (or n.) . *memory;* ns. W 51. [Cf. **ġe-munan.**]

ġe-myndiġ, adj. *mindful;* nsm. W 6.

myne, m. *thought, intention; remembrance, favor, affection;* as. W 27 (according to the traditional emendation, [mīn] **myne wisse,** *might show me favor, feel affection for me*—an adaptation of *Beowulf* 169, itself of doubtful meaning; here the MS. reading is taken as **mīne wisse;** see **mīn** and **witan.**)

N

nā (ne ā), adv. *never, not (at all);* M 21, 258, 268, 325; W 54, 66, 96; S 66.

naca, wk.m. *boat, ship;* gs. —n, S 7.

næbbe (ne hæbbe), see **habban.**

næfre (ne æfre), adv. *never;* W 69, 112.

næġl or **næġel,** m. *nail;* dip. **næġlum,** R 46.

næġled, pp. adj. *nailed, studded.* **næġled-cnearr,** m. *nailed ship;* dip. —um, B 53.

næniġ (ne æniġ), pron. and adj. *not any, none;* as pron. w. part. gen., nsm. S 25.

næs (ne wæs), see **bēon-wesan.**

nāg (ne āg), see **āgan.**

nama, wk.m. *name;* ns. M 267; D 37; ds. —n, R 113 (in a phrase imitative of the Bible, **for dryhtnes naman,** *for the Lord's [name's] sake*) .

ġe-nāme, ġe-nāmon, see **ġe-niman.**

nān (ne ān), pron. (and adj.) , *not one, none;* as pron. w. part. gen., nsm. W 9; dp. —um, B 25.

nāp, ġe-nāp, see **nipan, ġe-nīpan.**

ne or **nē,** negative particle. *not, nor.* (a) as adv., *not;* B 24, etc. (5 times) ; R 10, etc. (7 times) ; M 21, etc. (18 times) ; W 15, etc. (5 times) ; S 12, etc. (8 times) ; D 8, 11; at head of series, *neither,* W 66a, S 95a. (b) as conj., *nor;* B 46; M 259; W 16, 66b-69 (7 times) ; S 40 (twice) , 41 (twice) , 44b, 45 (twice) , 46, 82, 83, 95b, 96 (twice) . [Negative affix in **nā, næbbe, næfre,** etc.]

nēah, adv. *near;* M 103; W 26.

ġe-neahhe, adv. *frequently;* M 269; W 56; D 25, 32.

nealles (ne ealles), adv. *not at all;* W 32, 33.

nearon (ne earon), see **bēon-wesan.**

nearu, adj. wa-stem. *narrow, close;* (fig.) *anxious;* nsf. S 7.

ġe-nēat, m. *follower, retainer;* ns. M 310. [Cf. **heorþ-ġenēat.**]

-nebba, wk.m. *beaked one*, formed from adjectival -NEBB, *beaked*, corresponding to NEBB, n. ja-stem. *bill, beak, nose, face.* See hyrned-nebba.

nefne (ne efne), conj. (following a negative). *unless,* W 113; *except, but,* S 46.

nēotan, v.2, w. gen. *make use of;* inf. M 308. [NĒOTAN, NĒAT, NUTON, NOTEN.]

ġe-nerian, wk.v.I. *save;* pret. 3s. ġenerede, B 36.

nīed, f. i-stem. *need, (dire) necessity;* dis. —e, B 33; pl., *constraints, fetters;* ap. —a, D 5.

ġe-nīewian, wk.v.II. *renew;* pp. ġenīewod, nsm. R 148; nsf. W 50, 55.

niht, f. (orig. a cons.-stem). *night;* ds. —e, R 2. niht-helm, m. *cover of night;* as. W 96. niht-scua, wk. m. *shadow of night;* ns. W 104; S 31. niht-wacu, f. *night-watch;* ns. S 7.

niman, v.4. *take; receive,* inf. M 39; *take off, kill,* inf. M 252; w. dat. or instr. *take on, assume,* pres. 3p. nimaþ, S 48 (**bearwas blostmum nimaþ,** *the groves take on blossoms, burst into bloom*—for the idiom, Mrs. Gordon compares fōn w. dat.; see her note). [NIMAN, NAM, NĀMON, NUMEN; cf. be-, for-niman.]

ġe-niman, v.4. *take; lay hold of,* pret. 3p. ġenāmon, R 30, 60; *receive,* pret. 3s. subj. ġenāme, M 71.

nipan, v.1. *grow dark, darken;* pres. 3s. nipeþ, W 104; pret. 3s. nāp, S 31. [NĪPAN, NĀP, NIPON, NIPEN.]

ġe-nipan, v.1. *become dark, vanish;* pret. 3s. ġenāp, W 96.

nis (ne is), see bēon-wesan.

nīþ, m. *violence, enmity, malice;* as. S 75.

ġe-nōg, adj. *enough;* npm. —e, R 33; (by understatement, *many*).

nolde, noldon, nolden, see nyllan.

norþ, adv. (*in, to the*) *north;* B 38.

norðan, adv. *from the north;* W 104; S 31.

norðerne, adj. ja-stem. *northern;* nsm.wk. norðerna, B 18.

nū, adv. *now,* C 1; R 78, 80, 84, 95, 126, 134; M 93, 175, 215, 316; W 9, 75, 97; S 33, 58, 82, 90; D 39; —conj. *now that,* M 57, 222, 232, 250.

nyllan (ne willan), anom.v. *will not;* pres. 1s. nylle, M 246; 3s. nyle, S 99 (MS. **wille**); pret. 3s. nolde, M 6, 9, 275; 3p. noldon, M 81, 185; 3p. subj. nolden, M 201.

O

of, prep. w. dat. *from, of, out of;* R 30, 49, 61, 66, 120, 133; M 7, 108, 149, 150, 154, 162, 221; W 113; S 107.

ofer, prep. w. acc. *over.* (a) of motion: *over, across, through;* B 15, 19, 26, 55, 71; M 88, 91, 97, 98; W 24, 57, 82; S 60, 64; *over, beyond,* S 58; ofer bæc, *to the rear, back,* M 276. (b) of distribution or extent: *throughout,* R 12, 82; S 39. (c) of intensity and extent: ofer eall, *over all* (louder than all else and to all parts: so all could hear), M 256. (d) of degree: *above, more than,* R 91, 94. (e) of crossing someone's will or command: *contrary to, in disregard of,* R 35.

ōfer, m. *bank, shore;* ds. ōfre, M 28.

ofer-cuman, v.4. *overcome;* pret. 3p. ofercōmon, B 72; —impers. w. gen., *pass over;* pp. ofercumen, nsn. D 26 (þæt þæs cynerīċes o. wǣre, *that it had passed over with respect to that kingdom: that that kingdom were no more*—cf. the similar impersonal use of **ofergān**, D 7, etc.). [Cf. **cuman**.]

ofer-gān, anom. v., impers. w. gen. *pass over, go by;* pret. 3s. **oferēode**, D 7, 13, 17, 20, 27, 42 (**þæs o.**, it *passed over with respect to that: that has passed*—cf. **ofer-cuman**, above, at D 26). [Cf. **gān**.]

ofer-mōd, n. *great pride, overconfidence;* ds. —**e**, M 89. [Cf. **mōd**.]

of-ġiefan, v.5. *give up, relinquish, leave;* pret. 3p. **ofġēafon**, W 61. [Cf. **a-, for-ġiefan**.]

ofostlīċe, adv. *speedily,* M 143. [Cf. **efstan**.]

of-scēotan, v.2. *kill by shooting or hurling a weapon;* pret. 3s. **ofscēat**, M 77, *struck dead* (with a cast of his spear). [Cf. **scēotan**.]

oft, adv. *often;* B 8; M 188, 212, 296, 321; W 1, 8, 17, 20, 40, 53 (MS. —emended to **eft**), 90; S 3, 6, 24, 29; D 4; —comp. **oftor**, R 128.

on, prep. *in, on,* etc.

    1. w. dat. or instr. (a) of position: *in, on;* B 27, etc. (8 times) ; R 9, etc. (28 times; postpos. at 98) ; M 25, etc. (37 times) ; W 12, etc. (11 times—either dat. or acc. at 42) ; S 5, etc. (9 times) ; D 9, 29; *in* (transl. *from*) , M 125; *in* (transl. *of*) , M 142; *in* (transl. *among*) , M 217, 266. —(b) of condition, state: *in,* S 85; D 25. —(c) of respect: *in,* S 41. —(d) of hostile action: *on, at the expense of,* M 129, 259. —(e) of an inclusive source: **gelang on**, *comprehended in, inseparable from,* S 121. —(f) of trust: *in,* S 108 (or acc. —see **meaht**) . —(g) of con-

trolling mood: *in, with,* W 105. —(h) of time: *in,* W 35, 44; S 40; *on,* R 105.

    2. w. acc. (a) of motion: *into, to, on, onto, upon, toward;* B 36, 38, 54; R 5, 32b, 34 (postpos.) , 40, 103, 104, 125 (MS. dat.) , 152; M 58, 78, 163, 178, 194, 270, 291, 322; W 81 (MS. dat.) ; S 32, 47, 52, 63, 120; D 5, 6. —(b) of time: *in,* B 14; R 68; **on ealle tīd**, *during (for) all time,* S 124; **on dæġ**, *on a (certain) day,* M 198. —(c) in various phrases where motion is sometimes but not always clearly implicit: **on bēot**, *threateningly,* M 27 (see Gordon's note) ; **on ellen**, *valiantly,* M 211; **on flot**, *afloat, into (deep) water, to sea,* B 35; M 41; **on . . . hand**, *on . . . hand,* M 112; **on . . . healfe**, *on . . . side,* R 20; **on lāst**, *on the track, in pursuit,* B 22; **on hira selfra dōm**, *as they themselves shall decide,* M 38. —(d) **bēodeþ sorge on brēost-hord**, *forebodes sorrow in the heart* (implying that sorrow will enter into the heart?), S 55.

    on-weġ, prep. phrase as adv. *away;* W 53; S 74.

on, adv. *on, onward;* S 91 (**ieldu him on fareþ**, *old age catches up to him, overtakes him:*—Mrs. Gordon points out that if **on** were the postpos. prep. it ought to be preceded by acc. **hine**).

on-bierġan, wk.v.I, w. gen. *taste (of), partake (of)* ; inf. R 114. [Cf. **bierġan**.]

on-ċierran, wk.v.I. *turn, change;* refl., *turn aside or be changed;* pres. 3s. **onċierreþ**, S 103 (**for þon hīe sēo molde onċierreþ**, *before which [the terrible power of God] the* *earth will turn aside;* — so Mrs. Gordon, citing *Apocalypsis* xx, 11: *a cuius conspectu fugit terra*) .

on-cnāwan, v.7. *perceive;* inf. M 9. [CNĀWAN, CNĒOW, CNĒOWON, CNĀWEN.]

on-cweðan, v.5. w. dat. of person, *reply to, answer;* pret. 3s. oncwæþ, M 245; S 23. [Cf. cweðan.]

on-drǣdan, v.7, w. refl. dat. and acc. *dread;* pres. 3s. ondrǣdeþ, S 106. [-DRǢDAN, DRĒD (DREORD), DRĒDON, DRǢDEN.]

on-efen, prep. w. dat. *close by, beside,* M 184.

ōnettan, wk.v.I. *hasten on;* pres. 3s. ōnetteþ, S 49. [From Gmc. *ONHAITJAN; stress on first syll. early obscured the compound.]

on-fand, see on-findan.

on-fēng, see on-fōn.

on-findan, v.3. *find, find out, perceive;* pret. 3s. onfunde, M 5; *experience, come to know;* pret. 3s. on-fand, D 4. [Cf. findan.]

on-fōn, contr. v.7. *receive;* pret. 3s. onfēng, M 110 (w. acc.). [Cf. fōn.]

on-funde, see on-findan.

on-gann, see on-ġinnan.

on-ġēan, adv. *again; in return,* M 49; *back, out again,* M 137; eft o., *back again,* M 156.

on-ġēan, prep. w. dat. *against,* M 100.

on-ġēaton, see on-ġietan.

on-ġierwan, wk.v.I. *unclothe, strip;* pret. 3s. (refl.), onġierede, R 39. [The prefix here is negative; cf. ġierwan.]

on-ġietan, v.5. *perceive, apprehend, realize;* inf. R 18; W 73; pret. 3p. onġēaton, M 84; pp. onġieten, uninfl., D 10. [ĠIETAN, ĠEAT, ĠEATON, ĠIETEN; cf. be-ġietan.]

on-ġinnan, v. 3. *begin, undertake;* pres. 3p. subj. onġinnen, R 116; pret. 3s. ongann, R 19, 27, 73; M 12, 17, 89, 91, 228, 265; pret. 3p. ongunnon, R 65, 67; M 86, 261. [-ĠINNAN, GANN, GUNNON, GUNNEN; recorded only with be- or on-.]

on-hrēran, wk.v.I. *stir, move;* inf. S 96. [Cf. hrēran.]

on-liesan, wk.v.I. *liberate, redeem;* pret. 3s. onliesde, R 147. [Cf. liesan.]

on-sendan, wk.v.I. *send on, send forth;* pres. 3s. onsendeþ, W 104; pp. onsended, uninfl., R 49 (*yielded up*). [Cf. sendan.]

on-stellan, wk.v.I. *establish;* pret. 3s. onstealde, C 4 (var.). See a-stellan.

on-wæcnan, v.6 (irreg.). *wake up;* pres. 3s. onwæcneþ, W 45. [WÆCNAN, WŌC, WŌCON, WÆCNED.]

on-weġ, adv., see on.

on-wendan, wk.v.I, trans. *change;* pres. 3s. on-wendeþ, W 107. [Cf. wendan.]

on-wrēon, contr.v.1. *uncover, disclose;* imper.sg. onwrēoh, R 97. [The prefix here is negative; cf. be-wrēon.]

open, adj. *open;* npm. opene, R 47.

ōr, n. *beginning;* as. C 4.

ord, m. *point; point of origin, beginning,* as. C 4 (var.); *point of a weapon* (usually a spear), ns. M 60, 146, 157, 253 (ord and īren—see īren); as. M 47, 110; ds. —e, M 124, 226; *battle-line,* ns. M 69 (or *the flower, pick?*); *forefront of the battle,* ds. —e, M 273.

orne, adj. ja-stem. *not mean; excessive.* See un-orne.

oþ, conj. *until;* B 16.

oþ, prep. *to, up to, till.* oþ-þæt, conj. *until,* R 26, 32; M 278, 324; W 71, 86; D 39.

oþ-beran, v.4. *carry off;* pret. 3s.
oþbær, W 81. [oþ- here has the
sense of *away; cf.* beran.]

ōðer, adj. and pron. *other, another.*
(a) adj., asm. —ne, M 234; dsn.
ōðrum, M 64. (b) pron., nsm. M
282; asm. —ne, M 143; dsm. ōð-
rum, M 70, 133; ōðer, (asn.) twēġa,
one of two things, M 207.

oþþe, conj. *or,* R 36; M 208, 292;
W 26, 28; S 70 (twice), 114.

oþ-þringan, v.3. *wrest away;* pres. 3s.
oþ-þringeþ, S 71. [Cf. ġe-þringan.]

P

-pāda, wk. m. *coated one,* formed
from adjectival -PĀD, *coated,* cor-
responding to PĀD, f. *coat.* See
hasu-, sealwiġ-pāda; also hyrned-
nebba, isiġ-feðra, ūriġ-feðra.

plega, wk.m. *play, sport, fight.* See
gūþ-, hand-, wiġ-plega.

plegian, wk.v.II. *play;* pret. 3p. pleg-
odon, B 52.

prass, m. *proud array;* ds. —e, M 68.

R

rād, see rīdan.

ġe-ræċan, wk.v.I. *reach;* pret. 3s. ġe-
ræhte, *reached with a weapon,
pierced,* M 158, 226; feorh ġ.,
reached the life, pierced fatally,
M 142.

rædan, wk.v.I. *give counsel, instruct;*
pret. 3s. rædde, M 18. [Cf. ĠE-RĀD,
adj. *wise, skillful;* also RĒD, n.
counsel, advice; and RĒDAN, v.7
(pret. RĒD or REORD), *advise,* etc.]

ġe-rædan, wk.v.I. *decide;* pres. 2s.
ġerædest, M 36.

ġe-rædu, n. ja-stem pl. *trappings;*
dp. —m, M 190. [Cf. RĀD, f. *riding;
harness;* and rīdan, v.1.]

ræran, wk.v.I. *rear, raise.* See a-
ræran.

ræs, m. *rush, onset, attack.* See
beadu-, gār-ræs.

rand, m. *boss of a shield* (the metal
center); *shield;* ap. —as, M 20.

rēaf, n. *raiment;* as. M 161 (coat of
mail?) [Another meaning, *spoil,
booty,* seems less appropriate.]

rēċan (later reċċan), wk.v.I, w. gen.
care about; pret. 3p. rōhton, M
260. [RĒĊAN (from *RŌCJAN),
RŌHTE, RŌHT.]

recene, adv. *quickly,* M 93; W 112.

ġe-reġnian, wk.v.II. *adorn, orna-
ment;* pp. ġereġnod, asn. M 161.

reord, f. (or n.) *voice, speech;* dis. —
e, S 53 (of a bird). reord-berend,
m. nd-stem. *speech-bearer* (a peri-
phrasis for a human being as one
endowed with speech; it appears
in several of the religious poems,
sometimes, as here, with point);
np. R 3; dp. —um, R 89. [Cf.
RĒDAN, v.7. *advise,* redupl. pret. s.
REORD.]

rest, f. jō-stem. *resting-place, bed;*
as. —e, R 3 (obj. of wunodon:
were in bed) [Cf. wæl-rest.]

restan, wk.v.I. *rest, lie, remain;* pret.
3s. reste, R 64 (refl.), 69 (intrans.).

rīċe, n. ja-stem. *realm, kingdom;* ns.
W 106; as. R 119, 152; gs. —s, S
81; D 23. [Cf. cyne-, heofon-,
weorold-rīċe.]

rīċe, adj. ja-stem. *powerful;* as. rīcne,
R 44; gp. rīċra, R 131; rīċost,
superl., nsm. M 36.

rīdan, v.1. *ride;* inf. M 291; pret. 3s.
rād, M 18, 239. [RĪDAN, RĀD, RIDON,
RIDEN.]

riht, n. *right, privilege, just title.*
See land-riht.

riht, adj. *right, proper, true;* nsn.
M 190; asm. —ne, R 89.

ġe-rihtan, wk.v.I. *direct;* pp. ġeriht,
nsf. R 131.

rihte, adv. *rightly, correctly,* M 20.

rinc, m. *warrior, man;* dp. —um, M
18. [Cf. fierd-, gūþ-, hilde-, sǣ-
rinc.]

risan, v.I. *rise.* See a-rīsan.

rōd, f. *rood, cross;* ns. R 44, 136;
ds. —e, R 56, 131; as. —e, R 119.
[Original sense *twig, branch,
pole.*]

rodor, m. *the heavens, sky.* See upp-
rodor.

rōhton, see rēċan.

rūn, f. *(private) counsel;* ds. in sun-
dor æt rūne, (*apart at counsel;* or,
apart in private meditation), W
111.

ġe-rȳman, wk.v.I. *open* (a way); pret.
ls. ġerȳmde, R 89; pp. ġe-rȳmed,
nsn. M 93. [Base-word RŪM, adj.
spacious.]

S

sǣ, m. or f. i-stem. *sea* (applied to
large bodies of water, usually salt
but occasionally fresh); as. (f.) W
4; (m.) S 14, 18. sǣ-fōr, f. *sea-voy-
age;* gs. or ds. —e, S 42. sǣ-lida,
wk. m. *seafarer;* vs. M 45; as. —n,
M 286. sǣ-mann, m. *seaman;* dp.
—um, M 38, 278; np. —menn, M
29. sǣ-rinc, m. *sea-warrior, viking;*
ns. M 134.

sæċċ, f. jō-stem. *strife, battle;* ds. —
e, B 4, 42.

sæd, adj. *sated;* nsm. B 20 (w. gen.,
sated with). [Cognate w. Lat.

SATIS; mod. "sad" has shifted its
meaning.]

sæġde, ġe-sæġde, sæġe, sæġeþ, see
secgan, ġe-secgan.

sæl, n. *hall.* See wīn-sæl.

sǣl, m. i-stem (or f.). *time, occasion;*
ns. R 80; (*happy time,*) *joy,
pleasure,* dip. —um, D 28.

sǣlan, wk.v.I. *fasten, bind, tie;* inf.
W 21. [From SĀL, m. or f. *rope.*]

ġe-sǣliġ, adj. *prosperous, fortunate;*
see weorold-ġesǣliġ.

sæt, see sittan.

ġe-sæt, see ġe-sittan.

sāg, see sīgan.

samod, adv. *together, jointly, in
unison;* W 39.

sang, m. *song;* as. S 19.

sang, v. see singan.

sār, n. *pain;* as. S 95.

sār, adj. *sore, painful, grievous;* nsm.
D 9; npf. —e, W 50 (sāre æfter,
sore with longing for); gp. —ra,
R 80.

sāre, adv. *sorely,* R 59.

ġe-sāwe, see ġe-sēon.

sāwol, f. *soul;* ns. R 120; M 177;
ds. sāwle, S 100.

ġe-sāwon, see ġe-sēon.

scacan, v.6. *shake;* see a-scacan.

scadu, f. wō-stem. *shadow, darkness;*
ns. R 54.

scaða, wk.m. *one who does harm;
ravager, enemy, warrior.* See fǣr-,
hell-scaða.

scēaf, see scūfan.

sceaft, m. *shaft* (of spear); ns. M
136.

ġe-sceaft, f. i-stem. *creature, creation;*
ns. B 16; R 12, 55, 82; wyrda
ġesceaft, *the operation of the
fates,* ns. W 107. [Cf. forþ-
ġesceaft; related to SCEAP-, base
of scieppan, q.v.]

-sceaftiġ, adjectival component, *having possessions* (?). See fēa-sceaftiġ.

sceal, see sculan.

scealc, m. *retainer, warrior;* np. —as, M 181.

sceard, adj., w. gen. *bereft (of)* ; nsm. B 40.

scearp, adj. *sharp.* See mylen-scearp.

scēat, m. *surface, region, expanse;* ap. —as, R 37; S 61, 105; dp. —um, R 8, 43. [The meaning in R is sometimes taken to be *corner,* but *surface* is appropriate at all three places.]

scēat, v. see scēotan.

sceatt, m. *coin; tax;* dp. —um, M 40, 56 *(tribute-money).*

scēaþ, f. *sheath;* ds. —e, M 162.

scēawian, wk.v.II. *see, behold; look at;* pret. 1s. scēawode, R 137. [Cf. ġeond-scēawian.]

ġe-scēawian, wk.v.II. *show, display;* pres. 3s. ġescēawaþ, D 33.

scēotan, v.2. *shoot, hurl; hit with a missile;* pret. 3s. scēat, M 143 *(pierced* with a spear), 270 *(shot* an arrow); pp. scoten, nsm. B 19 *(shot* by an arrow or *pierced* by a dart). [SCĒOTAN, SCĒAT, SCUTON, SCOTEN; cf. of-scēotan.]

scield, m. *shield;* as. B 19; ds. —e, M 136; ap. —as, M 98. scield-burg, f. cons.-stem. *wall of shields;* ns. M 242.

scieppan, v.6. *create;* pret. 3s. scōp, C 5 (var. ġescōp). [SCIEPPAN, SCŌP, SCŌPON, SCEAPEN.]

scieppend, m. nd-stem. *(the) Creator;* ns. C 6; W 85.

scieþþan, v.6. *injure;* inf. R 47. [SCIEÞÞAN, SCŌD, SCŌDON, SCEADEN. The present stem is recorded only as SCEÞ- (seemingly an Anglian spelling) and, once,

LWS. SCYÞ- (corresponding to EWS.*SCIEÞ-) . The past participle is recorded only once, in *Genesis* 869, where it is *sceapen* instead of the expected SCEADEN.]

scīma, wk.m. *light, radiance;* as. —n, R 54.

scīnan, v.1. *shine;* inf. R 15. [SCĪNAN, SCĀN, SCINON, SCINEN.]

scip,n. *ship;* ds. —e, M 40, 56. scip-flota, wk.m. *sailor, seaman;* np. —n, B 11.

scīr, adj. *bright, clear;* asn. M 98; asm. —ne, R 54.

scolde, scolden, scoldon, see sculan.

scop, m. *court poet and singer;* ns. D 36.

scōp, see scieppan.

scoten, see scēotan.

scræf, n. *pit, cavern, grave.* See eorþ-scræf.

scua, wk.m. *shade, shadow.* See niht-scua.

scūfan, v.2. *shove, thrust;* pret. 3s. scēaf, M 136. [SCŪFAN, SCĒAF, SCUFON, SCOFEN.]

sculan, pret.-pres. v. *shall, must, have to, be destined to;* w. inf. except as indicated; pres. 3s. sceal, R 119; M 60, 252; W 37, 56, 70, 73, 112; S 109; —w. bēon understood, *must be,* M 312, 313; W 65, 66; —1p. sculon, C 1; 2p. scule (ġē), M 59; 3p. sculon, M 54, 220; 3s. subj. scyle, S 74 (v. of motion understood: *must go).* 111 *(should, ought to);* pret. 1s. scolde, *had to,* R 43; W 8, 19; S 30; 3s. scolde, M 16 *(had occasion to, was called upon to);* 3s. subj. scolde, W 3 *(may have had to);* D 12 (v. of action understood: *ought to act);* pret. 3p. scoldon, M 19 *(should, ought to),* 105 *(were to, were destined to)* ;

3p. subj. **scolden**, M 291, 307 (*should*). [SCULAN, SCEAL, SCULON, SCOLDE.]

scūr, m. *shower;* dip. —**um**, S 17.

scyle, see **sculan**.

sē, sēo, þæt, dem. adj., def. art. and pron. *that, the, that one.* (a) as adj. and def. art., **sē** or (weakly stressed) **se**, nsm. B 37; R 13, etc. (7 times); M 6, etc. (15 times); W 16, 82; S 12, etc. (5 times);— **sēo**, nsf. B 16; M 104, 144, 284; W 95, 100, 115; S 103, 107; D 16; —**þæt**, nsn. R 6; S 94; asn. B 64; R 18, 21; M 22, 102, 137, 168, 194; S 108; —**þæs**, gsm. R 49; M 131, 141, 160, 165; gsn. M 8, 148, 202; D 26; —**þære**, gsf. M 95; dsf. R 21, 112, 131; M 8, 220; S 100;— **þām** or **þam**, dsm. or dsn. B 29; R 9, etc. (11 times); M 10, etc. (19 times); S 122; dp. R 59, 143, 154; M 40, 190, 278; —**þone**, asm. B 61, 62; R 127; M 19, etc. (10 times) ; —**þā**, asf. R 20, 68, 119; M 48, 72, 74, 78, 139, 163, 325; W 113; S 120; in **þā hwīle þe**, M 14, 83, 235, 272 (see **hwīl**); np. B 53, 57; R 46, 61; M 96, 182, 261, 305; W 77, 78; S 10, 56, 87; ap. M 82, 145, 196, 277, 322; S 57; — **þāra**, gp. M 174, 212. (b) as dem. pron. *that (one), those, (he, she, it, they)* etc., **sē**, nsm. M 75, 150, 157, 227, 310; S 104; —**þæt**, nsn. R 28a, 39, 74; M 76, 223, 325; S 99; D 19, 23 (pointing to a person); asn. R 28b, 58, 66; M 5, 36, 84, 246; S 12, 24, 55, 74 (obj. of **ġewyrċe**, anticipating clause at 77), 109; D 12, 35; —**þæs**, gsn. M 120 (w. **þanc**, *for that*), 239; S 122 (w. **þanc**); *as to that, with respect to that*, D 7, 13, 17, 20, 27, 42; **to þæs**, *to that extent*, S 40b, 41

(twice); alone as adv., *to that extent*, S 39, 40a; —**þām**, dsm. R 129; dsn. M 9, 34; —**þā**, np. M 81; S 50; —**þȳ**, isn. as adv. w. comp., *by that, the*, B 46; M 146; W 49; correlatively, M 312, 313 (3 times w. comp., once as conj., *the . . . as*). (c) as rel. pron., *who, which*, etc., **sē**, nsm. R 107; M 27, 153; —**þæt**, asn. M 289 (= **þæt þæt**, *that which*); D 41; —**þæs**, gsn. B 51 (= **þæs-þe**; see note); —**þā**, np. M 184; — **þon**, isn. S 103 (w. **for**, *before which, for which*). (d) as indef. pron. *he who, whoever*, **sē**, nsm. W 88. (e) w. **þe**, as compound rel. pron. *he who*, etc., **sē-þe**, nsm. R 98, 113, 145; M 258, 316; W 29, 37, 112; S 27, 47, 106a, 107; — **sēo-þe**, nsf. R 121; —**þām- þe**, dsm. W 31, 56, 114; S 51; dp. R 149, 154; —**þone-þe**, asm. W 27; — **þāra-þe**, gp. B 26; R 86. (f) **þæs-þe**, gsn. as conj., *according to what, as*, B 68.

ġe-seah, see **ġe-sēon**.

sealde, ġe-sealde, ġe-sealdon, see **sellan, ġe-sellan**.

sealt, n. *salt*. **sealt-ȳþ**, f. jō-stem. *salt seawave;* gp. —**a**, S 35.

sealwiġ, adj. *dark-colored*. **sealwiġ-pāda**, wk.m. *dark-coated one;* ap. —**n**, B 61 (referring to the raven, the eagle, and the wolf; stylistically less satisfactory if treated as as., referring only to the raven). [On the form, see **pāda**.]

sēarian, wk.v.II. *grow sere, wither, fade;* pres. 3s. **sēaraþ**, S 89.

sēaþ, m. pit; ds. —**e**, R 75.

sēċan, wk.v.I. *seek;* —(a) *set out for, seek out, go to, come to;* inf. B 55; R 104, 127 (*resort to*); pret. 3p. **sōhton**, B 58, 71 (*invaded*); R 133; M 193; —(b) *search for, try*

to find; pret. 1s. **sōhte**, W 25; —(c)
try to obtain; pres. 3s. **sēċeþ**, W
114. [SĒĊAN (from *SŌCJAN),
SŌHTE, SŌHT.]

ġe-**sēċan**, wk.v.1. *seek, go to, come to;*
inf. R 119; M 222; pres. 1s. subj.
ġe**sēċe**, S 38; pret. 3s. ġe-**sōhte**, M
287 (*sank to*); 3p. ġe-**sōhton**, B 27.

se**ċg**, m. ja-stem. *retainer, man,
warrior;* ns. B 17; M 159; S 56;
D 24; ap. —**as**, M 298; gp. —**a**, B
13; W 53; dp. —**um**, R 59. [From
*SAGJA-, cognate w. Lat. SOCIU-S.
Cf. sele-secg.]

secgan, wk.v.III. *say, tell, relate;* inf.
R 1; M 30; S 2; D 35; imper. sg.
sæġe, M 50; pres. 3s. **sæġeþ**, M 45;
3p. **secgaþ**, B 68; 2s. subj. **secge**,
R 96; pret. 3s. **sæġde**, M 147. [SEC-
GAN, SÆĠDE, SÆĠD; cf. a-secgan.]

ġe-**secgan**, wk.v.III. *say;* pret. 3s. ġe-
sæġde, M 120 (w. þanc, *gave
thanks*).

sefa, wk. m. *mind, spirit, heart;* as.
—**n**, W 57; S 51; ds. —**n**, D 9, 29.
[Cf. mōd-sefa.]

sēft-, combining-form corresponding
to SĒFTE, adj. *soft.* **sēft-ēadiġ**, adj.
blessed with comfort; nsm. S 56
(Grein's emendation, for MS. *eft
eadig*).

seld, n. *hall.* See cear-seld.

ġe-**selda**, wk.m. *companion, fellow-
retainer;* ap. —**n**, W 53 (or *fa-
miliar spirit?*) [Lit. "one of the
same dwelling"; V. Salmon sug-
gests an allusion to an old belief
that men's spirits, though nor-
mally in the same dwelling, the
body, could be sent alone in
quest of friends or enemies.]

seldliċ, adj. *rare, wonderful;* nsm. R
13: comp. **seldliċre**, asn. R 4 (*ex-
ceedingly rare?*) .

sele, m. i-stem. *hall;* perhaps as sepa-
rate word, as. W 25; but see **sele-
drēoriġ** below. **sele-drēam**, m. *hall-
joy, festivity in the hall;* np. —**as**,
W 93. **sele-drēoriġ**, adj. *sad for
want of a hall, homesick,* nsm. W
25 (see note). **sele-secg**, m. *hall-
warrior, retainer;* ap. —**as**, W 34.

sēlest, adj. superl. *best;* asn. (w.
part. gen.), R 118; nsm.wk —**a**,
R 27. [Comp. SĒL, adv., **sēlra**, adj.;
positive lacking; from *SŌLI-.]

self, adj. *self;* nsm. S 35; nsm.wk.—
a, R 105; asf. —**e**, R 92; gsf. —**re**,
D 9; dsm. —**um**, S 1; D 29 (him
understood), 35; gp. —**ra**, M 38.

sellan, wk.v.I. *give;* inf. M 38, 46
(*hand over, pay*) ; pres. 1p. subj.
sellen, M 61 (*pay*); pret. 3s. **sealde**,
M 271 (*gave, inflicted*). [SELLAN,
SEALDE, SEALD.]

ġe-**sellan**, wk.v.I. *give;* pret. 3s. ġe-
sealde, M 188 (*gave, presented*) ;
D 41 (the same); pret. 3p. ġe-
sealdon, M 184 (*gave, yielded up*) .

sēlra, adj. comp. *better;* asm. —**n**,
D 6. [Cf. sēlest.]

ġe-**sēman**, wk.v.I. *reconcile, decide
the terms between;* inf. M 60.
[Base-word SŌM, f. *agreement.*]

sendan, wk.v.I. *send;* inf. M 30; W
56; pret. 3s. **sende**, M 134; 3p.
sendon, M 29. [SENDAN, SENDE,
SENDED; base-word SAND, f. *a send-
ing, message;* cf. on-sendan.]

sēo, see sē.

seofian, wk.v.II. *lament, sigh;* pret.
3p. **seofodon**, S 10.

seofon, num. adj. *seven;* npm. —**e**,
B 30.

seolfor, n. *silver;* dis. **seolfre**, R 77.

ġe-**sēon**, contr.v.5. *see;* pres. 3s. ġe-
siehþ, W 46; pret. 1s. ġe**seah**, R
14, 21, 33, 36, 51; 3p. ġe**sāwon**,

M 84, 203; 1s. subj. ġesāwe, R 4.
[SĒON (*SEHWAN), SEAH, SĀWON,
SEWEN.]

ġe-set, n. seat; np. ġesetu, W 93.

setl, n. seat; ds. —e, B 17.

ġe-settan, wk.v.I. set, seat, place;
pret. 3p. ġesetton, R 67; pp.
ġeseted, nsn. R 141. [SETTAN,
SETTE, SETED; cf. a-settan, sittan.]

sē-þe, see sē.

sīde, wk.f. side; ds. sīdan, R 49.

sīde, adv. widely; wīde and sīde, far
and wide, R 81.

sīe, see bēon-wesan.

ġe-siehþ, see ġe-sēon.

sīen, f. i-stem. sight, spectacle. See
wǣfer-sīen, and cf. an-sīen.

ġe-sīene, adj. ja-stem. visible; npm.
R 46. [Cf. ġe-sēon.]

ġe-sierwed, pp. adj. armed; nsm. M
159. [As from ġe-SIERWAN, wk.v.I,
unrecorded in other forms; base-
word SEARU, f. wō-stem. equip-
ment.]

sīgan, v.l. sink; pret. 3s. sāg, B 17.
[SĪGAN, SĀG, SIGON, SIĠEN.]

siġe, m. i-stem. victory. siġe-bēam, m.
tree of victory (the cross); ns. R
13; as. R 127.

sigor, m. victory; gp. —a, R 67.
sigor-fæst, adj. victorious; nsm. R
150.

ġe-sihþ, f. jō-stem. sight, vision; ds.
—e, R 21, 41, 66; as. —e, R 96.

simble, adv. ever, always; S 68.

sinc, n. treasure; as. M 59; gs. —es,
W 25; ds. —e, R 23. sinc-ġiefa, wk.
m. giver of treasure, bountiful
lord; as. —n, M 278. sinc-þegu, f.
receiving of treasure; as. —þeġe,
W 34.

sind, sindon, see bēon-wesan.

sin-gāl, adj. ever-living, perpetual;
nsf. R 141. [sin-, always (Lat.

SEMPER, OE sim-ble), gāl, lusty,
hence vigorous, alive; hardly felt
as a compound; cf. gāl, win-gāl.]

singan, v.3. sing; pres. part. sing-
ende, asm. uninfl., S 22; pres. 3s.
singeþ, S 54; pret. 3s. sang, M 284.
[SINGAN, SANG, SUNGON, SUNGEN.]

sinu, f. wō-stem. sinew. sinu-bend,
f. jō-stem. sinew-bond (a bond
made by cutting a sinew, ham-
stringing); ap. —a, D 6.

sittan, v.5. sit; pres. 3s. siteþ, D 28;
pret. 3s. sæt, D 24. [SITTAN, SÆT,
SǢTON, SETEN.]

ġe-sittan, v.5. sit; pret. 3s. ġe-sæt, W
111.

sīþ, m. journey, voyage, venture; ds.
—e, S 51; experience, trial, ap.
—as, S 2. sīþ-fæt, m. expedition;
ds. —e, R 150. [Cf. bealu-sīþ.]

ġe-sīþ, m. companion; ds. —e, D 3.

sīðian, wk.v.II. travel, journey, pass;
inf. R 68; M 177; pres. 1s. subj.
sīðie, M 251.

siþþan, adv. afterwards, R 142; S 78;
—conj. after, B 13, 69; R 3, 49, 71
(MS.; emended to stefn, q.v.); W
22; D 5.

slǣp, m. sleep; ns. W 39; is. slǣp'
for slǣpe, D 16.

slāt, see slītan.

sleaht, m. or n. (var. of slieht, i-
stem), slaughter. See wæl-sleaht,
and cf. bill-ġe-slieht.

slēan, contr.v.6. strike; pret. 3s. slōg,
M 163, 285; 3s. subj. slōge, M 117.
[SLĒAN (*SLEAHAN), SLŌG, SLŌGON,
SLǢGEN; cf. be-slēan.]

ġe-slēan, contr.v.6. obtain by striking,
win; pret. 3p. ġeslōgon, B 4.

ġe-slieht, m. or n. i-stem. slaughter.
See bill-ġeslieht, and cf. sleaht and
slēan.

slītan, v.l. lacerate, tear, rend; pret.

3s. **slāt,** S 11. [SLĪTAN, SLĀT, SLITON, SLITEN.]

slīðen, adj. *cruel, dire, fierce;* nsf. W 30.

slōg, slōge, ġe-slōgon, see **slēan, ġe-slēan.**

smiþ, m. *smith;* see **wīġ-smiþ.**

snāw, m. *snow;* as. W 48.

snell, adj. *keen, bold;* np. —e, M 29.

snīwan, v.1, with wk. pret. *snow;* pret. 3s. **snīwde,** S 31.

snottor, adj. *wise, discerning;* nsm. W 111 (as noun). [Both **snotor** and **snottor** appear to be metrically substantiated in different poems.]

sōfte, adv. *easily;* M 59. [Cf. the mutated **sēft-.**]

sōht-, ġe-sōht-, see **sēċan, ġe-sēċan.**

sorg, f. *sorrow;* ns. W 30, 39, 50; as. —e, S 42 (*anxiety?*), 54; D 3; gp. —a, R 80; dip. —um, R 20, 59; D 24. **sorg-ċeariġ,** adj. *troubled by sorrow, sorrowful;* nsm. D 28 (as noun, or modifying indef. "someone" understood). **sorg-lēoþ,** n. *song of sorrow, dirge;* as. R 67. **sorg-lufu,** f. *sorrowful love;* ns. D 16.

sōþ, n. *truth;* ds. —e, W 11 (to s., *for a truth, indeed*). **sōþ-ġiedd,** n. ja-stem. *lay of truth* (as opposed to legendary matter); as. S 1.

ġe-spann, n. *fastening, joint.* See **eaxl-ġespann.**

spēdan, wk.v.I. *be prosperous, be wealthy;* pres. 2p. **spēdaþ,** M 34 (*ġif ġē* s. *to þām, if you have that much wealth, if you are good for the necessary amount*—see Gordon's note). [Base-word **SPĒD,** f. i-stem (from *SPŌDI-), *success, wealth.*]

spēdiġ, adj. *successful;* nsm. R 151.

spell, n. *message;* as. M 50.

spere, n. i-stem. *spear;* as. M 137 (*spear-head*); ap. **speru,** M 108. [Cf. **wæl-spere.**]

spillan, wk.v.I. *destroy;* inf. M 34 (*ūs spillan, slaughter each other*).

sprang, see **springan.**

sprecan, v.5, intrans. or trans. *speak;* with a clause, *say;* inf. R 27; pres. 3s. **spriċeþ,** W 70; pret. 3s. **spræc,** M 211, 274; 1p. **spræcon,** M 212; 3p. M 200. [SPRECAN, SPRÆC, SPRÆCON, SPRECEN.]

sprenġan, wk.v.I. *cause to spring or quiver;* pret. 3s. **sprenġde,** M 137 (the subject may be **se sceaft** rather than **Byrhtnōþ**). [Based on SPRANG, 2nd grade of **springan.**]

springan, v.3. *spring;* pret. 3s. **sprang,** M 137. [SPRINGAN, SPRANG, SPRUNGON, SPRUNGEN.]

stæf, m. *sign, letter of the alphabet; verbal formula.* See **glēo-stafas.**

stæþ, n. *bank, shore;* ds. —e, M 25. [Cf. **ēa-stæþ.**]

ġe-stāg, see **ġe-stīgan.**

stān, m. *stone;* ds. —e, R 66. **stān-clif,** n. *rocky cliff, crag;* ap. —u, S 23. **stān-hliþ,** n. *rocky slope; stone declivity;* ap. —u, W 101 (fig. for high stone walls, or transition from image of a ruined citadel to weatherbeaten cliffs of the earth itself?).

standan, v.6. *stand, remain, endure;* inf. R 43, 62; M 19; pres. 3s. **stent,** M 51; **standeþ,** W 74, 97, 115; 3p. **standaþ,** W 76; S 67; pret. ls. **stōd,** R 38; 3s. **stōd,** M 25, 28, 145, 152, 273; 1p. **stōdon,** R 71; 3p. **stōdon,** R 7; M 72, 79, 100, 127, 182, 301; W 87; 3p. subj. **stōden,** M 63. [STANDAN, STŌD, STŌDON, STANDEN; cf. **be-, wiþ-standan.**]

ġe-standan, v.6. *stand, stand up;* inf.
M 171; pret. 3p. ġestōdon, R 63
(w. refl. dat., *took their stand?*—
see note).

stang, see stingan.

-stapa, wk.m. *stepper, treader.* See
eard-stapa.

staðol, m. *(fixed) position; founda-
tion;* ds. —e, R 71; dp. —um, S
109 (healdan on s., *keep in place,
control*—Mrs. Gordon).

ġe-staðolian, wk.v.II. *establish, con-
firm, make steadfast;* pres. 3s.
ġestaðolaþ, S 108; pret. 3s. ġe-
staðolode, S 104.

steall, m. *standing-place.* See weall-
steall.

ġe-steall, n. *foundation, resting
place?* ns. W 110 (eorðan g.,
earthly resting place, habitation?)

stēam, m. *moisture, blood;* dis. —e,
R 62.

stearn, m. *tern* (perhaps not the
modern tern or sea-swallow but a
small species of seagull—see Mrs.
Gordon's note); ns. S 23.

stede, m. i-stem. *place, position;* as.
M 19. stede-fæst, adj. *steadfast,
unyielding;* npm. —e, M 127, 249.
[Cf. camp-, folc-, mæðel-stede.]

stefn, m. i-stem. *stem.* (a) *prow or
stern of a ship;* ds. —e, B 34; (b)
trunk of a tree; ds. —e, R 30.

stefn, f. *voice;* ns. R 71 (not in MS.,
which has *siþþan*) .

stefna, wk.m. *stem of ship, prow or
stern;* ds. —n, S 7 (prow, as the
place for a look-out, or stern,
where one steers?).

stefnettan, wk.v.I, *stand firm;* pret.
3p. stefnetton, M 122.

stellan, wk.v.I. *place.* See a- and on-
stellan.

stent, see standan.

steppan, v.6. *step, go, advance;* pret.
3s. stōp, M 8, 78, 131. [STEPPAN,
or STÆPPAN, STŌP, STŌPON, STAPEN.]

stīeran, wk.v.I, w. dat. *steer, control;*
inf. S 109.

ġe-stīgan, v.1. *climb up, mount,
ascend;* inf. R 34; pret. 3s. ġe-stāg,
R 40. [STĪGAN, STĀG, STIGON,
STIĠEN; cf. a-stīgan.]

stihtan, wk.v.I. *direct;* pret. 3s. stihte,
M 127.

stingan, v.3. *stab, pierce;* pret. 3s.
stang, M 138. [STINGAN, STANG,
STUNGON, STUNGEN.]

stīþ, adj. *hard, firm, stubborn,
severe;* nsn. M 301; apm. —e, S
104.

stīþ-hycgende, pres. part. adj. ja-
stem. *firm of purpose, resolute;*
npm. M 122.

stīþ-mōd, adj. *brave, unflinching;*
nsm. R 40.

stīþlīċe, adv. *sternly, harshly;* M 25.

stōd, stōden, stōdon, see standan.

ġe-stōdon, see ġe-standan.

stōl, m. *seat, high-seat, throne.* See
ġief-stōl.

stōp, see steppan.

storm, m. *storm;* np. —as, W 101;
S 23.

stōw, f. *place.* See wæl-stōw.

strǣl, m. or f. *arrow;* dip. —um, R
62.

strang, adj. *strong;* nsm. R 40; dsn.
—um, S 109 (*headstrong*); npm.
—e, R 30.

strēam, m. *stream;* as. M 68; in pl.,
seas, ocean; ap. —as, S 34. [Cf.
lagu-strēam.]

strēgan, wk.v.I. *strew, spread;* inf. S
97. [A non-West-Saxon form oc-
curring only here. Related W-S
forms are STREWIAN and
STRĒAWIAN, wk.II.]

stund, f. *a time, (short) while;* as. —e, M 271. See **ymb.**

styrian, wk.v.I. *stir, move.* See a-**styrian.**

sum, pron. and adj. (a) pron., *one, a certain one;* w. part. gen., nsm. M 149, 164; nsn. S 68; asn. M 285; —without gen., in a series of singulars, *one . . . another,* etc.; asm. —ne, W 81, 82, 83; —in pl., *some, a number;* apm. —e, W 80 (preceding the series of singulars; understatement for "many"?); dp. —um, D 34; *certain ones,* npm. —e, S 56 (þā **sume,** *those particular ones*—not *some of those;* see Mrs. Gordon's note). (b) adj. *some, a;* asf. —e, M 271.

sumor, m. (here a-stem; sometimes u-stem). *summer;* gs. —es, S 54.

sundor, adv. *separately, apart;* him **sundor,** *by himself,* W 111.

sunne, wk. f. *sun;* ns. B 13.

sunu, m. u-stem. *son;* ns. R 150; M 76, 115, 298; as. B 42.

sūðerne, adj. ja-stem. *southern;* asm. (-rne for -rnne), M 134 (*of southern make*).

swā, adv. *so; in such manner; in like manner; accordingly;* M 33, 59, 122, 132, 198, 209, 243, 280, 319, 320, 323; W 6, 19, 62, 85, 111; S 51; D 7, 13, 17, 20, 27, 42; correl. w. the conj., *so, as,* D 9a; —conj. *as,* C 3; B 7; R 92, 108, 114; M 290; W 14, 43, 75; S 90; correl. w. the adv., D 9b; w. subj., *as if,* W 96.

swǣs, adj. *dear, beloved;* asm. —ne, W 50 (as noun, *loved one*).

swǣtan, wk.v.I. *bleed;* inf. R 20. [Base-word **swāt,** m. *blood.*]

swancor, adj. *supple;* apf. **swancre,** D 6.

swāt, m. *blood;* gs. —es, R 23; dis. —e, B 13.

sweart, adj. *dark, black;* asm.wk. —an, B 61.

swebban, wk.v.I. *put to sleep; kill.* See a-**swebban.**

swefn, n. (*sleep,*) *dream, vision;* gp. —a, R 1.

swēġ, m. i-stem. *sound;* (bird's) *song* or *cry;* as. S 21.

swelċ, rel. pron. *such as;* np. —e, S 83. [swā plus līċ.]

swelċe, conj. adv. *likewise, and also;* B 19, 30, 37, 57; R 8; S 53. **swelċe swā,** conj. *just as,* R 92.

swelgan, v.3. *swallow;* see **for-swelgan.**

sweltan, v.3. *die, perish;* inf. M 293. [SWELTAN, SWEALT, SWULTON, SWOLTEN.]

swenġ, m. i-stem. *blow, stroke;* gs. —es, M 118.

sweorcan, v.3. *become gloomy;* pres. 3s. **sweorceþ,** D 29. [SWEORCAN, SWEARC, SWURCON, SWORCEN.]

ġe-**sweorcan,** v.3. *grow dark, gloomy;* pres. 3s. subj. ġe**sweorce,** W 59.

sweord, n. *sword;* ns. M 166; as. M 15, 161, 237; gs. —es, B 68; ds. —e, M 118; ap. **sweord,** M 47; gp.—a, B 4; dip. —um, B 30.

sweostor, f. r-stem. *sister;* gs. M 115.

sweotule, adv. *clearly,* W 11.

swēte, adj. ja-stem. *sweet;* asn. S 95 (as noun). [Cf. unmutated ¡swōt, *sweet.*]

swīcan, v.1. *deceive, fail, desert.* See be-**swīcan.**

swillan, wk.v.I. *wash.* See be-**swillan.**

swimman, v.3. *swim;* pres. 3p. **swimmaþ,** W 53 (fig. ?—or partly literal, the spirits of the vision fading into sea-birds?). [SWIMMAN, SWAMM, SWUMMON, SWUMMEN.]

ġe-**swinċ,** n. i-stem. *toil.* ġe**swinċ**-

dagas, m.pl. *days of toil or hardship;* dip. —dagum, S 2.

swiþ, adj. *strong;* comp. swiðre, nsf. S 115; asf. in on þā swiðran healfe, *on the right (the stronger) side,* R 20.

swiðe, adv. *greatly, very; fiercely, severely;* M 115, 118, 282; W 56.

symbel, n. *feast, banquet;* ds. symble, R 141; gp. symbla, W 93.

synn, f. jō-stem. *sin;* gp. —a, S 100; dp. —um, R 99, 146; dip. —um, R 13.

T

tǣċan, wk.v.I. *show, direct, teach;* pret. 3s. tǣhte, M 18. [TǢCAN, TǢHTE, TǢHT; cf. TĀCN, n. *token, sign.*]

tǣsan, wk.v.I. *lacerate, rive;* pret. 3s. tǣsde, M 270.

tēoġan, wk.v.II (contr.). *adorn, prepare, create;* pret. 3s. tēode, C 8. [The inf. is conjectural; apparently from *TEHOJAN, then *TEOHOJAN, contr. to TĒOJAN; pret. TĒODE, pp. TĒOD.]

tīd, f. i-stem. *time, hour; period of time;* ns. M 104; as. S 124; *lifetime,* in tīd-dæġ, m. *last day of one's life, final hour,* ds. —e, S 69 (Grein's emendation for MS. *tide ge;* tīd-dæġ is recorded only in *Genesis* 1165, where it may mean either *last day* or *life-span*). [Cf. ǣfen-, morgen-tīd.]

til, adj. *good;* asm. —ne, D 38; *praiseworthy, commendable,* nsm. W 112.

til, prep. w. dat. *for,* C 6 (Moore MS.—the rest have to).

tilian, wk.v.II. *strive, endeavor;* pres. 1p. subj. tilien, S 119.

tīr, m. *glory;* ns. M 104; as. B 3.

tō or to, prep. w. dat., instr., rarely gen., *to, for, at,* etc.

  1. w. dat. or instr. (a) where the meaning is still expressed by "to" (in various senses), B 17, 28, 34; R 42, etc. (9 times); M 8, etc. (20 times); W 36; S 51, 61; to þām, *to that extent,* M 34; to hwon (instr.), *to what (end, service, fate),* S 43; —(b) marking purpose, function, service, value, effect: *for, as,* C 6; R 31, 102, 153; M 46, 131, 197, 245; W 11, 30; S 20, 69 (to twēon, *as an occasion for uncertainty*), 101; D 3; —(c) marking sphere of action or juxtaposition: *at, in,* R 141, M 12; —(d) marking object of thought: *on, of,* M 4 (twice), 128; *(thought) for, (delight) in,* S 44 (twice), 45 (twice); —(e) marking object inspiring awe or desire: *toward, of, for,* R 86, 129; —(f) marking source of help: *from,* W 115; —(g) marking time: *at, toward,* R 2; to ealdre, *for ever,* S 79; —(h) fōn to *(take to,) seize upon, take up,* M 10.

  2. w. uninflected inf. (often dat.), *to,* S 37.

  3. w. gen., to þæs, *to that extent,* S. 40, 41 (twice).

tō, prep. as adv. *thither, to that place;* S 119.

tō, adv. *too* (w. adj. or adv., denoting excess); M 55, 66, 90, 150, 164; W 66 (twice), 67 (twice), 68 (3 times), 69, 112.

to-berstan, v.3. *burst asunder, be shattered;* pret. 3s. tobærst, M 136, 144. [Cf. berstan.]

to-brecan, v.4. *break apart, break through;* pp. tobrocen, nsf. M 242. [Cf. brecan.]

to-gædere, adv. *together,* M 67. [Cf.
æt-gædere.]

to-ġēanes, prep. w. dat. *against;* S 76
(postpos.)

ġe-toht, n. *battle;* ds. —e, M 104.

torn, n. *passion, anger;* 2s. W 112.

to-twæman, wk.v.I. *divide, split in
two;* pp. totwæmed, nsn. M 241.
[Base-word TWĀM, dat. of twēġen,
q.v.]

trem, m. or n. *step, space;* as. M 247
(adverbial acc., marking extent).

trēo, n. wa-stem. *tree, cross;* as. R 4,
14, 17, 25. [Cf. ġealg-trēo.]

trēow, f. wō-stem. *good faith, pledge,
agreement;* as. —e, W 112.

trymian or trymman, wk.v.I. *make
firm, encourage; put in order,
marshal, array;* inf. trymian, M
17; pret. 3p. trymedon, M 305.
[Base-word TRUM, adj. *firm, strong.*]

ġe-trymian, wk.v.I. same as pre-
ceding; pp. ġetrymed, M 22 (per-
haps both *drawn up in order* and
encouraged: arrayed for battle).
[MS. getrymmed is irregular but
perhaps intended for meter.]

tū, see bū-tū and twēġen.

tungol, n. *star;* ns. B 14.

twæman, wk.v.I. *divide;* see to-
twæman.

twēġen, m., twā, f., tū, n. *two;* nom.
twēġen, M 80; gen. twēġa, M 207.
[Cf. bū-tū.]

twēo, wk. m. *doubt, uncertainty;* ds.
—n, S 69 (to twēon weorðeþ, *be-
comes an occasion for uncer-
tainty*).

þ

þā, adv. and conj.—(a) as adv., *then,
after that, next;* C 7; R 27, etc.
(10 times); M 2, etc. (35 times);

—(b) as rel. conj., *when,* R 36, 41,
42, 68, 151, 155; M 5, 10, 16, 22,
84, 121, 165, 199, 239, 276. þā-
ġiet, adv. *still,* M 168, 273.

þā, dem. adj., def. art. and pron.,
see sē.

þær, adv. and conj.—(a) as adv.,
there, B 17, 32, 37; R 8, etc. (17
times); M 17, etc. (19 times); W
54; S 18, 23a; (perhaps) *there-
upon, then,* R 30, 31, 32, 57, 60;
—(b) as rel. conj., *where,* R 123,
139, 140, 141, 142, 156; M 23, 24,
28; W 115; S 6, 23b, 121; —
(vaguely logical) *whereas, while,*
S 10. þær-on, adv. *therein,* R 67.

þǣre, þæs, þæs-þe, see sē.

þæt, conj. *that.* — (a) in substantive
clauses (subject, object, apposi-
tive), B 8; R 4, etc. (7 times);
M 6, etc. (20 times); W 12, 13,
41; S 67, 77 (explaining þæt, pron.,
74), 123 (explaining þæs, pron.);
D 10, 11, 14 (introducing clause
as obj. of ġefrugnon), 26, 30, 31,
36; —(b) in apposition with a
noun signifying a time: *that,
when,* R 81; M 105; — (c) in
causal clauses: *in that, for, be-
cause;* B 48; R 19, 34, 107; M 221,
243, 251; — (d) the clause equiva-
lent to a noun in gen. governed
by a noun or adj. in the main
clause: *that,* M 176, 180; —(e) the
clause stating what is urged or
asked; *that,* M 229, 257, 263, 307;
— (f) in a clause of purpose: *that,
in order that,* M 177; S 34, 37,
119; — (g) in clauses of result or
manner: *that, so that,* M 63, 119,
135, 136, 137, 142, 144, 150, 157,
226, 227, 286; S 42; D 16.

þæt, dem. adj., def. art., and pron.,
see sē.

þām, þām-þe, see sē.

þanan, adv. *thence,* W 23.

þanc, m. and n., w. gen. *thanks (for);* ns. S 122; as. M 120, 147.

ġe-þanc, m. or n. *thought;* as. M 13 (gōd ġ., *an unflinching spirit*). [Cf. mōd-ġeþanc.]

ġe-þancian, wk.v.II, w. dat. of person. *thank, give thanks to;* pres. 1s. ġeþancie, M 173.

þāra, see sē.

þās, see þēs.

þe, þē, indecl. particle, serving as rel. pron., any case, number, or gender. *who, which, that,* etc.; R 111, 118, 137; M 36, etc. (19 times; at 190, obj. of on understood); S 57, 100; þe . . . him, dsm. *to whom,* W 10; S 13; in þā hwīle þe, conj. *while* (lit. *the time in which*), M 14, 83, 235, 272. [Also in combination with þēah, q.v., and with the dem. pron.: see sē. In the MSS. also isn. of the dem. pron., here normalized as þȳ; see sē.]

þē, pers. pron., see þū.

ġe-þeah, see ġe-þicgan.

þēah, adv. *though, however,* M 289.

þēah-þe, conj. *though,* W 2; S 97, 113.

þearf, f. (a) *need;* ns. M 233; as. —e, M 175; —(b) *(time of) need, distress;* ds. —e, M 201, 307; —(c) *what is needful, morally requisite or desirable;* ds. —e, M 232 (*our good, what we must do*).

þearf, see þurfan.

þearle, adv. *severely, sorely, grievously;* B 23; R 52; M 158.

þēaw, m. *custom, habit;* ns. W 12.

þeġn, m. *servant, minister;* esp. *a (noble) retainer;* as. M 151; np. —as, R 75 (*the Lord's servants*); M 205, 220; ap. —as, M 232; gp.

—a, S 68 (MS. þinga). [Cf. būr-, magu-þeġn.]

þeġnlīċe, adv. *as befitting a þeġn; loyally, nobly,* M 294.

-þegu, f. *receipt, receiving.* See hring-, sinc-þegu, and cf. ge-þicgan.

þenċan, wk.v.I. *think;* inf. S 96; pres. 3p. þenċaþ, R 115; —w. inf., *purpose, intend, desire (to);* pres. 1s. þenċe, M 319; 3s. þenċeþ, R 121; M 258, 316; S 51. [ÞENĊAN, ÞŌHTE, ÞŌHT; base-word þanc, *thought;* cf. ġeond-þenċan.]

ġe-þenċan, wk.v.I. *think, determine, reflect, consider;* —w. indirect question, *think why* or *how,* inf. W 58; S 118; D. 12; w. subst. clause, *reflect that,* inf. D 31.

þenden, conj. *while,* S 102.

þenian or þennan, wk.v.I. *stretch out;* inf. þenian, R 52 (w. God as object and unstated subject; equivalent to passive, *stretched out,* w. God as subject).

þēod, f. *people;* ds. —e, M 90, 220; gp. —a, M 173; dp. —um, B 22.

þēoden, m. *prince, lord;* ns. M 120, 232; vs. M 178; as. M 158; ds. þēodne, R 69; M 294; gs. þēodnes, W 95.

-þēodiġ, adj. combining-form. *of a people or country.* See el-þēodiġ.

þēs or þes, þēos, þis, dem. adj. and pron. *this;* — (a) as adj., þes, nsm. W 62; þēos, nsf. R 12, 82; S 86; þis, nsn. M 45; W 110; S 65; asn. W 89; þisne, asm. R 104; M 32, 52; W 75, 85, 88; þās, asf. R 96; W 58; S 87; D 31; ap. M 298; W 91, 101; þisse, gsf. W 74; dsf. M 221; þissum, dsn. R 83, 109, 138; þȳs, ism. M 316; isn. B 66. (b) as pron., þisses, gsn. (*as to this, with respect to this*), D 7, 13, 17, 20,

27, 42; þissum, dsn. B 67 (this, the present time).

ġe-þicgan, v.5. receive; pret. 3s. ġeþeah, D 40 (MS. geþah). [ÞICGAN, ÞEAH (occas. ÞAH), ÞǢGON, ÞEĠEN.]

þider, adv. thither, S 118.

þīestre, n. ja-stem. darkness; often pl., shades of night; np. þīestru, R 52. [An alternate þīestru, f. īn-stem, is also found and cannot always be distinguished from the neuter.]

þīn, poss. adj. thy, thine; asn. M 178; apm. —e, M 37; dp. —um, M 50.

þing, n. (thing,) state, condition; affair, trouble; ns. D 9; circumstance, gp. —a, S 68 (MS. þinga gehwylce, emended to þeġna ġehwelċum. See note.)

þingan, wk.v.I. determine. See un-þinġed.

þis, þisne, þisse, þisses, þissum, see þēs.

ġe-þōht, m. thought; as. D 22; is. —e, W 88; np. —as, S 34.

þolian, wk.v.II. (a) trans., suffer, undergo, endure; pret. 3p. þolodon, R 149; (b) intrans. endure, hold out; inf. M 201, 307. [Cf. for-þolian.]

ġe-þolian, wk.v.II, trans. endure, put up with; inf. M 6.

þon, pron., ism. and isn., see sē, pron., for, for-þon, ǣr-þon.

þone, þone-þe, see sē.

þonne, adv. and conj. —(a) as adv., then (temporal), R 107, 115, 117, 139, 142; W 45, 49; S 94a, 118, 119; D 31; then (consequential), therefore, W 88; —(b) as rel. conj., when, M 213; W 39, 51, 60, 70, 74, 103; S 8, 84, 94b (correl.), 102;

—(c) conj. w. comp., than, R 128; M 33, 195; S 65, 116.

þorfte, þorfton, see þurfan.

þrāg, f. (period of) time; ns. W 95.

ġe-þrang, n. throng, press; ds. —e, M 299.

þrīe, m., þrēo, f. and n. pl. three; gen. þrēora, M 299; S 68 (w. sum, one of three things).

ġe-þringan, v.3. press, constrict; pp. geþrungen, npm. uninflected (for geþrungne), S 8 (pinched). [ÞRINGAN, ÞRANG, ÞRUNGON, ÞRUN-GEN; cf. oþ-þringan.]

þrīste, adv. resolutely, unflinchingly, D 12.

þrītiġ, num. thirty; as subst. w. part. gen., acc. (extent of time), D 18.

þrōwian, wk.v.II. suffer; intrans., pret. 3s. þrōwode, R 84, 98, 145; trans., suffer, endure, pret. 1s. þrōwode, S 3.

ġe-þrungen, see ġe-þringan.

þrymm, m. ja-stem. glory, majesty; ns. W 95. þrymm-fæst, adj. glorious; nsm. R 84.

þrȳþ, f. i-stem. strength, power; often in plural w. reference to the powers of inanimate things, as here of spears: np. —e, W 99.

þū, pron. 2d pers. sg. thou; ns. R 78, 96; M 30, 36, 37, 45, 176, 231; þē, ds. M 29, 30, 177, 179; as. R 95; M 173. [See þīn, poss. adj., and ġē.]

þūhte, see þyncan.

þurfan, pret.-pres. v. need, have reason to (w. inf.); pres. 3s. þearf, R 117; 1p. þurfe (wē), M 34; 3p. þurfon, M 249; pret. 3s. þorfte, B 39, 44; 3p. þorfton, B 47. [ÞURFAN, ÞEARF, ÞURFON, ÞORFTE.]

þurh, prep. w. acc. through; — (a) of motion: through, R 18; M 141, 145, 151; — (b) expressing cause or agency: *through, by, by reason of, by means of;* R 10, 119; M 71; S 88.

þurh-drifan, v.1. *drive through, pierce;* pret. 3p. þurhdrifon, R 46. [DRĪFAN, DRĀF, DRIFON, DRIFEN.]

þurh-wadan, v.6. *pass through, pierce;* pret. 3s. þurhwōd, M 296. [Cf. wadan.]

þus, adv. *thus,* M 57.

þȳ, see sē.

ge-þyldig, adj. *patient;* nsm. W 65.

þynćan, wk.v.I, impers. w. dat. of person. *seem;* pres. 3s. þynćeþ, M 55; W 41; D 29; pret. 3s. þūhte, R 4; M 66. [þYNĆAN, þŪHTE, þŪHT; based on þUNC-, passive grade of the ablaut series *þINC-, *þANC-; *þUNC-; cf. þenćan.]

þȳs, see þēs.

U

ūhta, wk.m. *period before daybreak, early morning;* gp. ūhtna, W 8.

un-befohten, adj. *unopposed, without a fight;* npm. unbefohtne, M 57. [Cf. feohtan.]

unc, see wit.

under, prep. *beneath, under;* w. dat., R 55, 85; W 107; w. acc. (after a verb implying motion), W 96.

un-earg, adj. *undaunted, unflinching;* npm. —e, M 206.

un-forcūþ, adj. *undisgraced, reputable;* nsm. M 51.

un-forht, adj. *unafraid, undaunted;* nsm. R 110; npm. —e, M 79. [MS. has *unforht* at R 117, but with opposite meaning; see an-forht.]

ge-unnan, pret.-pres. v., w. gen. *grant;* pres. subj. 2s. ġeunne, M 176. [UNNAN, ANN, UNNON, ŪðE.]

un-orne, adj. ja-stem. *unpretentious, simple, humble;* nsm. M 256. [Cf. orne.]

un-rim, n. *countless number;* ns. B 31 (w. part. gen.). [RĪM, n. *number.*]

un-þinged, adj. *unprepared for, unexpected;* nsm. S 106. [þINĠAN, wk.v.I, *invite, determine upon.*]

un-wāclīce, adv. *without weakening;* M 308. [Cf. wāc, wācian.]

un-wearnum, adv. *irresistibly;* S 63. [wearn, f. *hindrance;* q.v.]

un-weaxen, adj. *not fully grown;* nsm. M 152. [weaxan, v.7, *grow.*]

upp, adv. *up;* B 13, 70; R 71; M 130.

upp-gang, m. *passage up on land, passage to shore;* as. M 87. upp-rodor, m. *high heaven, the heavens above;* as. S 105.

uppe, adv. *up,* R 9.

ūre, poss. adj. *our;* nsm. M 232, 240, 314; nsn. M 313; ūrne, asm. M 58; ūrum, dp. M 56. [For the pron. see wē.]

ūriġ, adj. *dewy.* ūriġ-feðra, wk.m. *dewy-feathered one;* ns. S 25. [A valid word though in a seemingly corrupt passage; a wk. noun or wk. adj. with subst. function, from strong adj. *ŪRIĠ-FEðER, *dewy-feathered;* see -feðra.]

ūs, ūsiċ, see wē.

ūt, adv. *out;* B 35; M 72.

ūþ-wita, wk.m. *wise man;* np. —n, B 69. [The stressed prefix is intensive; it may once have meant *beyond.* Cf. wita.]

W

wāc, adj. *weak* (morally or physically); nsm. W 67 (wāc wiġa, *weak in battles*) ; asm. —ne, M 43 (of a spear-shaft vigorously shaken: *pliant, slender*); comp. **wācra**, npm. −n, as noun, *the inferior, degenerate*, S 87. [Implies moral weakness in **un-wāclīċe**, q.v.]

wācian, wk.v.II. *weaken, prove soft;* inf. M 10.

wacu, f. *watch.* See **niht-wacu.**

wadan, v.6. (a) intrans., *pass, proceed, advance;* inf. M 140; pret. 1s. **wōd**, W 24; 3s. M 130, 253; 3p. **wōdon**, M 96, 295; −(b) trans., *tread, traverse;* inf. W 5. [WADAN, WŌD, WŌDON, WADEN; cf. **þurh-wadan.**]

ġe-wadan, v.6. *go, pass (all the way)* ; pret. 3s. **ġewōd**, M 157.

wæcnan, v.6 (irreg.). *awake.* See **on-wæcnan.**

wǣd, f. (or **wǣde**, n. ja-stem). *clothing, an article of clothing, covering;* dp. −um, R 15, 22 (the alternating vesture of the cross, now precious ornaments, possibly including silken streamers, now blood).

wǣfer-sīen, f. i-stem. *spectacle, show;* ds. −e, R 31. [**wǣfer** does not occur alone but is used in several compounds referring to theatrical exhibitions and is probably related to WĀFIAN, wk.v.II, *marvel at, gaze at.* Cf. **ġe-siene**, **an-sīen**, and **ġe-sēon.**]

wǣġ, m. i-stem. *wave, surf;* as. S 19; ap. −as, W 46.

wǣgon, see **wegan.**

wæl, n. *slaughter; the slain collectively, number of slain;* in compounds often translatable by *battle;* ns. B 65; M 126, 303; ds. −e, M 279, 300. **wæl-feld**, m. u-stem. *battlefield;* ds. −a, B 51. **wæl-ġīfre**, adj. *greedy for slaughter;* npn. −ġifru, W 100. **wæl-rest**,

f. *a resting-place among the slain;* as. −e, M 113. **wæl-sleaht**, n. (or m.) *deadly combat;* gp. −a, W 7, 91. **wæl-spere**, n. i-stem. *deadly spear;* as. M 322. **wæl-stōw**, f. *place of slaughter, battlefield;* gs. −e, M 95; ds. −e, B 43; M 293. **wæl-wulf**, m. *death-dealing wolf;* np. −as, M 96 (epithet for the vikings).

wǣpen, n. *weapon;* ns. M 252; as. M 130, 235; np. W 100;·gs. **wǣpnes**, M 168; ds. **wǣpne**, M 228; gp. **wǣpna**, M 83, 272, 308; dp. **wǣpnum**, M 10, 126. **wǣpen-ġewrixl**, n. *weapon-exchange, trading of blows;* gs. −es, B 51.

wǣr, f. *covenant, pledge;* dip. −um, S 110 (**ġewiss wǣrum**, *unfailing in its* [the mind's] *pledges;* MS. **werum** can also be taken as dp. of **wer:** *constant toward men;* but see note).

wǣre, **wǣron**, **wǣs**, see **bēon-wesan.**

wǣta, wk.m. *moisture, blood;* ds. −n, R 22.

wæter, n. *water;* as. B 55; M 91, 98; ds. −e, M 64, 96.

wamm, m. *blemish, iniquity;* dp. −um, R 14.

wan, adj. *lacking, wanting* (generally as first member of a compound). **wan-hȳġdiġ**, adj. *heedless, reckless, imprudent;* nsm. W 67.

wand, see **windan.**

wandian, wk.v.II. *turn aside, waver, flinch;* inf. M 258; pret. 3s. **wandode**, M 268. [Cf. **windan.**]

wang, m. *field, meadow;* ap. −as, S 49 (less probably np.) .

wann, adj. *dark;* nsm. W 103; nsf. R 55.

-ware, m.pl. (orig. f.pl. of WARU, *people*), *inhabitants, people.* See **bealu-**, **burg-ware.**

warian, wk.v.II. *guard, take charge of; attend* (as a guardian or ruling spirit); pres. 3s. waraþ, W 32.

wāt, see witan.

ġe-wāt, see ġe-witan.

waðum, m. *wave, stream, sea;* gp. —a, W 24, 57. (MS. *waðena, waþema.*)

wāwan, v.7. *blow, be blown about in the wind.* See be-wāwan.

wē, pron. 1st pers. pl. *we;* nom. C 1 (var.); R 70; M 33, 34, 35, 40, 61, 212, 213; S 117 (twice), 118, 119 (twice); D 14, 21; ūre, gen. M 234 (w. ǣġhwelċ); ūs, dat. B 68; R 147b; M 39, 40, 93, 233; W 115; acc. R 73, 75, 147a; M 34 (refl., *each other*), 60, 237. ūsiċ, acc. S 123. [See iċ, wit, and ūre, poss. adj.]

wēa, wk.m. *woe, misery;* as. —n, D 4; gs. —n, D 25; gp. —na, D 34.

ġe-wealc, n. *rolling, tossing;* as. S 6, 46.

weald, m. u-stem. *forest, woodland;* ds. —a, B 65.

ġe-weald, n. *control, prerogative, power;* as. R 107; M 178.

wealdan, v.7., w. gen. *wield;* inf. M 83, 168, 272; *hold, be master of,* inf. M 95. [WEALDAN, WĒOLD, WĒOLDON, WEALDEN.]

wealdend, m. nd-stem. *ruler;* esp. *the Lord;* ns. R 111, 155; vs. M 173 (w. gen.); as. R 67 (w. gen.); gs. —es, R 17, 53; ds. —e, R 121; in the secular sense, np. W 78.

weall, m. *wall;* ns. W 98; ds. —e, W 80; np. —as, W 76. weall-steall, m. *site of a wall, wall-stead, foundation;* as. W 88. [Cf. bord-weall.]

weard, m. *guardian, lord;* w. defining gen., (a) *God:* heofon-rīċes w., as. C 1; mann-cynnes w., ns. C 7;

(b) *the cuckoo:* sumeres w., ns. S 54. [Cf. brycg-weard.]

wearg, m. *criminal;* ap. —as, R 31.

wearn, f. *hindrance;* dp. —um, D 1 (be wearnum, *by hindrances,* an emendation for MS. *be wurman:* see note). [Cf. un-wearnum.]

wearþ, see weorðan.

weaxan, v.7. *grow, increase.* See un-weaxen. [WEAXAN, WĒOX, WĒOXON, WEAXEN.]

weġ, m. *way, path, road;* as. R 88. [Cf. eorþ-, flōd-, forþ-, hwæl-weġ, and on-weġ, adv. under on.]

wegan, v.5. *carry, bear;* pret. 3p. wǣgon, M 98. [WEGAN, WÆĠ, WǢGON, WEĠEN; cf. for-wegan.]

wēl, adv. *well, fully;* R 129, 143; as quasi-adj., wēl biþ, *it will be well, turn out well,* W 114.

wela, wk.m. *wealth;* ns. W 74. [Cf. eorþ-wela.]

wēman, wk.v.I. *allure, entertain;* inf. W 29.

wēn, f. i-stem. *expectation;* dp. —um, D 25.

wēnan, wk.v.I. (a) *believe, suppose;* wēnde, pret. 3s. M 239 (w. gen. þæs, and explanatory clause); (b) *expect, hope, look forward to;* pres. 1s. wēne, R 135 (w. refl. pron. dat. and clause).

wendan, wk.v.I. *turn;* (a) *change;* inf. R 22; (b) *go (away); go about;* inf. M 316; pres. 3s. wendeþ, D 32; 1s. subj. wende, M 252; pret. 3p. wendon, M 193; (c) w. forþ, *go forth, advance;* pret. 3p. wendon, M 205. [WENDAN, WENDE, WENDED; base-word WAND, corresponding to pret. of windan, q.v.; cf. on-wendan.]

wenian or wennan, wk.v.I. *accustom* (mod. "wean" with wider application); pret. 3s. wenede, W 36 (w.

to wiste, *accustomed him to the feast, was ever feasting him*). [Related to wunian, q.v.]

wēop, see wēpan.

weorc, n. *work; pain;* as. R 79 (*work or pain*) ; ap. C 3 (*works;* or as. *work*). [Cf. beadu-, dæġ-weorc.]

ġe-weorc, n. *a piece of construction, a work;* np. W 87.

weorod, n. *band of men, host, company;* ns. M 64, 97; as. M 102; ds. —e, R 152; M 51; is. —e, B 34; R 69, 124; gp. —a, R 51. [Cf. heorþ-weorod.]

weorold, f. i-stem. *world;* ns. S 49; as. W 58, 107; S 87; D 31; gs. —e, R 133; W 74; ds. —e, M 174; S 45. weorold-ġesǣliġ, adj. *blessed with this world's goods, prosperous;* nsm. M 219. weorold-rīċe, n. *kingdom of the world;* ds. W 65. [wer, *man;* ELD, *age, lifetime,* later supplanted by -old, -uld.]

weorðan, v.3. *become, be;* —(a) as independent verb: inf. W 64; pres. 3s. weorðeþ, W 110; S 69; pret. 3s. wearþ, M 113, 186 (w. on flēame, *took to flight;* E's transcript has pl. *wurdon*), 295 (*came to pass, there was*); 3p. wurdon, B 48 (beteran w., *were the better, had the better of it*); D 15; —(b) as auxiliary w. past part., forming passive, pret. 3s. wearþ, B 32, 65; M 106, 114, 116, 135, 138, 241, 288; 3s. subj. wurde, M 1; forming pluperfect, pret. 3s. wearþ, M 202. [WEORÐAN, WEARÞ, WURDON, WORDEN.]

ġe-weorðan, v.3. *become;* pp. ġeworden, nsm. R 87.

weorðian, wk.v.II. *honor, adore;* inf. R 129; pres. 3p. weorðiaþ, R 81.

ġe-weorðian, wk.v.II. *honor, exalt;* pret. 3s. ġeweorðode, R 90, 94; S 123; *adorn,* pp. ġeweorðod, asm. R 15.

weorþlīċe, adv. *splendidly, worthily, honorably;* R 17; M 279.

wēpan, v.7. *weep;* pret. 3s. wēop, R 55. [WĒPAN, WĒOP, WĒOPON, WŌPEN.]

wer, m. *man;* ns. W 64; gp. —a, S 21; dp. —um, S 110 (alt. reading: see wǣr).

werian, wk.v.I. *defend;* pret. 3p. weredon (w. refl. pron.), M 82, 283.

wēriġ, adj. *weary, exhausted, afflicted;* nsm. B 20; S 29; asm. —ne, W 57; npm. wērġe, M 303. wēriġ-mōd, adj. *weary in spirit, dejected;* nsm. as noun, W 15. (Can be taken separately, *a weary spirit,* but the compound improves the sense. See note.) [Cf. lim-, mere-wēriġ.]

wesan, see bēon-wesan.

west, adv. *west(ward),* M 97.

wēste, adj. ja-stem. *waste;* nsm. W 74.

wicg, n. ja-stem. *horse, steed;* ds. —e, M 240.

wīċing, m. *pirate, viking;* as. M 139; ap. —as, M 322; gp. —a, M 26, 73, 97; dp. —um, M 116. [Perhaps so called because the earliest pirates lived along the shores of bays: OE wīċ.]

wīde, adv. *widely, far;* S 60; D 22; wide and side, *far and wide,* R 81; superl. widost, *farthest, most widely,* S 57.

wiernan, wk.v.I. w. gen. of thing. *refuse, deny, withhold;* pret. 3s. wiernde, M 118; 3p. wierndon, B 24 (w. dat. of pers.). [Base-word wearn, f. *hindrance,* q.v.]

wīf, n. *woman;* ds. —e, S 45; gp. —a, R 94.

wīg, n. *war, battle;* ns. W 80; gs. —es, B 20, 59; M 73, 130; ds. —e, M 10, 128, 193, 235, 252; gp. —a, W. 67. wīg-haga, wk.m. *battle-hedge* (shield-wall); as. —n, M 102. wīg-heard, adj. *hardy in battle;* asm. —ne, M 75. wīg-ple₃a, wk.m. *play of battle;* ds. —n, M 268; is. —n, M 316. wīg-smiþ, m. *war-smith* (kenning for warrior); np. —as, B 72.

wiga, wk.m. *warrior;* ns. M 210; as. —n, M 75, 235; ds. —n, M 126; np. —n, M 79, 302; gp. wiġena, M 135. [Cf. byrn-wiga.]

wiġend, m. nd-stem. *warrior;* np. M 302.

willa, wk.m. *desire;* ns. R 129.

willan, anom. v. *be willing, desire, will* (w. inf. except as noted); pres. 1s. R 1; M 216, 247, 317 (fram ne w., *will not go away*); D 35; 3s. wile, R 107; M 52; 1p. willaþ, M 35, 40; 3p. willaþ, M 46; 1s. subj. wille, M 221; 2s. subj. wille, M 37; 3s. subj. wille, W 14 (hycgan understood), 72; S 43, 97, 113; pret. 3s. wolde, R 34, 41, 113 (or subj.); M 11, 129, 160; 3s. subj. wolde, W 28; pret. 3p. woldon, R 68; M 207.

win, n. *wine.* win-gāl, adj. *gay, or wanton, with wine;* nsm. S 29. win-sæl, n. *wine-hall;* np. —salu, W 78.

wind, m. *wind;* dis. —e, W 76.

windan, v.3. *wind;* —(a) intrans., *fly, speed; circle round;* inf. M 322; pret. 3p. wundon, M 106; —(b) trans., *wave, brandish;* pret. 3s. wand, M 43. [WINDAN, WAND, WUNDON, WUNDEN; cf. be-windan and wunden.]

wine, m. i-stem (treated as a-stem). *friend, loved-one, comrade, patron;* ns. M 250; as. S 115; ap.

winas, M 228. wine-dryhten, m. *lord and friend, patron;* as. M 248, 263; gs. —dryhtnes, W 37. wine-lēas, adj. *friendless, lordless;* nsm. W 45. wine-mǣġ, m. *beloved kinsman;* ap. —māgas, M 306; gp. —māga, W 7; dip. —māgum, S 16. [Cf. ġeō-, gold-wine.]

ġe-winn, n. *battle, struggle, agony;* as. M 214; ds. —e, R 65; M 248; 302. [Cf. ǣr-ġewinn.]

ġe-winnan, v.3, trans. *win* (by fighting), *conquer;* inf. M 125. [WINNAN, WANN, WUNNON, WUNNEN.]

winter, m. (elsewhere with u-stem forms), *winter;* as. S 15 (as adv., *in winter*); gs. —es, W 103; pl., in reckoning age, *years:* gp. wintra, W 65; D 18, 38; dip. wintrum, M 210. winter-ċeald, adj. *winter-cold;* asf. —e, D 4. winter-ċeariġ, adj. *winter-sad;* nsm. W 24.

wis, adj. *wise;* nsm. M 219; W 64; ism. —e, W 88.

wise, wk.f. *manner, way (of behaving);* dip. wīsum, S 110.

wisian, wk.v.II. *guide, direct;* pret. 3s. wisode, M 141.

wisliċ, adj. *certain, assured;* asm. —ne, D 34. [Cf. next word.]

ġe-wiss, adj. *trustworthy, unfailing;* asn. S 110.

wisse, see witan.

wist, f. *means of subsistence, food, feast;* ds. —e, W 36.

wit, pron. 1st pers. dual, *we two,* acc. unc, R 48. [See iċ, wē.]

wita, wk.m. *wise man, counselor;* ns. W 65.

witan, pret.-pres. v. *know, have knowledge of;* pres. 1s. wāt, W 11; 3s. wāt, M 94; W 29, 37; S 12, 55, 92; pret. 3s. wisse, M 24; subj. W 27 (mine wisse, *might know about my people;* for the traditional emendation, see **myne**). [WITAN, WĀT, WITON, WISSE, or WISTE.]

ġe-**witan**, v.1. *go, depart;* —(a) w. limiting adv. or prep. (for**þ**, **upp**, **ūt**, **þurh**, etc.); inf. S 52; pret. 3s. ġe**wāt**, B 35; R 71; M 72, 150; W 95; 3p. ġe**witon**, R 133; —(b) w. inf. specifying the manner of going or attendant action; pret. 3p. ġe**witon**, B 53 (w. refl. dat.); —(c) unmodified: pp. ġe**witen**, *departed;* npm. —e, S 80, 86. [WĪTAN, WĀT, WITON, WITEN; cf. ÆTWĪTAN, with different semantic development.]

wīte, n. ja-stem. *punishment, torment, torture;* ds. R 61; gp. **wīta**, R 87.

witiġ, adj. *wise;* nsm. D 32 (**w. dryhten**, *God in his wisdom*—Malone).

wiþ, prep. *with, against, towards,* etc. (a) w. gen., *towards,* M 8, 131; —(b) w. dat. *against,* M 103; *in exchange for,* M 31, 35, 39; — (c) w. acc. *against,* B 9, 52; M 82, 277, 298; S 75; *toward,* S 112 (twice); —(d) w. acc. or dat. *(in friendly rivalry) with,* M 290.

wiðer-lēan, n. *requital;* ns. M 116.

wiþ-standan, v.6. w. dat. *withstand;* inf. W 15. [Cf. **standan**.]

wlanc, adj. *proud, high-spirited, bold, lusty;* nsm. S 29; nsf. W 80; asm. —**ne**, M 139; dsn.wk. —**an**, M 240 (of a horse: *spirited,* or *proud, splendid?*); npm. —**e**, B 72; M 205. [Cf. **mōd-wlanc**.]

wlītan, v.1. *look;* pret. 3s. **wlāt**, M 172. [WLĪTAN, WLĀT, WLITON, WLITEN.]

wlitiġian, wk.v.II. *make beautiful, brighten;* pres. 3p. **wlitiġiaþ**, S 49.

(Less probably, *become beautiful.*) [WLITIĠ, adj., *beautiful.*]

wōd, **wōdon**, ġe-**wōd**, see **wadan**, ġe-**wadan**.

wolcen, m. or n. *cloud, sky;* dp. **wolcnum**, R 53, 55.

wolde, **woldon**, see **willan**.

wōma, wk.m. *noise, tumult* (or *proclaimer, herald?*); ns. W 103.

word, n. *word, speech, command;* as. R 35; M 168; ap. R 27; W 91; ds. —**e**, R 111; dip. —**um**, (as formal indication of speech: *with, in words*), R 97; M 26, 43, 210, 250, 306. [Cf. **ġielp-**, **lāst-word**.]

ġe-**worden**, see ġe-**weorðan**.

ġe-**worhtne**, ġe-**worhton**, see ġe-**wyrċan**.

wōrian, wk.v.II. *wander, go astray;* fig., *degenerate, go to ruin;* pres. 3p. **wōriaþ**, W 78 (*totter?*—Bosworth-Toller).

worn, m. *a great number, multitude;* as., w. part. gen., W 91.

wracu, f. *misery;* as. **wræce**, D 4.

wræc, n. *persecution, exile;* gs. —**es**, D 1. **wræc-lāst**, m. *path or track of exile;* ns. W 32; ap. —**as**, W 5; S 57 (w. **lecgaþ**, *lay tracks of exile: direct their exiled steps, travel*—Mrs. Gordon).

wræc, **wræce**, verb-forms, see **wrecan**.

wrāþ, adj. *hostile, cruel, angry;* gp. —**ra**, R 51; W 7.

wrecan, v.5. (a) w. acc. of person, *avenge (someone);* inf. M 248, 258; pret. 3s. **wræc**, M 279; 3s. subj. **wræce**, M 257; —(b) *utter, recite;* inf. S 1. [WRECAN, WRÆC, WRĒCON, WRECEN.]

ġe-**wrecan**, v.5, w. acc. of person. *avenge (someone);* inf. M 208, 263.

wreċċa, wk.m. *an exile;* gs. —**n**, S 15.

wrēon, contr.v.I. *cover.* See **be-, on-wrēon.**

ġe-**wrixl,** n. *exchange.* See **wæpen-ġewrixl.**

wudu, m. u-stem. *wood, forest;* ns. R 27; as. M 193. [Cf. **holt-wudu.**]

wuldor, n. *glory; the realm of glory, heaven;* gs. **wuldres,** R 14, 90, 97, 133; S 123; ds. **wuldre,** R 135, 143, 155. **wuldor-fæder,** m. r-stem. *glorious or heavenly Father,* gs. C 3.

wulf, m. *wolf;* ns. W 82; as. B 65. [Cf. **wæl-wulf.**]

wund, f. *wound;* as. —e, M 139, 271; dip. —um, B 43; M 293, 303.

wund, adj. *wounded;* nsm. M 113, 144.

wunden, pp. adj. *wound, twisted;* **wunden gold,** *twisted gold* (i.e. gold rings, ornamental gold, the traditional gift of the lord to his retainers); nsn. W 32. [Cf. **windan,** v.3.]

ġe-**wundian,** wk.v.II. *wound;* pp. ġe-**wundod,** nsm. M 135. [Cf. **for-wundian.**]

wundon, see **windan.**

wundor, n. *wonder;* gp. **wundra,** C 3; dip. **wundrum,** as adv. *wondrously,* W 98.

wunian, wk.v.II. (a) intrans., *dwell, live, remain;* inf. R 121, 143; pres. 3p. **wuniaþ,** R 135; S 87 (*remain*); pret. 3p. **wunodon,** R 155; —(b) trans., *remain on, dwell in;* pret. 1s. **wunode,** S 15; *occupy, be in,* pret. 3p. **wunodon,** R 3 (*reste w.,* *were in bed*). [Related to **wenian,** q.v.]

wurde, wurdon, see **weorðan.**

wurman (D 1, according to the MS.), see **wyrm.**

wuton or **uton,** hortatory auxiliary. *let us* (pres. 1p. subj., originally of **witan**); S 117.

wylfen, adj. *wolfish;* asm. —ne, D 22.

wynn, f. i-stem. *joy, delight, pleasure;* ns. W 36; S 45; as. S 27; dip. —um, R 15 (as adv., *beautifully*); W 29; gp. —a, M 174.

wyrċan, wk.v.I. *make, form;* inf. R 65; M 102.

ġe-**wyrċan,** wk.v.I. (a) *make, form;* pret. 3p. ġe**worhton,** R 31 (acc. mē understood); pp. ġe**worht,** asm. —ne, S 115 (**his ġ. wine,** *the friend he has made*); —(b) *bring about, work, accomplish;* inf. M 264; pres. 3s. subj. ġe**wyrċe,** S 74 (*let him bring it about*); —(c) **flēam** ġe**wyrċan,** lit. *make flight: take to flight;* inf. M 81.

wyrd, f. i-stem. *fate, destiny;* ns. R 74; W 5, 100 (personified, **wyrd sēo mære,** *Wyrd the renowned, Wyrd the mighty*); S 115; ds. —e, W 15; gp. —a, R 51; W 107. [Related to ***WURD**-, grade of **weorðan,** *become;* hence, *that which comes to pass.* Perhaps anciently regarded as a goddess.]

-**wyrde,** adjectival combining-form, ja-stem. *-worded, -spoken;* see **hræd-wyrde.** [Based on **word,** n., prehist. ***WURD-.**]

ġe-**wyrht,** f. i-stem (or n.). *deed.* See **eald-ġewyrht,** and cf. **wyrċan.**

wyrm, m. i-stem. *worm, snake, serpent;* dp. —um, D 1 (usual normalization of MS. *wurman,* here emended to **wearnum**). [Malone suggests that **be wurman** may refer to snake rings, gold rings made by Weland and coveted by Niþhad, or to swords with serpentine markings, instruments of the hamstringing.] **wyrm-līca,** wk. m. *likeness of a serpent;* dip. —līcum, W 98 (probably alluding to serpentine ornamentation such as was practiced by the Roman builders).

wȳscan, wk.v.I. *wish;* pret. 3s. **wȳscte,** D 25. [Gmc. *WUNSCJAN; cf. Germ. WUNSCH, WÜNSCHEN.]

Y

yfel, n. *evil, harm;* gs. —es, M 133 (dep. on **hogode.**)

ymb, or **ymbe,** prep. w. acc. — (a) *about, near, round about;* **ymbe,** B 5; M 249; **ymb,** S 11. (b) *about, concerning;* **ymbe,** M 214; S 46a; **ymb,** S 46b; D 12.. (c) governing words for periods of time: *after;* **ǣfre ymbe stunde,** *ever after a while, ever and anon,* M 271.

ymb-clyppan, wk.v.I. *embrace;* pret. 3s. **ymbclypte,** R 42. [Cf. **clyppan.**]

ȳþ, f. jō-stem. *sea-wave;* gp. —a, S 6, 46. [Cf. **sealt-ȳþ.**]

Proper Names

Most personal names among the Germanic peoples were compounds made of recognizable elements of the language and at least vaguely significant when put together. Such names in the list below are separated into their elements by hyphens, but no systematic effort has been made to expound their meaning. Sometimes the two elements in a name were selected in honor of different relatives, and only a vague propriety was demanded of the combination. Sometimes the entire name was that of an ancestor or ancient hero. Spellings in the manuscripts show that both elements in names, especially the weakly stressed second element, were subject to slurring, with loss of identity as words. In poetry, these elements could be given a restored dignity and treated like members of ordinary compounds, with strong secondary stress on the second member, particularly when it was followed by an inflectional syllable, as in *Byrht-nōðes*. Sometimes, however, even in such an ancient poem as *Beowulf,* the second member receives much less stress than it would be entitled to in an ordinary compound and ranks with syllables of the weakest grade.

The historical and legendary names in *Brunanburh, Maldon,* and *Deor* are summarily treated here. For several of them much fuller discussion is provided by the editions of Campbell, Gordon, and Malone respectively. For *Deor* Malone's later articles should also be consulted.

Ādam, Adam; gs. —**es**, R 100.

Ælf-here, one of the three defenders of the ford at Maldon; ns. M 80.

Ælf-nōþ, one of two retainers who fell beside Byrhtnoþ when he died; ns. M 183.

Ælf-rīc, father of Ælfwine, probably the ealdorman of Mercia who was banished in 985 or 986; gs. —**es**, M 209. See Gordon's ed.

Ælf-wine, scion of a distinguished Mercian family: kinsman of Byrhtnoþ, son of Ælfric, grandson of Ealhhelm. See Gordon's ed.

He sets the pattern of sacrifice after Byrhtnoþ's death. ns. M 211; vs. M 231.

Æsc-ferhþ, son of Ecglaf, a Northumbrian of noble family, a hostage in Byrhtnoþ's household; ns. M 267.

Æðel-gār, father of the virtuous Godric; gs. —es, M 320.

Æðel-rēd, Ethelred II, King of England 978–1016 ("the Unready," i.e. unwise or "Redeless"); gs. —es, M 53, 151, 203. [The second element of the name is RĒD, *advice, counsel,* which figures also in the traditional epithets.]

Æðel-rīc, retainer of Byrhtnoþ and brother of Sigebyrht, cited for valiant conduct in the last phase of the battle; ns. M 280. [On the possibility that he survived the battle, see Gordon's ed.]

Æðel-stān, Athelstan, King of England 924–939; ns. B 1.

Anlāf, leader of the Vikings from Dublin at Brunanburh; ns. B 46; gs. —es, B 31; ds. —e, B 26. [Early form of Old Norse Ólaf; on his identity see Campbell's edition.]

Beadu-hild, daughter of Niþhad, mother of the famous Widia by Weland; ds. —e, D 8.

Briten, f. Britain; as. —e, B 71. [The spelling of this name, ultimately from Lat. BRITANNIA, varies greatly; e.g. also BRYTEN, BRITON, BREOTON.]

Brūnan-burh, unidentified site of the battle of A.D. 937; as. B 5. [The second element is certainly BURG, f. cons.-stem, *fortress,* etc.; the first may be gs. of BRŪNA, wk.m., pr. name, Brown.]

Byrht-helm, father of Byrhtnoþ; gs. —es, M 92.

Byrht-nōþ, earl or ealdorman of Essex, A.D. 956–991. Gordon thinks he was born about 926, so that he was about 65 when he was killed at Maldon. See Gordon's introduction. ns. M 17, 42, 101, 127, 162; as. M 257; gs. —es, M 114. [BYRHT, var. of BEORHT, adj. *bright;* NōÞ, f. *daring.*]

Byrht-wold, the old retainer of Byrhtnoþ whose prescription for courage in defeat opens the last speech of the incomplete poem, 312 ff.; ns. M 309. [WOLD, half-stress form of WEALD, WALD, *power.*]

Čēola, father of the Wulfstan who led the defence of the ford at Maldon; gs. —n, M 76.

Constantinus, Constantine III, King of the united Picts and Scots at Brunanburh; ns. B 38.

Dene, m. i-stem pl. Danes (a name often applied to Scandinavians in general); dp. **Denum,** M 129 (chiefly Norwegians).

Dēor, known only as speaker of the poem of that name, who says he was formerly the scop of the Hedenings; ns. D 37.

Dinges Mere, the otherwise unknown name of some part of the sea off the coast of Britain, probably an estuary between northern England and Ireland; as. (less probably ds.), B 54. [See mere in the main glossary.]

Dunnere, a simple freeman at Maldon. ns. M 255.

Dyflin, Dublin, where Anlaf ruled a Norse kingdom at the time of the battle of Brunanburh; as. B 55.

Ēad-mund, Prince Edmund, younger brother of Athelstan, who ruled after him, 939–946; ns. B 3.

Ēad-rīċ, a retainer of Byrhtnoþ's; ns. M 11.

Ēad-weard, (1) Edward the Elder, King of Wessex 899–924, son of Alfred and father of Athelstan; gs. —es, B 7, 52. (2) a retainer of Byrhtnoþ's; ns. M 117. (3) Ēadweard se langa, the Tall, a retainer of Byrhtnoþ's, perhaps the same as 2; ns. M 273.

Ēad-wold, a retainer of Byrhtnoþ's, brother of Oswold; ns. M 304.

Eahl-helm, grandfather of Ælfwine, father-in-law of Ælfric; ealdorman of Mercia ca. 940–950; ns. M 218. [EALH, m. *temple.*]

Ēast-Seaxe, m. i-stem pl. the East Saxons, centered in Essex; gp. Ēast-Seaxna, M 69.

Ecg-lāf, a Northumbrian nobleman, father of Æscferhþ; gs. —es, M 267.

Engle, m. i-stem pl. the Angli, Angles as contrasted with Saxons; np. B 70.

Eorman-rīċ, the Ermanaric of history, ruler of the Goths in the third quarter of the fourth century, who died ca. 375 when the Huns invaded his empire, centered near the mouth of the Danube. Known in legend as a violent man, and eventually as a tyrant who meted out savage punishment for imagined crimes; gs. —es, D 21.

Gadd, kinsman of Offa; gs. —es, M 287.

Ġēat, legendary hero, perhaps originally a god, lover of Mæþhild; gs. —es, D 15.

God-rīċ, (1) son of Odda; leader of the flight from the battle of Maldon; ns. M 187, 237, 325. (2) son of Æðelgar; a retainer of Byrhtnoþ's who, unlike the preceding, fought to the last; ns. M 321.

God-wiġ, son of Odda; a fugitive with his brothers Godric (1) and Godwine; ns. M 192.

God-wine, son of Odda; a fugitive with his brothers Godric (1) and Godwig; ns. M 192. (E's transscript calls him *Godrine*.)

Gotan, wk.m.pl. the Goths; in the time of Ermanaric they had not yet separated into Ostrogoths and Visigoths; gp. **Gotena,** D 23.

Hedeningas, m.pl. the people ruled by Heden, a legendary Germanic king, wooer of Hagen's daughter, Hild, and once the lord of Deor; gp. —a, D 36.

Heorrenda, a scop of Heden, celebrated in one of the versions of the Hild saga; according to Deor, his successful rival; ns. D 39.

Īras, m.pl. the Irish; gp. **Īra,** B 56.

Lēof-sunu, retainer of Byrhtnoþ, probably from Sturmer in Essex; the third to speak after Byrhtnoþ's death; ns. M 244.

Maccus, one of the three defenders of the ford at Maldon; ns. M 80.

Mǣringas, m.pl. an unidentified people ruled by the unidentified Þeodric; gp. **Mǣringa,** D 19.

Mǣþ-hild, a legendary lady, beloved by Ġēat; probably the one who was threatened with rape by a river demon; gs. —e, D 14.

Māria, the Virgin Mary; as. —n, R 92.

Mierce, m. i-stem pl. the Mercians; np. B 24; dp. **Miercum,** M 217.

Niþ-hād, legendary king, persecutor of Weland; ns. D 5.

Norþ-Hymbre, m. i-stem pl. the Northumbrians; dp. —**Hymbrum,** M 266.

Norþ-mann, m. cons.-stem, Norseman; np. **Norþ-menn,** B 53; gp. -**manna,** B 33.

Odda, father of the fugitives, Godric (1), Godwig and Godwine; gs. —**n,** M 186, 238. [See Gordon's glossary for the possible origin of the name, Scandinavian or English.]

Offa, an officer of Byrhtnoþ's, apparently second in command under him; his speech after B's death, M 231 ff., seems to indicate that he is now the leader; ns. M 198, 230, 286, 288; gs. —**n,** M 5.

Ōs-wold, a retainer of Byrhtnoþ's, brother of Eadwold; ns. M 304.

Pante, wk.f. the river near Maldon, in Essex, now called Blackwater, though the old name Pant (pron. Pont) survives for the part below Maldon. See Gordon's glossary. gs. **Pantan,** M 68; as. **Pantan,** M 97.

Scottas, m.pl. the Scots; gp. **Scotta,** B 11, 32. [The spelling *Sceotta* in MS. A suggests that at least in the South the *sc* was palatalized; but perhaps only by a few.]

Scyttisc, pr. adj. Scottish; nsm. B 19.

Seaxe, m. i-stem pl. the Saxons, as distinguished from the Angles; np. B 70. [The reference is to the invasion of the fifth century as recounted by Bede and the Anglo-Saxon Chronicle.]

Siġe-byrht, brother of Æðelric, one of Byrhtnoþ's retainers. It is not definitely stated that Sigebyrht was present at the battle; gs. —**es,** M 282.

Stūr-mere, a pool (**mere**) in the river Stour in Essex, from which the village of Sturmer takes its name. (See Gordon's glossary.) as. M 249.

Þēod-rīċ, a ruler of uncertain identity; held by some to be Theodoric the Ostrogoth, in later legend Dietrich von Bern; by others, including Malone, to be the king of the Franks, the Hug-Dietrich, father of Wolf-Dietrich, of later legend. Perhaps he is neither. ns. D 18.

Þur-stān, father of Wistan; gs. —**es,** M 298. [The name is adapted, according to Gordon, from OE Scand. þURSTÆIN; the first element may be þŪR, OE variant of þUNOR, Old Norse þÓR, the god.]

Wealh, m. a Welshman (originally a foreigner), Briton; ap. **Wēalas,** B 72.

Wēland, legendary smith; ns. D 1.

West-Seaxe, m. i-stem pl. the West-Saxons; np. B 20; gp. **West-Seaxna,** B 59.

Wiġ-helm, father of an unidentified warrior at Maldon; gs. —**es,** M 300. [Gordon suggests that **Wiġ-helmes bearn** is Offa, but this seems unlikely. Perhaps we should read **mǣġ** for **bearn** and conclude that Wistan was not only the son of Þurstan but a nephew or grandson of Wighelm.]

Wī-stān, one of Byrhtnoþ's retainers, son of Þurstan; ns. M 297. [Gordon suggests that the first element may be either wiġ, *war,* or, by way of Scandinavian, wīн, wēoн, *idol, shrine;* if he was named for Wighelm, q.v., the element is wiġ.]

Wulf-mǣr, (1) son of Byrhtnoþ's sister; ns. M 113. (2) Wulfmǣr se Ġeonga, W. the Young, a retainer of Byrhtnoþ's, son of Wulfstan; ns. M 155, 183.

Wulf-stān, chief defender of the ford at Maldon, son of Ceola, father of Wulfmǣr (2); ns. M 75; gs. —es, M 155; ds. —e, M 79.

The Library of Literature

CRANE, STEPHEN, *The Red Badge of Courage*, ed. Frederick C. Crews, 6

DICKENS, CHARLES, *Great Expectations*, ed. Louis Crompton, 2

HAWTHORNE, NATHANIEL, *The Scarlet Letter*, ed. Larzer Ziff, 1

MELVILLE, HERMAN, *Moby Dick*, ed. Charles Feidelson, 5

One Hundred Middle English Lyrics, ed. Robert D. Stevick, 7

SWIFT, JONATHAN, *Gulliver's Travels*, ed. Martin Price, 3

TWAIN, MARK, *The Adventures of Huckleberry Finn*, ed. Leo Marx, 4

Sinfully mine

KENDALL RYAN

Sinfully Mine

Book 2 in the LESSONS WITH THE DOM Series

Copyright © 2015 Kendall Ryan

Edited and Formatted by Pam Berehulke,
Bulletproof Editing

Cover design and Photography by Sara Eirew